Red Power

Red Power

The American Indians' Fight for Freedom

SECOND EDITION

Edited by Alvin M. Josephy Jr., Joane Nagel,

and Troy Johnson

University of Nebraska Press Lincoln & London

Acknowledgments for the use of
previously published materials appear
on page 293–94, which constitutes an
extension of the copyright page.

Library of Congress
Cataloging-in-Publication Data
Josephy, Alvin M., 1915–
Red power : the American Indians' fight for freedom /
edited by Alvin M. Josephy Jr., Joane Nagel, and Troy
Johnson. — 2nd ed.
    p.   cm.
Includes bibliographical references and index.
ISBN 0-8032-2587-3 (cl: alk. paper). —
ISBN 0-8032-7611-7 (pa: alk. paper).
1. Indians of North America—Government relations.
2. Indians of North America—Social conditions.   I. Nagel,
Joane.   II. Johnson, Troy R.   III. Title
E93.J67   1999
323.1′197073—dc21   98-39661
                          CIP

This book is dedicated to

the renewing spirit of activism.

Through protest and resistance,

we become authors of ourselves.

Contents

Illustrations

Acknowledgments

This new edition of *Red Power* was a collaborative effort across both space and time. When Troy Johnson and Joane Nagel began working together in 1992, they had never met. They were introduced by Duane Champagne, director of the American Indian Studies Center at the University of California, Los Angeles, who knew they were each working independently on studies of American Indian activism. Duane's generosity established one link in the collaboration reflected in these pages. Troy and Joane had both read and been influenced by Alvin M. Josephy Jr.'s 1971 classic work on Indian activism — the first edition of *Red Power*. So when Gary Dunham, Native Studies editor for the University of Nebraska Press, contacted them about the possibility of working with Alvin Josephy on a new edition, they were thrilled and delighted. These pages are the result of these long-distance introductions by Duane Champagne and Gary Dunham, and the long-distance writing, commenting, revising, commenting, and re-revising that has taken place among the three editors in the six years since the first of those introductions was made.

This new edition is also a creation of both the electronic age and the mismatch of technology. Alvin Josephy was wise enough to stick to hard copy for his portions of this collaboration — a medium that still interfaces well with all other technologies. Joane Nagel and Troy Johnson, however, are now completely chained to their computers. This is not usually a problem in collaboration, except that Joane uses a PC and Troy uses a Mac. Anyone who has tried to cross this great divide knows about the frustrations and challenges involved. We were all saved, however, by the internet. Virtually [!] all of the text here was transmitted via the net. The universal net language of data packets translated text from Mac to PC and back again several times, with English-language versions interjected in between. By this method we were able to communicate yet remain imbedded in the technology of our choice.

There was also other human agency in this work, agency for which we are very grateful. Tony Clark helped us locate background information and documents on Women of All Red Nations and prepared the index, George Lundskow helped prepare the manuscript, and Su Lee dug through official archives to locate many of the new documents included here. The University of Nebraska Press gave us a travel advance that permitted us to meet at an early crucial point in the conception and organization of the new edition. We are grateful to the individuals and organizations who granted us permission to include their words and documents in this work. Without these voices and without the daring, bravery, and vision of the many activists and supporters of the Red Power movement, this story of Native American resistance and resurgence could never have been told. This new edition is dedicated to their spirit and their sacrifice.

Greenwich, Connecticut
Lawrence, Kansas
Long Beach, California

Red Power

Introduction: "You Are on Indian Land!"

It has been more than a quarter century since the first edition of *Red Power: The American Indians' Fight for Freedom* was published in 1971. Much has happened in Indian country since Vine Deloria proclaimed in 1970: "This country was a lot better off when the Indians were running it." The selection of Deloria's article by the same name as the end piece of the first edition of this book marks the point where our work on the new edition begins. When Vine Deloria Jr. spoke those words, Alcatraz Island was still occupied by the group called Indians of All Tribes, Deloria himself was just finishing law school, and many things were to come.

Since 1971 we have seen the rise of a widespread protest movement by Native Americans in cities and on reservations, a proliferation of native newspapers, organizations, and associations supporting American Indian interests and representing Indian communities, a series of landmark tribal land claims and reservation resource rights decisions that have reaffirmed Indian treaty rights, a legislative and judicial reaffirmation of tribal rights to self-determination and sovereignty that has opened the way for tribal economic development including casino gaming, a blossoming of cultural and spiritual renewal on many reservations and in urban Indian communities, an emerging intertribal urban Indian culture and community in U.S. cities, and an upsurge in the American Indian population as more and more Americans reassert their native ancestry.

PROTESTS

The occupation of Alcatraz Island by Indians of All Tribes from 1969 to 1971 marked the beginning of the decade-long Indian activist movement known as "Red Power." The 1970s were the most intense years of Native American protest during the twentieth century, and the activism occurred both in cities and on reservations. Many protests of the early 1970s followed the model of the Alcatraz occupation, with Indians taking over possession of federal land and claiming it for educational and cultural uses. Most post-Alcatraz protests were much briefer, however, and often took the form of seizures of unused or abandoned federal property or demonstrations at government buildings or in national parks or

1

monuments such as Mount Rushmore or Plymouth Rock. Many of these protest events involved members of the American Indian Movement (AIM).

As the decade proceeded, American Indian protests lasted longer, and some took on a more serious, sometimes violent, tone, revealing the depth of grievances and difficulty of solving problems centuries in the making. Perhaps best known of these later protests was the seventy-one-day siege at Wounded Knee on the Pine Ridge Reservation in the spring of 1973. Other reservation-based protests continued throughout the 1970s and revealed a growing diversity inside Native America — between urban and reservation Indians and within reservation communities — and included two occupations of the Bureau of Indian Affairs in Washington DC, the takeover of property on the Menominee Reservation by the Menominee Warrior Society, and a shootout on Pine Ridge followed by the imprisonment of Leonard Peltier.

The "Longest Walk," in July 1978, was the last major event of the Red Power era. Several hundred Native Americans marched into Washington DC to dramatize the forced removal of Native Americans from their aboriginal homelands, to bring attention to the continuing problems of American Indians, and to expose and confront the backlash movement against Indian treaty rights that was gaining strength in the Great Lakes and Pacific Northwest regions of the United States. Unlike the events of the mid-1970s, the Longest Walk was seen as a peaceful and spiritual event that ended without violence. Red Power had come full circle from the festive Alcatraz days, through a cycle of violent confrontation, to the spiritual unity that marked the end of the Longest Walk. Since 1980 the Native American rights struggle has moved increasingly into the courts and the halls of U.S. and tribal governments. But activists have continued to challenge stereotypes and exploitation of Indians by protesting the use of Indian mascots by athletic teams, to defend tribal treaty rights by protesting the continued failure to return such Indian lands as the Black Hills, and to protest violations of Indian human rights by demanding the repatriation of Indian burial remains and sacred objects and the protection of native burial and other sacred grounds.

ORGANIZATIONAL GROWTH

The Indian protests of the last three decades have been accompanied by a dramatic growth in the number and variety of organizations designed to represent Indian interests, to build bridges among reservation communities, to link together tribally diverse urban Indians, and to provide a communication network to connect Native Americans around the country and around the world. Dozens of American Indian newspapers and periodicals were founded during the late 1960s and 1970s, including the American Indian Historical Society's *The Indian Historian* and *Wassaja*, the National Indian Youth Council's *ABC: Americans Before Columbus*, and the influential *Akwesasne Notes*, published by the Mohawk Nation. The voices of many of the most militant activists were published in *Warpath*, edited by Leighman Brightman. These periodicals joined the ranks of older, more established newspapers and journals such as the *Navajo Times* and the *Indian Leader*, published by Haskell Indian Junior College (now Haskell Indian Nations University) in Kansas. In addition to the growth in publications, Native American history and culture became a topic of serious study during the 1960s, and this new academic focus was reflected in educational institutions. American Indian Studies centers were established at over one hundred universities around the United States, and nearly two dozen reservation community colleges were established in the decade following the 1968 founding of the first tribally controlled institution of higher education, Navajo Community College.

A number of important legal, political, and economic national organizations were also established during this period. In addition to the National Indian Youth Council (founded in 1961) and the American Indian Movement (founded in 1968), there were the National Indian Education Association (founded in 1969), the Native American Rights Fund (founded in 1970), the National Tribal Chairman's Association (founded in 1971), and the Council of Energy Resource Tribes (founded in 1975). These organizations provided lines of communication among American Indian communities and represented Indian interests at various levels of government. National organizations with members from different Indian tribes and communities contributed to an increasing awareness of common problems and interests shared by many tribes as well as by the growing urban Indian population.

LAND CLAIMS AND RESOURCE RIGHTS

Many important decisions about treaty rights and land claims were made during the past three decades. In particular, during the 1980s a number of major tribal land claims settlements and resource rights decisions were made by Congress and the U.S. federal courts. While land claims awards varied in amount and in the extent to which they were judged to be fair, the claims-making process encouraged many Indian communities to research their histories as they organized their cases for litigation. As a result of the increased knowledge of and interest in tribal history and the financial resources obtained from land claims, a number of successful claimants were able to reestablish and revitalize tribal community economic and cultural life. For instance, the Passamaquoddies of Maine invested a portion of the proceeds from their multimillion-dollar land claims settlement in a variety of community enterprises including a housing manufacturing firm and timber mill as well as in educational programs in Passamaquoddy language and culture. Decisions to permit tribal control of economic enterprises opened the way for the Mashantuckett Pequots of Connecticut to establish the extraordinarily successful Foxwoods High Stakes Bingo and Casino, many proceeds of which have been used to purchase reservation land and to research and reconstruct tribal history and traditions. Despite these and other land claims settlements (e.g., to the Warm Springs, Yavapai-Apaches, Havasupais, Yakamas, Siletzes, Penobscots), all land disputes have not been settled and continue to generate controversy and protest. The occupation of Yellow Thunder Camp in the disputed Black Hills during the 1980s symbolized unresolved land disputes between the Sioux and the United States.

The exploitation of Indian resources has been the most consistent theme marking Indian-white relations since European contact. The acquisition of Indian land by colonial and U.S. governments through the use of Indian treaties was, for the most part, a successful strategy in that it reduced Indian landholdings to an infinitesimal portion of the continent. Treaties, however, were not without their costs to non-Indian governments. The consequences of the treaty-making strategy for U.S. political and economic interests manifested itself in the past three decades in a variety of legislative and court decisions upholding and expanding tribal rights to develop and control resources and economic development. In addition to the 1975 Indian Self-Determination and Education Assistance Act, there were the 1979 Archaeological Resources Protection Act, the 1983 Radioactive Waste Disposal Act, the 1983 Land Consolidation Act, and the 1988 Indian Gaming Regulatory Act, all of which extended tribal sovereignty over the decision making and control of reservation land and resources.

We will argue that one legacy of Red Power activism was the reversal of three decades of post–Second World War federal Indian "termination" policy in which the federal government sought to "terminate," once and for all, Indian treaty rights and tribal trust status. Instead of termination, the 1970s brought to Indian country a new era of "Self-Determination." The 1973 Menominee Restoration Act explicitly reversed Congress' earlier decision to terminate the Menominee tribe of Wisconsin and reinstated the tribe's trust status and tribal government. This was followed by the landmark 1975 Indian Self-Determination and Education Assistance Act, which paved the way for tribal governments to contract for services outside the direct control of the Bureau of Indian Affairs. The 1975 Self-Determination Act was the beginning of a variety of legislation ushering in the self-determination era, including a number of laws reshaping the federal-tribal relationship in the direction of more self-rule. Among these were the 1972 Indian Education Act, the 1974 Indian Financing Act, the 1976 Indian Health Care Improvement Act, the 1978 Indian Child Welfare Act, the 1978 Tribally Controlled Community College Assistance Act, the 1978 American Indian Religious Freedom Act, the 1990 Native American Languages Act, the 1990 Native American Graves Protection and Repatriation Act, the 1990 Indian Arts and Crafts Act, and the 1994 American Indian Religious Freedom Act Amendments.

Linked to these legislative changes, the 1970s, 1980s, and 1990s have been decades of much change on Indian reservations. Tribal government jurisdiction and the assertion of tribal rights have been reaffirmed and expanded. Reservation communities are developing tribal court systems, establishing tribal education systems including tribal colleges, extending tribal sovereignty and control over resources and taxation, securing and enforcing tribal hunting, fishing, and water rights, and building tribal economic development programs, most recently in the areas of gaming, natural resources, and recreation.

CULTURAL AND SPIRITUAL RENEWAL

The rise of Indian protest and the reaffirmation of tribal sovereignty during the past three decades has a distinct political and economic character. But this is not the whole picture of what has happened in Indian country since the 1960s. The militancy and legal sophistication of Indian leaders has been strengthened and deepened by a reaffirmation of the centrality of spirituality and a recommitment to native traditions. Many court cases have been fought over Indian religious freedom in schools, prisons, and native churches. Legal cases such as *Pollock v. Marshall* (1988), *Lyng v. Northwest Indian Cemetery Protective Association* (1988), and *Employment Division, Department of Human Resources of Oregon v. Smith* (1990) are examples of the increasing attacks on native religions, traditions, and cultures. *Pollock v. Marshall* denied Indian prisoners the right to wear long hair. *Lyng v. Northwest Indian Cemetery Protective Association* was a direct assault on the protection and preservation of Indian sacred sites. Despite the American Indian Religious Freedom Act of 1978 and a study which showed that a proposed logging road would have devastating effects on traditional Indian religious practices, the U.S. Supreme Court ruled that the First Amendment's Free Exercise of Religion clause did not prohibit the government from constructing a proposed road through the sacred land. In *Employment Division, Department of Human Resources of Oregon v. Smith*, the U.S. Supreme Court ruled that the First Amendment does not protect the religious use of peyote by Indian people. Four years later, however, President Clinton nullified the impact of the Supreme Court ruling when he signed Public Law 103-344 (the American Indian Religious Freedom Act Amendments of 1994), which guaranteed American Indians the right to use the sacrament of peyote in traditional religious ceremonies. The effectiveness of Public Law 103-344 protection will no doubt be tested soon, since, in 1997, the Supreme Court found unconstitutional the 1993 Religious Freedom Restoration Act — a law which was passed in response to the *Oregon v. Smith* decision in an effort to protect the religious practices of all U.S. citizens. Another major issue of cultural and spiritual renewal is the continuing struggle over the repatriation of Indian ancestral remains. The strongly voiced demand of Indian people for the right to control and protect their cultural heritage indicates a growing spiritual concern and commitment that resulted in the passage of the 1990 National Museum of the American Indian Act and the 1990 Native American Graves Protection and Repatriation Act, which set up procedures for the return of Indian burial remains and sacred objects to Indian tribes.

As a material manifestation of cultural renewal, there has been a flourishing of American Indian art and cultural organizations and activity during the past three decades. Since the 1960s there has been the creation of many new tribal museums, the thriving growth of tribal and urban Indian powwows and arts festivals, the establishment of tribal language programs and craft centers, an explosion of Native American literature, music, and film, and the founding of the National Museum of the American Indian (NMAI). The NMAI is an institution that represents an important move away from the past — a museum about Indians controlled by Indians.

URBAN INDIAN COUNTRY

Urban Indian communities have grown rapidly during the last three decades. In 1960 just 28 percent of Indians lived in urban areas. This figure rose to 44 percent in 1970, increased to 50 percent in 1980, and by 1990 more than half of American Indians lived in cities. The growth of the urban Indian population, particularly during the period from 1960 to 1980, contributed to the emergence of the Red Power national Indian protest movement. The urbanization of Indian America had just begun to escalate when the first edition of *Red Power* was published; the decades since then have seen the growth of intertribal communities and the blossoming of pan-Indian culture in U.S. cities — a trend that has had profound consequences for American Indian identity and unity.

The last quarter century has produced an interesting set of countervailing trends in Indian America, the roots of which can be traced to the pre-1970 period. There has been a "detraditionalization" of Indian individuals and communities as Native Americans have moved into the urban American mainstream. However, there also has been a "retraditionalization" of Indian individuals and communities, as many of these same urban (and reservation) Indians have returned to reservations and to traditional practices in an effort to reconnect with their native roots. These apparently contradictory trends are partly the result of demographic and social changes in the Indian population: increased levels of intermarriage, urbanization, and education. On the one hand, we can see the emergence of "new Indians" — native people living away from reservation communities, often intermarried with non-Indians or with Indians from other tribes, whose children are of mixed tribal and non-Indian ancestry, who do not speak an Indian language, and who are more educated and more likely to be employed than many of their reservation counterparts. All of these changes mark a path toward the creation of an intertribal "Indian" identity and community, more assimilated into the American mainstream, more "ethnic" than tribal. On the other hand, we can also see the maintenance of "old Indian ways." The reassertion of tribal sovereignty and the building of tribal resources have fostered a continued and strengthened sense of tribal identity and affiliation and a renaissance of tribal culture, spirituality, and community on reservations and in cities.

Thus, a consequence of urbanization and reservation revitalization has been both the "detribalization" and the "retribalization" of American Indians. The tension between these two trends has produced many interesting debates in Indian country about issues of tribal membership and rights, individual and collective ethnic authenticity, misrepresentations or fraudulent claims about individual ancestry or tribal affiliation, and legitimate claims to cultural production rights (who can legitimately produce Indian literature or Indian art; who has genuine knowledge of or should be able to teach Indian spirituality), and it has generated debates about the future of Native American social, cultural, political, and economic life.

INDIAN POPULATION RESURGENCE

At the beginning of the twentieth century, the American Indian population reached its nadir, falling to fewer than 250,000. During the ensuing century, particularly in the decades after 1960, there was a dramatic growth in the number of Native Americans and an accompanying revitalization of tribal and urban Indian communities. During the Red Power decade of the 1970s, the number of Americans in the U.S. census who reported their "race" to be American Indian increased from 792,730 in 1970 to 1,364,033 in 1980 — a 72-percent increase (an additional 5 million Americans reported some Indian ancestry in 1980). This growth in the Indian population could not be explained using the usual demographic tools (increased birthrates, decreased death rates, immigration). Researchers concluded that many individuals had changed their primary identities from non-Indian (most likely "white") to American Indian from one census to the next, and that many of these "new" Indians were likely living in urban areas, often away from traditional Indian communities.

While the growth in the number of American Indians assured the continuation of native communities, a continuation that was in doubt at the beginning of the century, the nontraditional origins and mixed ancestry of many native people posed a challenge to tribal communities and native leaders as the end of the twentieth century approached. That challenge involved questions that paralleled those posed by the urbanization of the Native American population: who could make legitimate tribal membership claims, who had a right to participate in tribal decision making, who should share tribal and other Indian resources, who spoke for Indian rights, and who represented Indian interests?

[THE FUTURE RED ROAD]

The trends and changes in American Indian protest and politics since 1970 that we have outlined above set the agenda for the documents we have selected for the new edition of *Red Power*. We have replaced and added a number of documents, many of them in the voices of native scholars, activists, leaders, and individuals, covering such topics as tribal sovereignty, reservation economic development, protest activism, health, education, environment, religious freedom, repatriation and protection of sacred sites, self-determination and self-governance, urban Indians, Indian identity, native culture and spirituality, and ethnic authenticity.

The post–Second World War era has been a revolutionary period in American Indian history, marked most importantly, we think, by Native American activism. During this period American Indians have organized themselves to articulate and pursue their rights, have educated themselves to seek legal remedies to past injustices, and have mobilized their urban and reservation members to use protest, politics, and the media to ensure that their grievances and demands are heard. The new edition of *Red Power* covers the early, watershed days of this dynamic and important period of recent American Indian history and examines the entire Red Power era and its aftermath. We hope that this updated and expanded edition will extend the saga of Native American activism and capture the spirit of Indian resistance and renewal that flourished in the final decades of the twentieth century and that marked the path forward into the next millennium — the future Red Road.

1 Red Power Protest

Declaration of Indian Purpose

American Indian Chicago Conference

June 13–20, 1961

The words "Red Power" were first used in public gatherings in the mid-1960s. Among the earliest reported uses of the term were declarations by Mel Thom and other National Indian Youth Congress members at the 1964 American Indian Capital Conference on Poverty in Washington DC, and by Vine Deloria Jr. during the 1966 convention of the National Congress of American Indians (NCAI). The NCAI was founded in 1944 and represented mainly Indian tribes and nations. The National Indian Youth Council was a newer and more activist organization that grew out of a history-making American Indian conference in Chicago in 1961. In June 1961, 420 Indians from sixty-seven tribes gathered at the University of Chicago for the American Indian Chicago Conference. During the week-long meeting, these Native Americans voiced their opinions and desires on every aspect of contemporary Indian affairs. Committees were formed, organized their thinking, and prepared resolutions and statements. The final drafts, including a great number of recommendations, were drawn up as a "Declaration of Indian Purpose" and were passed by the entire conference. The declaration began with the following resolution:

In order to give due recognition to certain basic philosophies by which the Indian people and all other people endeavor to live, We, the Indian people, must be governed by high principles and laws in a democratic manner, with a right to choose our own way of life. Since our Indian culture is slowly being absorbed by the American society, we believe we have the responsibility of preserving our precious heritage; recognizing that certain changes are inevitable. We believe that the Indians should provide the adjustment and thus freely advance with dignity to a better life educationally, economically, and spiritually.

The resolution was followed by a statement of beliefs, presented as a Creed:

WE BELIEVE in the inherent right of all people to retain spiritual and cultural values, and that the free exercise of these values is necessary to the normal development of any people. Indians exercised this inherent right to live their own lives for thousands of years before the white man came and took their lands. It is a more complex world in which Indians live today, but the Indian people who first settled the New World and built the great civilizations which only now are being dug out of the past, long ago demonstrated that they could master complexity.

WE BELIEVE that the history and development of America show that the Indian has been subjected to duress, undue influence, unwarranted pressures, and policies which have produced uncertainty, frustration, and despair. Only when the public understands these conditions and is moved to take action toward the formulation and adoption of sound and consistent policies and programs will these destroying factors be removed and the Indian resume his normal growth and make his maximum contribution to modern society.

WE BELIEVE in the future of a greater America, an America which we were the first to love, where life, liberty, and the pursuit of happiness will be a reality. In such a future, with Indians and all other Americans cooperating, a cultural climate will be created in which the Indian people will grow and develop as members of a free society. . . .

It has long been recognized that one Commissioner cannot give the personal attention to all tribal matters which they deserve. He cannot meet all callers to his office, make necessary visits to the field, and give full attention to the review of tribal programs and supporting budget requests. In view of these conditions, we most urgently recommend that the present organization of the Bureau of Indian Affairs be reviewed and that certain principles be considered no matter what the organizational change might be.

The basic principle involves the desire on the part of Indians to participate in developing their own programs with help and guidance as needed and requested, from a local decentralized technical and administrative staff, preferably located conveniently to the people it serves. . . . The Indians as responsible individual citizens, as responsible tribal representatives, and as responsible Tribal Councils want to participate, want to contribute to their own personal and tribal improvements and want to cooperate with their Government on how best to solve the many problems in a businesslike, efficient, and economical manner as rapidly as possible. . . .

We believe that where programs have failed in the past, the reasons were lack of Indian understanding, planning, participation, and approval.

A plan of development should be prepared by each Indian group, whose land or other assets are held in trust, whether such lands or assets are fully defined or not; such plans to be designed to bring about maximum utilization of physical resources by the dependent population and the development of that population to its full potential; such plans to be prepared by the Indians of the respective groups, with authority to call upon the agencies of the federal government for technical assistance, and the ultimate purpose of such planning to be the growth and development of the resources and the people;

That requests for annual appropriations of funds be based on the requirements for carrying into effect these individual development plans, including credit needs and capital investment, and the annual operating budget for the Bureau of Indian Affairs to include sufficient funds to cover the costs of preparing plans and estimates similar in operation to a Point IV plan.

"We Are Not Free"

Clyde Warrior, president, National Indian Youth Council

February 2, 1967

In general, in the late 1960s the most articulate and insistent arguments for Indian self-determination were made by young, college-educated Indians. They were a new generation, proud of their Indian heritage, unwilling to share their elders' acceptance of white paternalism, and contemptuous of white society, which everywhere around them seemed to be falling into disarray.

Increasingly they appeared at university seminars, at meetings of national organizations, and at hearings of government agencies whose affairs touched Indian life. Their speeches and testimony, essentially demands for self-determination for Indians, comprised simultaneous attacks on many fronts: on the colonialist bureaucrats and white "Indian experts"; on their own "red apple" (red on the outside and white on the inside) elders and tribal leaders; and on the collusion between self-seeking or fearful Indians and whites that continued to keep control and power in the hands of the Indians' oppressors.

On February 2, 1967, the same day that older Indians in Washington were presenting President Johnson with a cautious reproof of the administration's proposed "omnibus bill," Clyde Warrior, an eloquent young Ponca Indian from eastern Oklahoma who had become president of the National Indian Youth Council, testified at a hearing of the President's National Advisory Commission on Rural Poverty in Memphis, Tennessee. His statement is typical of many utterances and writings that made him almost a legendary hero to young Indians throughout the country even before his untimely death in 1968. It is a moving plea for Indian freedom, and at its heart is a perceptive linking of Indian poverty with white society's continuing unwillingness to allow Indians to run their own affairs. White bureaucrats and "experts" from both government and private (university, foundation, church, state, and local political and business) sectors of the country were moving in authoritatively on the control and management of government-funded antipoverty programs. The trend was undermining the Indian self-government aspects of those projects that had seemed so promising during the first days of the OEO and threatening to negate a similar potential for self-government, envisioned by Senator McGovern, in the operation of other governmental agency programs that would come to the reservations. Warrior's statement reflects this development.

His theme, the major thrust of many of his speeches, struck a responsive chord among young Indians: tribal leaders had to recognize that white "experts" could not end poverty or solve other problems on the reservations; only "the poor, the dispossessed, the Indians" could decide what was best for them.

Following is the principal portion of his presentation to the commission.

Most members of the National Indian Youth Council can remember when we were children and spent many hours at the feet of our grandfathers listening to stories of the time when the Indians were a great people, when we were free, when we were rich, when we lived the good life. At the same time we heard stories of droughts, famines, and pestilence. It was only recently that we realized that there was surely great material deprivation in those days, but that our old people felt rich because they were free. They were rich in things of the spirit, but if there is one thing that characterizes Indian life today it is poverty of the spirit. We still have human passions and depth of feeling (which may be something rare in these days), but we are poor in spirit because we are not free — free in the most basic sense of the word. We are not allowed to make those basic human choices and decisions about our personal life and about the destiny of our communities which is the mark of free mature people. We sit on our front porches or in our yards, and the world and our lives in it pass us by without our desires or aspirations having any effect.

We are not free. We do not make choices. Our choices are made for us; we are the poor. For those of us who live on reservations these choices and decisions are made by federal administrators, bureaucrats, and their "yes men," euphemistically called tribal governments. Those of us who live in non-reservation areas have our lives controlled by local white power elites. We have many rulers. They are called social workers, "cops," school teachers, churches, etc., and now o e o employees. They call us into meetings to tell us what is good for us and how they've programmed us, or they come into our homes to instruct us and their manners are not always what one would call polite by Indian standards or perhaps by any standards. We are rarely accorded respect as fellow human beings. Our children come home from school to us with shame in their hearts and a sneer on their lips for their home and parents. We are the "poverty problem" and that is true; and perhaps it is also true that our lack of reasonable choices, our lack of freedoms, our poverty of spirit is not unconnected with our material poverty.

The National Indian Youth Council realizes there is a great struggle going on in America now between those who want more "local" control of programs and those who would keep the power and the purse strings in the hands of the federal government. We are unconcerned with that struggle because we know that no one is arguing that the dispossessed, the poor, be given any control over their own destiny. The local white power elites who protest the loudest against federal control are the very ones who would keep us poor in spirit and worldly goods in order to enhance their own personal and economic station in the world.

Nor have those of us on reservations fared any better under the paternalistic control of federal administrations. In fact, we shudder at the specter of what seems to be the forming alliances in Indian areas between federal administrators and local elites. Some of us fear that this is the shape of things to come in the War on Poverty effort. Certainly, it is in those areas where such an alliance is taking place that the poverty program seems to be "working well." That is to say, it is in those areas of the country where the federal government is getting the least "static" and where federal money is being used to bolster the local power structure and local institutions. By "everybody being satisfied," I mean the people who count and the Indian or poor do not count.

Let us take the Head Start Program as an instance. We are told in the not-so-subtle racist vocabulary of the modern middle class that our children are "deprived." Exactly what they are deprived of seems to be unstated. We give our children love, warmth, and respect in our homes and the qualities necessary to be a warm human being. Perhaps many of them get into trouble in their teens because we have given them too much warmth, love, passion, and respect. Perhaps they have a hard time reconciling themselves to being a number on an IBM card. Nevertheless, many educators and politicians seem to assume that we, the poor, the Indians, are not capable of handling our own affairs and even raising our own children and that state institutions must do that job for us and take them away from us as soon as they can. My grandmother said last week, "Train your child well now for soon she will belong to her teacher and the schools." Many of our fears about the Head Start Program which we had from listening to the vocabulary of educators and their intentions were not justified, however. In our rural areas the program seems to have turned out to be just a federally subsidized kindergarten which no one seems to take too seriously. It has not turned out to be, as we feared, an attempt to "re-thread" the "twisted head" of the child from a poor home. Head Start, as a program, may not have fulfilled the expectations of elitist educators in our educational colleges, and the poor may not be ecstatic over the results, but local powers are overjoyed. This is the one program which has not upset any one's apple cart and which has strengthened local institutions in an acceptable manner, acceptable at least to our local "patrons."

Fifty years ago the federal government came into our communities and by force carried most of our children away to distant boarding schools. My father and many of my generation lived their childhoods in an almost prison-like atmosphere. Many returned unable even to speak their own language. Some returned to become drunks. Most of them had become white haters or that most pathetic of all modern Indians — Indian haters. Very few ever became more than very confused, ambivalent, and immobilized individuals — never able to reconcile the tensions and contradictions built inside themselves by outside institutions. As you can imagine, we have little faith in such kinds of federal programs devised for our betterment nor do we see education as a panacea for all ills. In recent days, however, some of us have been thinking that perhaps the damage done to our communities by forced assimilation and directed acculturative programs was minor compared to the situation in which our children now find themselves. There is a whole generation of Indian children who are growing up in the American school system. They still look to their relatives, my generation, and my father's to see if they are worthy people. But their judgment and definition of what is worthy is now the judgment most Americans make. They judge worthiness as competence and competence as worthiness. And I am afraid me and my fathers do not fare well in the light of this situation and judgment. Our children are learning that their people are not worthy and thus that they individually are not worthy. Even if by some stroke of good fortune, prosperity was handed to us "on a platter," that still would not soften the negative judgment our youngsters have of their people and themselves. As you know, people who feel themselves to be unworthy and feel they cannot escape this unworthiness turn to drink and crime and self-destructive acts. Unless there is some way that we as Indian individuals and communities can prove ourselves competent and worthy in the eyes of our youngsters there will be a generation of Indians growing to adulthood whose reaction to their situation will make previous social ills seem like a Sunday School picnic.

For the sake of our children, for the sake of the spiritual and material well-being of our total community we must be able to demonstrate competence to ourselves. For the sake of our psychic stability as well as our physical well-being we must be free men and exercise free choices. We must make decisions about our own destinies. We must be able to learn and profit by our own mistakes. Only then can we become competent and prosperous communities. We must be free in the most literal sense of the word — not sold or coerced into accepting programs for our own good, not of our own making or choice. Too much of what passes for "grassroots democracy" on the American scene is really a slick job of salesmanship. It is not hard for sophisticated administrators to sell tinsel and glitter programs to simple people — programs which are not theirs, which they do not understand, and which cannot but ultimately fail and contribute to already strong feelings of inadequacy. Community development must be just what the word implies, Community Development. It cannot be packaged programs wheeled into Indian communities by outsiders which Indians can "buy" or once again brand themselves as unprogressive if they do not "cooperate." Even the best of outside programs suffer from one very large defect — if the program falters helpful outsiders too often step in to smooth over the rough spots. At that point any program ceases to belong to the people involved and ceases to be a learning experience for them. Programs must be Indian creations, Indian choices, Indian experiences. Even the failures must be Indian experiences because only then will Indians understand why a program failed and not blame themselves for some personal inadequacy. A better program built upon the failure of an old program is the path of progress. But to achieve this experience, competence, worthiness, sense of achievement, and the resultant material prosperity Indians must have the responsibility in the ultimate sense of the word. Indians must be free in the sense that other more prosperous Americans are free. Freedom and prosperity are different sides of the same coin and there can be no freedom without complete responsibility. And I do not mean the fictional responsibility and democracy of passive consumers of programs; programs which emanate from and whose responsibility for success rests in the hands of outsiders — be they federal administrators or local white elitist groups.

Many of our young people are captivated by the lure of the American city with its excitement and promise of unlimited opportunity. But even if educated they come from powerless and inexperienced communities and many times carry with them a strong sense of unworthiness. For many of them the promise of opportunity ends in the gutter on the skid rows of Los Angeles and Chicago. They should and must be given a better chance to take advantage of the opportunities they have. They must grow up in a decent community with a strong sense of personal adequacy and competence.

America cannot afford to have whole areas and communities of people in such dire social and economic circumstances. Not only for her economic well-being but for her moral well-being as well. America has given a great social and moral message to the world and demonstrated (perhaps not forcefully enough) that freedom and responsibility as an ethic is inseparable from and, in fact, the "cause" of the fabulous American standard of living. America has not however been diligent enough in promulgating this philosophy within her own borders. American Indians need to be given this freedom and responsibility which most Americans assume as their birthright. Only then will poverty and powerlessness cease to hang like the sword of Damocles over our heads stifling us. Only then can we enjoy the fruits of the American system and become participating citizens — Indian Americans rather than American Indians.

Perhaps, the National Indian Youth Council's real criticism is against a structure created by bureaucratic administrators who are caught in this American myth that all people assimilate into American society, that economics dictates assimilation and integration. From the experience of the National Indian Youth Council, and in reality, we cannot emphasize and recommend strongly enough the fact that no one integrates and disappears into American society. What ethnic groups do is not integrate into American society and economy individually, but enter into the mainstream of American society as a people, and in particular as communities of people. The solution to Indian poverty is not "government programs" but in the competence of the person and his people. The real solution to poverty is encouraging the competence of the community as a whole.

[The] National Indian Youth Council recommends for "openers" that to really give these people, "the poor, the dispossessed, the Indians," complete freedom and responsibility is to let it become a reality not a much-heard-about dream and let the poor decide for once, what is best for themselves. . . .

American Indian Warriors:
Fishing Rights and the Vietnam War

Statements of Sidney Mills and Woodie Kipp

1968 and 1973

The struggle over fishing rights in the Pacific Northwest during the mid-1960s marked the early stirrings of the Red Power national Indian activist movement of the late 1960s and early 1970s. The "fish-ins" of this period were a response to a 1957 Washington Supreme Court decision in which the court split four to four over the case of Robert Satiacum, a Puyallup and Yakama who had been arrested for fishing steelhead out of season with fixed gill nets. On the basis of this decision, Washington state and local law enforcement efforts to restrict tribal fishing activities escalated in the 1960s. As Indian fishermen continued to cast their nets, the fish-in movement was launched. Eventually the dispute over fishing rights reached the federal courts and the tribes prevailed, when, in 1974, Federal District Judge George H. Boldt interpreted the 1855 Camp Stevens treaty to mean that Indians and whites were to share equally all fishing rights.

For Sidney Mills, the son of a Yakama and a Cherokee, and an enrolled member of the Yakama tribe of Washington, who was also a private first class in the U.S. Army, the fishing rights struggle created an untenable situation. He was being asked to fight for his country in Vietnam to defend the rights of Vietnamese, yet the rights of his own people were being violated in the United States. Mills's comments reflect the growing bitterness shared by many Native American veterans and servicemen of the post–Second World War era, who saw themselves as warriors defending a country in which their own people were treated unjustly.

"I am a Yakama and Cherokee Indian, and a Man"
Sidney Mills
October 13, 1968

I am Yakama and Cherokee Indian, and a man. For two years and four months, I've been a soldier in the United States Army. I served in combat in Vietnam — until critically wounded. I recently made a decision and publicly declare it today — a decision of conscience, of commitment and allegiance.

I owe and swear first allegiance to Indian people in the sovereign rights of our many Tribes. Owing to this allegiance and the commitment it now draws me to, I HEREBY RENOUNCE FURTHER OBLIGATION IN SERVICE OR DUTY TO THE UNITED STATES ARMY.

My first obligation now lies with the Indian people fighting for the lawful Treaty Right to fish in usual and accustomed waters of the Nisqually, Columbia and other Rivers of the Pacific Northwest, and in serving them in this fight in any way possible.

Anyone fully aware of the facts and issues involved in this fight can understand that my decision is not difficult. What is difficult to understand is why these United States, and the State of Washington in particular, make it necessary for such decisions to be made. Why do the United States and the State of Washington command me to such a decision by their actions in seeking to effectively destroy the Indian people of this State and our way of life by denying rights that are essential to our existence?

This fight is real — as is the threat to Indian existence under the enforced policy objectives of the State of Washington, as permitted by the compromised position and abdication of responsibilities by the U.S. Government.

The defense of Indian people and a chosen way of life in this fight for unrelinquished fishing rights is more compelling and more demanding of my time and commitment than any duty to the U.S. military. I renounce, and no longer consider myself under, the authorities and jurisdiction of the U.S. Army.

I have served the United States in a less compelling struggle in Vietnam and will not be restricted from doing less for my people within the United States. The U.S. would have accepted sacrifice of my life in Vietnam in a less legitimate cause — in fact, nearly secured such sacrifice and would have honored such death. Yet I have my life and am now prepared to stand in another battle, a cause to which the United States owes its protection, a fight for people who the United States has instead abandoned. My action is taken with the knowledge that the Nation that would have accepted an honored death by its requirement may now offer only severe consequence and punishment because I now choose to commit my life to Indian people. I have given enough to the U.S. Army — I choose now to serve my people.

My decision is influenced by the fact that we have already buried Indian fishermen returned dead from Vietnam, while Indian fishermen live here without protection and under steady attack from the power processes of this Nation and the States of Washington and Oregon. I note that less than a month ago, we counted the death of another Indian fisherman, Jimmy Alexander, because of the conditions imposed upon our people to secure a livelihood while avoiding arrest. These conditions continued off Cook's Landing on the Columbia River, where Jimmy drowned, largely because the President of the United States ignored a direct appeal to intervene in the arrest case of Army Sergeant Richard Sohappy, a friend and fellow fisherman of Jimmy Alexander.

Sergeant Sohappy is back in Vietnam on his third tour of duty there. He was arrested three times in June for illegal net fishing, while home on recuperative furlough recovering from his fourth series of combat wounds and while attempting to secure income for his large family. For his stand in Vietnam, this Nation awarded him a Silver Star and Bronze Star, among others. For fighting for his family and people, this Nation permitted a professional barber acting as Justice of the Peace to interpret his Treaty, to ignore his rights, and to impose punishment and record under criminal conviction. His Commander-in-Chief, Lyndon Johnson, routinely referred the appeal for intervention to the Department of Interior, which routinely refused to act on basis of false information and facts — and on basis of a presumption of guilt on the part of Sergeant Sohappy. He now continues to fight for this Nation in Vietnam, his fellow Yakama tribesman Jimmy Alexander is dead, and the United States stands indifferent while his people and their rights are destroyed.

Equally, I have been influenced by the fact that many Indian women and children have become obligated by conditions and necessity to sustain a major burden in this fight. These women and children have sustained some of the most brutal and mercenary attacks upon their lives and persons that have been suffered by any Indian people since prior Indian wars.

Just three years ago today, on October 13, 1965, 19 women and children were brutalized by more than 45 armed agents of the State of Washington at Frank's Landing on the Nisqually River in a vicious, unwarranted attack. It is not that this is the anniversary of that occasion that brings us here or which prompts my declaration on this day — but rather the fact that such actions have gained a frequency in occurrence and have come to be an everyday expectation in their lives. As recently as last night, we have witnessed the beating or injury of women simply because they are among the limited numbers who will not surrender our limited rights.

This consideration, as much as any, gives immediacy to my decision and prompts me to act upon it now. I will not be among those who draw pride from a past in which I had no part nor from a proud heritage I will not uphold. We must give of ourselves today — and I will not be content to have women or children fighting in my stead. At the least, I will be among them — at the least, they will not be alone.

The disturbing question is, "Why must our Indian people fight?"

Why can't an Al Bridges or Lewis Squally fish on the Nisqually without placing their lives and property in jeopardy, when 45,000 non-Indian citizens of this State draw their income from the commercial salmon industry? Why can't a Bob Satiacum or Frankie Mounts continue their ancestral way of life in fishing, when 500,000 sports fishermen pleasure themselves upon this resource? Why must the life patterns of a Richard Sohappy be altered and the subsistence of a family be denied, when two to three times the total annual salmon catch by Indians of this State are alone escaping past Bonneville Dam and as many being caught by non-Indians below it? Why must a Jimmy Alexander lose his life under unnatural conditions, when non-Indians were able to catch 11,000,000 salmon to the Indians' half million in the last year before restrictions were enforceably imposed upon my people?

Is it because the U.S. Constitution, which declares all Treaties made to be the Supreme Law of the Land and contradictory state laws void, is almost 200 years old? But treaties are still being made under force of that document. Or, is it because the Indian Treaties involved here are slightly more than one hundred? Or is it because the non-Indian population has increased in that century in this area from 3,900 to more than 3,000,000?

Citizenship for the Indian has too frequently been used as a convenience of government for deprivation of rights and property held owing to our being Indians. We did not generally become citizens of this Nation nor lawful residents of its States until June 2, 1924 — and not when all other people gained nationality and citizenship under the Fourteenth Amendment in 1868, the "due process" and "equal protection of law" amendment. Indians did not become citizens under this Act since it was immediately held in the U.S. Supreme Court that Indians were born unto the allegiance of their Tribes and not unto the allegiance of the United States. The granting of citizenship was not to act negatively upon Indian allegiance nor rights.

It is such first Allegiance that I now declare and embrace in making total commitment to the Indian Cause and the immediate fight for undiminished Fishing Rights.

There is no reason why Indian people should not be permitted to fish in the waters where these rights exist. There is no reason why Indians should spend their lives in the courts, in jail, or under the dominion of fear. There is no legitimate reason why this Nation and the State of Washington cannot respect the equitable interests and rights of Indian people and be responsive to our needs.

The oldest skeletal human remains ever found in the Western Hemisphere were recently uncovered on the banks of the Columbia River — the remains of Indian fishermen. What kind of government or society would spend millions of dollars to pick upon our bones, restore our ancestral life patterns, and protect our ancient remains from damage — while at the same time eating upon the flesh of our living people with power processes that hate our existence as Indians, and which would now destroy us and the way of life we now choose — and by all rights are entitled to live?

We will fight for these Rights and we will live our life!

Woodie Kipp, a member of the Blackfeet tribe, was also in the U.S. military service during the Vietnam War. The former marine found himself facing a different enemy when he went to Wounded Knee, South Dakota, in 1973 during the seventy-one-day siege on the Pine Ridge Reservation. Kipp found that his former allies were flying missions over the reservation and he and his fellow Indians on the ground were potential targets. He provides a chilling and ironic account of this realization and its meaning to him as an Indian and a man in this excerpt from *American Indian Culture and Research Journal*.

"The Eagles I Fed Who Did Not Love Me"
Woodie Kipp
1973

The two F4-B Phantom jets came in low, very low, at about two hundred feet, probably traveling at somewhere around five hundred miles an hour. Five hundred was just cruising speed for these birds. I had seen them go faster in Vietnam. I had seen them twist and turn and hurl fiery death toward the ground in the form of 250-, 500-, and 1,000-pound bombs.

They were, as we say in the Blackfeet, *stoonatopsi*, dangerous. For the twenty months I had spent as a support combat engineer with the First Marine Air Wing on the outskirts of the Vietnamese city of DaNang, the sleek killing machines had been on my side. Now they were not on my side; now they were hunting me. . . .

I guess I felt like the dog owner who feeds and coddles his Doberman Pinscher only to wake one day to find the dog at his throat. I had fed these machines so they could do their killing work in both North and South Vietnam. Now I could appreciate the terror felt by the Viet Cong and the North Vietnamese who were on the receiving end of these sleek, dangerous planes whose nose cone radar costs several million dollars. . . .

I was nineteen when I sailed for Vietnam on the U.S.S. *General John Mitchell*. I was told I was going to fight communist aggression. Nineteen-year-olds can be fed a lot of hype and they believe it. I attended school through high school in Cut Bank, Montana. In Cut Bank, we were taught that the communists were trying to take over the world and enslave us all. . . . It did not occur to me as an Indian youth that my people had already undergone enslavement. . . . The communists had replaced the local Blackfeet as the bogeyman. . . .

And now, here, on the Plains of the great Sioux Nation, in the current state of South Dakota, the fighter bombers, the F4-B Phantoms that I, for twenty long months, had identified with, were looking for me. I knew these birds of prey: They never make social calls; they're always business, always serious as a heart attack. They belong to my uncle. Sam. Hey, Uncle! Uncle Sam, look, it's me, your nephew Woody; it's me who fed your birds while you were negotiating or doing whatever it is you big shots do during a war. . . .

Actually, Uncle, I feel much closer to those ideals when I am fighting for my own people here in my home country, where I'm more sure about what the war is trying to accomplish. We Indians lack freedom. We know freedom because, before you came here, we lived freedom. It was a way of life, not just a buzzword to be used to decimate peoples because of their color or their beliefs. Granted, even before you sallied onto the scene we had wars. But in those wars, there was still an element of honor, of the sanctity of life created by the Great Mystery. In Vietnam, in your war zone, there was no honor.

This Country Was a Lot Better Off
When the Indians Were Running It

Vine Deloria Jr., March 8, 1970

The voices of the National Indian Youth Conference and Clyde Warrior were heard and heeded by Native Americans across the country, many of whom were stirred to action. This was a time of many struggles in the United States — for civil rights, against the Vietnam war; it was an era in which many groups took to the streets in an effort to redefine the places and the rights of women, youth, racial and ethnic groups, the disabled, gays and lesbians, the poor.

Native Americans had seen their land and their rights steadily eroded for centuries. By the 1960s, Indian country was reeling from the federal policy of "Termination," designed to end tribal treaty rights and assimilate Indians into the dominant U.S. culture. More than one hundred tribes had been terminated (the Klamaths, the Menominees, and the Alabama-Coushattas, among others), and both reservation and urban Indians saw no end to the loss of sovereignty and the threats to cultural survival. It was time for action. The fish-ins in the Pacific Northwest during the mid-1960s foretold of a larger, national Indian movement. That protest movement and a decade of activism were launched in the early morning hours of November 20, 1969, when "Indians of All Tribes" set out for Alcatraz Island. Their nineteen-month occupation was the beginning of the end of Termination and a major step toward Self-Determination.

Vine Deloria Jr., a Standing Rock Sioux, captured the spirit of that time in this essay, first published in the *New York Times Magazine* on March 8, 1970, at the height of the Alcatraz occupation. He articulates with eloquence, wit, and anger the attitudes, frustrations, and hopes of great numbers of Indians in every part of the country. The following article is Deloria's personal appraisal of the strengths and values that sustained the Indian people through dark days and that continued to support them as they caught the "scent of victory in the air."

On Nov. 9, 1969, a contingent of American Indians, led by Adam Nordwall, a Chippewa from Minnesota, and Richard Oakes, a Mohawk from New York, landed on Alcatraz Island in San Francisco Bay and claimed the 13-acre rock "by right of discovery." The island had been abandoned six and a half years ago, and although there had been various suggestions concerning its disposal nothing had been done to make use of the land. Since there are Federal treaties giving some tribes the right to abandoned Federal property within a tribe's original territory, the Indians of the Bay area felt that they could lay claim to the island.

For nearly a year the United Bay Area Council of American Indians, a confederation of urban Indian organizations, had been talking about submitting a bid for the island to use it as a West Coast Indian cultural center and vocational training headquarters. Then, on Nov. 1, the San Francisco American Indian Center burned down. The center had served an estimated 30,000 Indians in the immediate area and was the focus of activities of the urban Indian community. It became a matter of urgency after that and, as Adam Nordwall said, "it was GO." Another landing, on Nov. 20, by nearly 100 Indians in a swift midnight raid secured the island.

The new inhabitants have made "the Rock" a focal point symbolic of Indian people. Under extreme difficulty they have worked to begin repairing sanitary facilities and buildings. The population has been largely transient, many people have stopped by, looked the situation over for a few days, then gone home, unwilling to put in the tedious work necessary to make the island support a viable community.

The Alcatraz news stories are somewhat shocking to non-Indians. It is difficult for most Americans to comprehend that there still exists a living community of nearly one million Indians in this country. For many people, Indians have become a species of movie actor periodically dispatched to the Happy Hunting Grounds by John Wayne on the "Late, Late Show." Yet there are some 315 Indian tribal groups in 26 states still functioning as quasi-sovereign nations under treaty status; they range from the mammoth Navajo tribe of some 132,000 with 16 million acres of land to tiny Mission Creek of California with 15 people and a tiny parcel of property. There are over a half a million Indians in the cities alone, with the largest concentrations in San Francisco, Los Angeles, Minneapolis and Chicago.

The take-over of Alcatraz is to many Indian people a demonstration of pride in being Indian and a dignified, yet humorous protest against current conditions existing on the reservations and in the cities. It is this special pride and dignity, the determination to judge life according to one's own values, and the unconquerable conviction that the tribes will not die that has always characterized Indian people as I have known them.

I was born in Martin, a border town on the Pine Ridge Indian Reservation in South Dakota, in the midst of the Depression. My father was an

Indian missionary who served 18 chapels on the eastern half of the reservation. In 1934, when I was 1, the Indian Reorganization Act was passed, allowing Indian tribes full rights of self-government for the first time since the late eighteen-sixties. Ever since those days, when the Sioux had agreed to forsake the life of the hunter for that of the farmer, they had been systematically deprived of any voice in decisions affecting their lives and property. Tribal ceremonies and religious practices were forbidden. The reservation was fully controlled by men in Washington, most of whom had never visited a reservation and felt no urge to do so.

The first years on the reservations were extremely hard for the Sioux. Kept confined behind fences they were almost wholly dependent upon Government rations for their food supply. Many died of hunger and malnutrition. Game was scarce and few were allowed to have weapons for fear of another Indian war. In some years there was practically no food available. Other years rations were withheld until the men agreed to farm the tiny pieces of land each family had been given. In desperation many families were forced to eat stray dogs and cats to keep alive.

By World War I, however, many of the Sioux families had developed prosperous ranches. Then the Government stepped in, sold the Indians' cattle for wartime needs, and after the war leased the grazing land to whites, creating wealthy white ranchers and destitute Indian landlords.

With the passage of the Indian Reorganization Act, native ceremonies and practices were given full recognition by Federal authorities. My earliest memories are of trips along dusty roads to Kyle, a small settlement in the heart of the reservation, to attend the dances. Ancient men, veterans of battles even then considered footnotes to the settlement of the West, brought their costumes out of hiding and walked about the grounds gathering the honors they had earned half a century before. They danced as if the intervening 50 years had been a lost weekend from which they had fully recovered. I remember best Dewey Beard, then in his late 80's and a survivor of the Little Big Horn. Even at that late date Dewey was hesitant to speak of the battle for fear of reprisal. There was no doubt, as one watched the people's expressions, that the Sioux had survived their greatest ordeal and were ready to face whatever the future might bring.

In those days the reservation was isolated and unsettled. Dirt roads held the few mail routes together. One could easily get lost in the wild back country as roads turned into cowpaths without so much as a backward glance. Remote settlements such as Buzzard Basin and Cuny Table were nearly inaccessible. In the spring every bridge on the reservation would be washed out with the first rain and would remain out until late summer. But few people cared. Most of the reservation people, traveling by team and wagon, merely forded the creeks and continued their journey, almost contemptuous of the need for roads and bridges.

The most memorable event of my early childhood was visiting Wounded Knee where 200 Sioux, including women and children, were slaughtered in 1890 by troopers of the Seventh Cavalry in what is believed to have been a delayed act of vengeance for Custer's defeat. The people were simply lined up and shot down much as was allegedly done, according to newspaper reports, at Songmy. The wounded were left to die in a three-day Dakota blizzard, and when the soldiers returned to the scene after the storm some were still alive and were saved. The massacre was vividly etched in the minds of many of the older reservation people, but it was difficult to find anyone who wanted to talk about it.

Many times, over the years, my father would point out survivors of the massacre, and people on the reservation always went out of their way to help them. For a long time there was a bill in Congress to pay indemnities to the survivors, but the War Department always insisted that it had been a "battle" to stamp out the Ghost Dance religion among the Sioux. This does not, however, explain bayoneted Indian women and children found miles from the scene of the incident.

Strangely enough, the Depression was good for Indian reservations, particularly for the people at Pine Ridge. Since their lands had been leased to non-Indians by the Bureau of Indian Affairs, they had only a small rent check and the contempt of those who leased their lands to show for their ownership. But the Federal programs devised to solve the national economic crisis were also made available to Indian people, and there was work available for the first time in the history of the reservations.

The Civilian Conservation Corps set up a camp on the reservation and many Indians were hired under the program. In the canyons north of Allen, S.D., a beautiful buffalo pasture was built by the C.C.C., and the whole area was transformed into a recreation wonderland. Indians would come from miles around to see the buffalo and leave with a strange look in their eyes. Many times I stood silently watching while old men talked to the buffalo about the old days. They would conclude by singing a song before respectfully departing, their eyes filled with tears and their minds occupied with the memories of other times and places. It was difficult to determine who was the captive — the buffalo fenced in or the Indian fenced out.

While the rest of America suffered from the temporary deprivation of its luxuries, Indian people had a period of prosperity, as it were. Paychecks were regular. Small cattle herds were started, cars were purchased, new clothes and necessities became available. To a people who had struggled along on $50 cash income per year, the C.C.C. was the greatest program ever to come along. The Sioux had climbed from absolute deprivation to mere poverty, and this was the best time the reservation ever had.

World War II ended this temporary prosperity. The C.C.C. camps were closed; reservation programs were cut to the bone and social services became virtually nonexistent; "Victory gardens" were suddenly the style, and people began to be aware that a great war was being waged overseas.

The war dispersed the reservation people as nothing ever had. Every day, it seemed, we would be bidding farewell to families as they headed west to work in the defense plants on the Coast.

A great number of Sioux people went west and many of the Sioux on Alcatraz today are their children and relatives. There may now be as many Sioux in California as there are on the reservations in South Dakota because of the great wartime migration.

Those who stayed on the reservation had the war brought directly to their doorstep when they were notified that their sons had to go across the seas and fight. Busloads of Sioux boys left the reservation for parts unknown. In many cases even the trip to nearby Martin was a new experience for them, let alone training in Texas, California or Colorado. There were always going-away ceremonies conducted by the older people who admonished the boys to uphold the old tribal traditions and not to fear death. It was not death they feared but living with an unknown people in a distant place.

I was always disappointed with the Government's way of handling Indian servicemen. Indians were simply lost in the shuffle of 3 million men in uniform. Many boys came home on furlough and feared to return. They were not cowards in any sense of the word but the loneliness and boredom of stateside duty was crushing their spirits. They spent months without seeing another Indian. If the Government had recruited all-Indian outfits it would have easily solved this problem and also had the best fighting units in the world at its disposal. I often wonder what an all-Sioux or Apache company, painted and singing its songs, would have done to the morale of élite German panzer units.

After the war Indian veterans straggled back to the reservations and tried to pick up their lives. It was very difficult for them to resume a life of poverty after having seen the affluent outside world. Some spent a few days with the old folks and then left again for the big cities. Over the years they have emerged as leaders of the urban Indian movement. Many of their children are the nationalists of today who are adamant about keeping the reservations they have visited only on vacations. Other veterans stayed on the reservations and entered tribal politics.

The reservations radically changed after the war. During the Depression there were about five telephones in Martin. If there was a call for you, the man at the hardware store had to come down to your house and get you to answer it. A couple of years after the war a complete dial system was installed that extended to most of the smaller communities on the reservation. Families that had been hundreds of miles from any form of communication were now only minutes away from a telephone.

Roads were built connecting the major communities of the Pine Ridge country. No longer did it take hours to go from one place to another. With these kinds of roads everyone had to have a car. The team and wagon vanished, except for those families who lived at various "camps" in inaccessible canyons pretty much as their ancestors had. (Today, even they have adopted the automobile for traveling long distances in search of work.)

I left the reservation in 1951 when my family moved to Iowa. I went back only once for an extended stay, in the summer of 1955, while on a furlough, and after that I visited only occasionally during summer vacations. In the meantime, I attended college, served a hitch in the Marines, and went to the seminary. After I graduated from the seminary, I took a job with the United Scholarship Service, a private organization devoted to the college and secondary-school education of American Indian and Mexican students. I had spent my last two years of high school in an Eastern preparatory school and so was probably the only Indian my age who knew what an independent Eastern school was like. As the program developed, we soon had some 30 students placed in Eastern schools.

I insisted that all the students who entered the program be able to qualify for scholarships as students and not simply as Indians. I was pretty sure we could beat the white man at his own educational game, which seemed to me the only way to gain his respect. I was soon to find that this was a dangerous attitude to have. The very people who were supporting the program — non-Indians in the national church establishments — accused me of trying to form a colonialist "élite" by insisting that only kids with strong test scores and academic patterns be sent east to school.

They wanted to continue the ancient pattern of soft-hearted paternalism toward Indians. I didn't feel we should cry our way into the schools; that sympathy would destroy the students we were trying to help.

In 1964, while attending the annual convention of the National Congress of American Indians, I was elected its executive director. I learned more about life in the N.C.A.I. in three years than I had in the previous 30. Every conceivable problem that could occur in an Indian society was suddenly thrust at me from 315 different directions. I discovered that I was one of the people who were supposed to solve the problems. The only trouble was that Indian people locally and on the national level were being played off one against the other by clever whites who had either ego or income at stake. While there were many feasible solutions, few could be tried without whites with vested interests working night and day to destroy the unity we were seeking on a national basis.

In the mid-nineteen sixties, the whole generation that had grown up after World War II and had left the reservations during the fifties to get an education was returning to Indian life as "educated Indians." But we soon knew better. Tribal societies had existed for centuries without going outside themselves for education and information. Yet many of us thought that we would be able to improve the traditional tribal methods. We were wrong.

For three years we ran around the conference circuit attending numerous meetings called to "solve" the Indian problems. We listened to and spoke with anthropologists, historians, sociologists, psychologists, economists, educators and missionaries. We worked with many Government agencies and with every conceivable doctrine, idea and program ever created. At the end of this happy round of consultations the reservation people were still plodding along on their own time schedule, doing the things they considered important. They continued to solve their problems their way in spite of the advice given them by "Indian experts."

By 1967 there was a radical change in thinking on the part of many of us. Conferences were proving unproductive. Where non-Indians had been pushed out to make room for Indian people, they had wormed their way back into power and again controlled the major programs serving Indians. The poverty programs, reservation and university technical assistance groups were dominated by whites who had pushed Indian administrators aside.

Reservation people, meanwhile, were making steady progress in spite of the numerous setbacks suffered by the national Indian community. So, in large part, younger Indian leaders who had been playing the national conference field began working at the local level to build community movements from the ground up. By consolidating local organizations into power groups they felt that they would be in a better position to influence national thinking.

Robert Hunter, director of the Nevada Intertribal Council, had already begun to build a strong state organization of tribes and communities. In South Dakota, Gerald One Feather, Frank LaPointe and Ray Briggs formed the American Indian Leadership Conference, which quickly welded the educated young Sioux in that state into a strong regional organization active in nearly every phase of Sioux life. Gerald is now running for the prestigious post of Chairman of the Oglala Sioux, the largest Sioux tribe, numbering some 15,000 members. Ernie Stevens, an Oneida from Wisconsin and Lee Cook, a Chippewa from Minnesota, developed a strong program for economic and community development in Arizona. Just recently Ernie has moved into the post of director of the California Intertribal Council, a statewide organization representing some 130,000 California Indians in cities and on the scattered reservations of that state.

By the fall of 1967, it was apparent that the national Indian scene was collapsing in favor of strong regional organizations, although the major national organizations such as the National Congress of American Indians and the National Indian Youth Council continued to grow. There was yet another factor emerging on the Indian scene: the old-timers of the Depression days had educated a group of younger Indians in the old ways and these people were now becoming a major force in Indian life. Led by Thomas Banyaca of the Hopi, Mad Bear Anderson of the Tuscaroras, Clifton Hill of the Creeks, and Rolling Thunder of the Shoshones, the traditional Indians were forcing the whole Indian community to rethink its understanding of Indian life.

The message of the traditionalists is simple. They demand a return to basic Indian philosophy, establishment of ancient methods of government by open council instead of elected officials, a revival of Indian religions and replacement of white laws with Indian customs; in short, a complete return to the ways of the old people. In an age dominated by tribalizing communications media, their message makes a great deal of sense.

But in some areas their thinking is opposed to that of the National Congress of American Indians, which represents officially elected tribal governments organized under the Indian Reorganization Act as Federal corporations. The contemporary problem is therefore one of defining the meaning of "tribe." Is it a traditionally organized band of Indians following customs with medicine men and chiefs dominating the policies of the tribe, or is it a modern corporate structure attempting to compromise at least in part with modern white culture?

The problem has been complicated by private foundations' and Government agencies' funding of Indian programs. In general this process, although it has brought a great amount of money into Indian country, has been one of cooptation. Government agencies must justify their appropriation requests every year and can only take chances on spectacular programs that will serve as showcases of progress. They are not willing to invest the capital funds necessary to build viable self-supporting communities on the reservations, because these programs do not have an immediate publicity potential. Thus, the Government agencies are forever committed to conducting conferences to discover that one "key" to Indian life that will give them the edge over their rival agencies in the annual appropriations derby.

Churches and foundations have merely purchased an Indian leader or program that conforms with their ideas of what Indian people should be doing. The large foundations have bought up the well-dressed, handsome "new image" Indian who is comfortable in the big cities but virtually helpless at an Indian meeting. Churches have given money to Indians who have been willing to copy black militant activist tactics, and the more violent and insulting the Indian can be, the more the churches seem to love it. They are wallowing in self-guilt and piety over the lot of the poor yet funding demagogues of their own choosing to speak for the poor.

I did not run for re-election as executive director of the N.C.A.I. in the fall of 1967, but entered law school at the University of Colorado instead. It was apparent to me that the Indian revolution was well under way and that someone had better get a legal education so that we could have our own legal program for defense of Indian treaty rights. Thanks to a Ford Foundation program, nearly 50 Indians are now in law school, assuring the Indian community of legal talent in the years ahead. Within four years I foresee another radical shift in Indian leadership patterns as the growing local movements are affected by the new Indian lawyers.

There is an increasing scent of victory in the air in Indian country these days. The mood is comparable to the old days of the Depression when the men began to dance once again. As the Indian movement gathers momentum and individual Indians cast their lot with the tribe, it will become apparent that not only will Indians survive the electronic world of Marshall McLuhan, they will thrive in it. At the present time everyone is watching how mainstream America will handle the issues of pollution, poverty, crime and racism when it does not fundamentally understand the issues. Knowing the importance of tribal survival, Indian people are speaking more and more of sovereignty, of the great political technique of the open council, and of the need for gaining the community's consensus on all programs before putting them into effect.

One can watch this same issue emerge in white society as the "Woodstock Nation," the "Blackstone Nation" and the block organizations are developed. This is a full tribalizing process involving a nontribal people, and it is apparent that some people are frightened by it. But it is the kind of social phenomenon upon which Indians feast.

In 1965 I had a long conversation with an old Papago. I was trying to get the tribe to pay its dues to the National Congress of American Indians and I had asked him to speak to the tribal council for me. He said that he would but that the Papagos didn't really need the N.C.A.I. They were like, he told me, the old mountain in the distance. The Spanish had come and dominated them for 300 years and then left. The Mexicans had come and ruled them for a century, but they also left. "The Americans," he said, "have been here only about 80 years. They, too, will vanish but the Papagos and the mountain will always be here."

This attitude and understanding of life is what American society is searching for.

I wish the Government would give Alcatraz to the Indians now occupying it. They want to create five centers on the island. One center would be for a North American studies program; another would be a spiritual and medical center where Indian religions and medicines would be used and studied. A third center would concentrate on ecological studies based on an Indian view of nature — that man should live *with* the land and not simply *on* it. A job-training center and a museum would also be founded on the island. Certain of these programs would obviously require Federal assistance.

Some people may object to this approach, yet Health, Education and Welfare gave out $10 million last year to non-Indians to study Indians. Not one single dollar went to an Indian scholar or researcher to present the point of view of Indian people. And the studies done by non-Indians added nothing to what was already known about Indians.

Indian people have managed to maintain a viable and cohesive social order in spite of everything the non-Indian society has thrown at them in an effort to break the tribal structure. At the same time, non-Indian society has created a monstrosity of a culture where people starve while the granaries are filled and the sun can never break through the smog.

By making Alcatraz an experimental Indian center operated and planned by Indian people, we would be given a chance to see what we could do toward developing answers to modern social problems. Ancient tribalism can be incorporated with modern technology in an urban setting. Perhaps we would not succeed in the effort, but the Government is spending billions every year and still the situation is rapidly growing worse. It just seems to a lot of Indians that this continent was a lot better off when we were running it.

The Occupation of Alcatraz Island

Indians of All Tribes, 1969–1971

The American Indian occupiers and visitors to Alcatraz Island during the nineteen-month occupation represented a large number of Indian tribes, including Indian people from reservations as well as the cities. An intertribal community was established on the island, and the occupiers issued proclamations, held news conferences, powwows, and celebrations, and negotiated with federal officials for possession of the island to establish Indian educational and cultural centers. In the beginning months of the occupation, workers from the San Francisco Indian Center gathered food and supplies on the mainland and transported them to Alcatraz Island. However, as time went by, the occupying force, which generally numbered around one hundred, confronted increasing hardship as federal officials interfered with delivery boats and cut off the supply of water and electricity to the island and as tensions on the island grew.

The negotiations between Indians of All Tribes and the federal government eventually collapsed, and Alcatraz Island was never developed in accordance with the goals of Indian protesters. Despite the occupiers' failure to achieve their demands, the Alcatraz occupation captured the attention and imagination of many Native Americans, some of whom visited the island, as well as others who watched from a distance, awed by the power and vision of the occupiers. These native visitors and observers described the impact of the occupation on their lives and on Indian identity and pride:

> Every once in a while something happens that can alter the whole shape of a people's history. This only happens once in a generation or lifetime. The importance is that Alcatraz had a power to begin fundamental change. The big one was Alcatraz. (George Horse Capture, Gros Ventre)
>
> The movement gave me back my dignity and gave Indian people back their dignity. It started with Alcatraz, we got back our worth, our pride, our dignity, our humanity. If you have your dignity and your spirituality and you can pray, then you can wear a tie, carry a briefcase, work a job. If you don't have those things, then you are lost. (Lenny Foster, Navajo)
>
> I experienced the excitement of it all — the good feelings — the excitement of seeing and watching your people put their heads up. Before that you were not having that. You had full-bloods claiming they were half-bloods, half-bloods claiming they were quarter-bloods, quarter-bloods

claiming they were white. Power wasn't the feeling with me. It was more a sense of pride. (Leonard Peltier, Chippewa)

Many American Indians who reflected back on the Alcatraz occupation described it as the spark that ignited a flame that burned bright across Indian country, lighting many paths — to demand an end to Termination and the honoring of treaty rights, to return to traditional and spiritual ways, to rebuild and revitalize Indian communities:

Alcatraz was the rekindling of the spirit of native people. It reminds me of a flame that kind of died down, and was at just a very low, low flame. The flame never went out. And Alcatraz sort of relit that and out of that fire came all these different people, spread in all the different directions to do incredible work. The people from Alcatraz have had a profound impact on the lives of people throughout this country. (Wilma Mankiller, Cherokee)

The largest thing that I saw as a spiritual value to Alcatraz is that it revitalized our individual spirits when we went there. For me it was like going home. So there was that spiritual revitalization for us. Again, all of a sudden, we're together. We see that we're not as alone as it appeared that we were, and that we have our abilities, and here we are, we're the disenfranchised, but we can make a school, we can make a clinic, we can do the things they say we can't do. What ended up happening with Alcatraz, it's just the way that this flame roared — it brought heat, it brought warmth back to the collective spirit of us as a people. It was like a revitalization and a re-energizing. (John Trudell, Santee Sioux)

Indians of All Tribes
November 1969

PROCLAMATION:

To the Great White Father and All His People:

We, the native Americans, re-claim the land known as Alcatraz Island in the name of all American Indians by right of discovery.

We wish to be fair and honorable in our dealings with the Caucasian inhabitants of this land, and hereby offer the following treaty:

We will purchase said Alcatraz Island for twenty-four dollars ($24) in glass beads and red cloth, a precedent set by the white man's purchase of a similar island about 300 years ago. We know that $24 in trade goods for these 16 acres is more than was paid when Manhattan Island was sold, but we know that land values have risen over the years. Our offer of $1.24 per acre is greater than the 47 cents per acre the white men are now paying the California Indians for their land.

We will give to the inhabitants of this island a portion of that land for their own, to be held in trust by the American Indian Government — for as long as the sun shall rise and the rivers go down to the sea — to be administered by the Bureau of Caucasian Affairs (BCA). We will further guide the inhabitants in the proper way of living. We will offer them our religion, our education, our life-ways, in order to help them achieve our level of civilization and thus raise them and all their white brothers up from their savage and unhappy state. We offer this treaty in good faith and wish to be fair and honorable in our dealings with all white men.

We feel that this so-called Alcatraz Island is more than suitable for an Indian Reservation, as determined by the white man's own standards. By this we mean that this place resembles most Indian reservations, in that:

1. It is isolated from modern facilities, and without adequate means of transportation.
2. It has no fresh running water.
3. It has inadequate sanitation facilities.
4. There are no oil or mineral rights.
5. There is no industry so unemployment is great.
6. There are no health care facilities.
7. The soil is rocky and non-productive; and the land does not support game.
8. There are no educational facilities.
9. The population has always exceeded the land base.
10. The population has always been held as prisoners and kept dependent upon others.

Further, it would be fitting and symbolic that ships from all over the world, entering the Golden Gate, would first see Indian land, and thus be reminded of the true history of this nation. This tiny island would be a symbol of the great lands once ruled by free and noble Indians.

USE TO BE MADE OF ALCATRAZ ISLAND

What use will be made of this land?
Since the San Francisco Indian Center burned down, there is no place

for Indians to assemble and carry on our tribal life here in the white man's city. Therefore, we plan to develop on this island several Indian institutes:

1. A Center for Native American Studies will be developed which will train our young people in the best of our native cultural arts and sciences, as well as educate them to the skills and knowledge relevant to improve the lives and spirits of all Indian peoples. Attached to this center will be traveling universities, managed by Indians, which will go to the Indian Reservations in order to learn the traditional values from the people, which are now absent in the Caucasian higher educational system.

2. An American Indian Spiritual center will be developed which will practice our ancient tribal religious ceremonies and medicine. Our cultural arts will be featured and our young people trained in music, dance, and medicine.

3. An Indian center of Ecology will be built which will train and support our young people in scientific research and practice in order to restore our lands and waters to their pure and natural state. We will seek to de-pollute the air and the water of the Bay Area. We will seek to restore fish and animal life, and to revitalize sea life which has been threatened by the white man's way. Facilities will be developed to desalt sea water for human use.

4. A Great Indian Training School will be developed to teach our peoples how to make a living in the world, improve our standards of living, and end hunger and unemployment among all our peoples. This training school will include a center for Indian arts and crafts, and an Indian Restaurant serving native foods and training Indians in culinary arts. This center will display Indian arts and offer the Indian foods of all tribes to the public, so they all may know of the beauty and spirit of the traditional Indian ways.

5. Some of the present buildings will be taken over to develop an American Indian Museum, which will depict our native foods and other cultural contributions we have given to all the world. Another part of the Museum will present some of the things the white man has given to the Indians, in return for the land and the life he took: disease, alcohol, poverty, and cultural decimation (as symbolized by old tin cans, barbed wire, rubber tires, plastic containers, etc.). Part of the museum will remain a dungeon, to symbolize both Indian captives who were incarcerated for challenging white authority, and those who were imprisoned on reservations. The Museum will show the noble and the tragic events of Indian history, including the broken treaties, the documentary of the Trail of

Tears, the Massacre of Wounded Knee, as well as the victory over Yellow-Hair Custer and his army.

In the name of all Indians, therefore, we re-claim this island for Indian nations, for all these reasons. We feel this claim is just and proper, and that this land should rightfully be granted to us for as long as the rivers shall run and the sun shall shine.

SIGNED,

INDIANS OF ALL TRIBES

November 1969

San Francisco, California

The Twenty-Point Proposal of
Native Americans on the Trail of
Broken Treaties
Washington DC, October 1972

The end of the Alcatraz occupation in June 1971 marked the beginning of nearly a decade of Red Power activism. Immediately following Alcatraz, there were a number of occupations of federal property around the country — at Fort Lawton and Fort Lewis in Washington State, at Ellis Island in New York, at the Twin Cities Naval Air Station in Minneapolis, at former Nike Missile sites on Lake Michigan near Chicago, at Argonne, Illinois, and in Beverly Hills, California, at an abandoned Coast Guard lifeboat station in Milwaukee, and at an unused army communications center in Davis, California. A number of protest camps were also established during the early 1970s, including those at Mount Rushmore and the Badlands National Monument. During the same years, government buildings also became the sites of protest — at regional Bureau of Indian Affairs offices in San Diego, San Francisco, Missoula, Billings, Phoenix, Cleveland, Denver, Spokane, and Seattle, as well as the main headquarters of the BIA in Washington DC in 1971 and again in 1972.

The second, 1972, occupation of the BIA occurred at the end of the next major protest event after the Alcatraz occupation — "The Trail of Broken Treaties." The Trail began in the fall of 1972, when a caravan of Indian activists departed from California for Washington DC, planning to arrive in late October, just before the 1972 U.S. presidential election, in order to draw national attention to the grievances of Native Americans. On its cross-country journey Trail activists stopped at many reservations and urban Indian communities. The spirit of Alcatraz was felt by Trail participants and observers alike. Frances Wise, a Waco-Caddo from Oklahoma, traveled with the caravan en route to Washington DC:

> Many of the people with us were like me before Alcatraz. They didn't quite understand what was going on, but they were interested. A lot of people joined us. I remember driving around a freeway cloverleaf outside of Columbus, Ohio. All I could see were cars in front of us and behind us, their lights on, red banners flying from their antennas. It was hard to believe, really. We were that strong. We were really doing something. It was exciting and fulfilling. It's like someone who's been in bondage. Indian country knew that Indians were on the move.

When the activists reached Washington, their arrangements for accommodations fell through and they headed for the Bureau of Indian Affairs building and ended up staying there for a week! The Trail of Broken Treaties and the week-long occupation of the Bureau of Indian Affairs provided a forum for putting forth the activists' plan for federal Indian policy reform. Vine Deloria Jr. complimented their "Twenty Point Proposal":

> The Trail of Broken Treaties came along in the fall of 1972. By that time, the activists had devised the Twenty Points, which in my opinion, is the best summary document of reforms put forth in this century. Written primarily by Hank Adams, who supervised the fishing rights struggle until the Supreme Court ruled in favor of Indians, it is comprehensive and philosophical and has broad policy lines that can still be adopted to create some sense of fairness and symmetry in federal Indian policy.

A SUMMARY OF THE TWENTY POINTS

1. Restoration of Constitutional Treaty-making Authority: This would force federal recognition of each Indian nation's sovereignty.

2. Establishment of a Treaty Commission to Make New Treaties: Re-establishes all existing treaties, affirms a national commitment to the future of Indian people, and ensures that all Indians are governed by treaty relations without exception.

3. An Address to the American People and Joint Sessions of Congress: This would allow us to state our political and cultural cases to the whole nation on television.

4. Commission to Review Treaty Commitments and Violations: Treaty-based lawsuits had cost Indian people more than $40 million in the last decade alone, yet Indian people remain virtual prisoners in the nation's courtrooms, being forced constantly to define our rights. There is less need for more attorney assistance than for an institution of protections that reduce violations and minimize the possibilities for attacks on Indian rights.

5. Resubmission of Unratified Treaties to the Senate: Many nations, especially those in California, have made treaties that were never ratified. Treaty status should be formalized for every nation.

6. All Indians To Be Governed by Treaty Relations: Covers any exceptions to points 1, 2, and 5.

7. Mandatory Relief against Treaty Violations: Federal courts to automatically issue injunctions against non-Indians who violate treaties, eliminating costly legal delays.

8. Judicial Recognition of Indian Rights to Interpret Treaties: A new law requiring the U.S. Supreme Court to hear Indian appeals arising from treaty violations.

9. Creation of Congressional Joint Committee on Reconstruction of Indian Relations: Reconfigurement of all committees dealing with Indian affairs into a single entity.

10. Land Reform and Restoration of a 110-million-acre Native Land Base: Termination of all Indian land leases, reversion of all non-Indian titles to land reservations, consolidation of all reservation natural resources under local Indian control.

11. Restoration of Rights to Indians Terminated by Enrollment and Revocation of Prohibition against "Dual Benefits": An end to minimum standards of "tribal blood" for citizenship in any Indian nation, which serves to keep people with mixed Indian ancestors from claiming either heritage.

12. Repeal of State Laws Enacted under Public Law 280: Eliminates all state powers over Indians, thereby ending disputes over jurisdiction and sovereignty.

13. Resume Federal Protective Jurisdiction over Offenses against Indians: Since state and local courts have rarely been able to convict non-Indians of crimes against Indians, Indian grand juries should have the power to indict violators, who will then be tried in federal courts.

14. Abolition of the Bureau of Indian Affairs: The BIA is so much a prisoner of its past that it can never be expected to meet the needs of Indians. Better to start over with an organization designed to meet requirements of new treaties.

15. Creation of an Office of Federal Indian Relations and Community Reconstruction: With one thousand employees or fewer, this agency would report directly to the president and preserve equality between Indians and the federal government.

16. Priorities and Purpose of the Proposed New Office: The previous agency would address the breakdown in the constitutionally prescribed relationship between the United States and the Indian nations.

17. Indian Commerce and Tax Immunities: Eliminate constant struggles between Indian nations and the states over taxation by removing states' authority for taxation on reservations.

18. Protection of Indian Religious Freedom and Cultural Integrity: Legal protection must be extended to Indian religious expression, and existing statutes do not do this.

19. National Referendums, Local Options, and Forms of Indian Organization: An appeal to restrict the number of Indian organizations and to consolidate leadership at every level.

20. Health, Housing, Employment, Economic Development, and Education: Increased funding, better management, and local control.

Demands of the
Independent Oglala Nation
Wounded Knee, South Dakota, March 1973

Despite its symbolic importance as the first major protest event in the national Red Power movement, the nineteen-month Alcatraz occupation became over-shadowed by the seventy-one-day siege at Wounded Knee on the Pine Ridge Reservation in South Dakota from February to May 1973. The siege is some-times called "Wounded Knee II" to distinguish it from the massacre of some 200 Indian men, women, and children by U.S. Seventh Cavalry troops in De-cember 1890 — a massacre for which the U.S. Congress formally apologized to the Oglala Lakota people in October 1990 but for which no offers of repa-ration or restitution were made.

Briefly stated, the 1973 conflict at Wounded Knee involved a dispute within Pine Ridge's Oglala Lakota (Sioux) tribe over the controversial tribal chairman Richard Wilson. Wilson was viewed as a corrupt puppet of the BIA by some segments of the tribe, including those associated with the American Indian Movement (AIM). An effort to impeach Wilson resulted in a division of the tribe into opposing camps that eventually armed themselves and entered into a two-and-one-half-month conflict that involved tribal police and government; AIM; reservation residents; federal law enforcement officials; the BIA; local citizens; nationally prominent entertainment figures; national philanthropic, religious, and legal organizations; and the national news media. The siege began with the arrival of a caravan of approximately 250 AIM supporters led by Dennis Banks and Russell Means on the evening of February 27, 1973. Al-though the armed conflict that followed AIM's arrival is generally character-ized as a standoff between AIM and its supporters and the Wilson government and its supporters, including the U.S. federal government, the siege at Wounded Knee was really only one incident in what had been a long history of political instability and factional conflict on the Pine Ridge Reservation. The next weeks were characterized by shootouts, roadblocks, negotiations, visit-ing delegations, and the movement of refugees out of various fire zones. In mid-March, halfway through the siege, a group of occupiers along with some local members of the Pine Ridge community declared an Independent Oglala Nation, swore in 350 new citizens, and announced plans to send a delegation to the United Nations.

When the siege ended on May 9, 1973, two Indians were dead and an unknown number on both sides were wounded, including casualties among federal government forces. Dick Wilson remained in office, though he was challenged at the next election and eventually voted out of office; he died in 1990. Many of the AIM members involved in the siege spent the next years in litigation, in exile, and in prison as a result of the siege and several armed conflicts that followed in its wake. The most celebrated of those later conflicts involved Leonard Peltier, who was tried and convicted for the deaths of two FBI agents who were shot on the Pine Ridge Reservation in 1975.

The following list of demands was presented to federal officials by representatives of the Independent Oglala Nation during the siege.

Communicate this to whoever is in charge. We are operating under the provisions of the 1868 Sioux Treaty [of Laramie]. This is an act of war initiated by the United States.

Demands:

I. Senator WILLIAM FULBRIGHT to convene Senate Foreign Relations Committee immediately for hearings on treaties made with American Indian Nations and ratified by the Congress of the U.S.

II. Senator EDWARD KENNEDY to convene Senate Sub-Committee on Administrative Practices and Procedures for immediate, full-scale investigations and exposure of the Bureau of Indian Affairs and the Department of the Interior from the Agency, reservation offices, to the area offices, to the central office in Washington, D.C.

III. Senator JAMES ABOUREZK to convene the Senate Sub-Committee on Indian Affairs for a complete investigation of all Sioux Reservations in South Dakota.

People we will negotiate with:

1. Mr. EHRLICHMAN of the White House.

2. Senators KENNEDY, ABOUREZK, and FULBRIGHT — or their top aides.

3. The Commissioner of the BIA and the Secretary of the Interior.

The only two options open to the United States of America are:

1. They wipe out the old people, women, children and men, by shooting and attacking us.

2. They negotiate our demands.

Signed:

Oglala Sioux Civil Rights Organization

President VERN LONG

Vice-Pres. PEDRO BISSONETTE
Secretary EDDIE WHITE WOLF
American Indian Movement Leader: RUSSELL MEANS
Before we took action this day we asked for and received complete direction and support of medicine men and chiefs of the Oglala Nation:
FRANK FOOLS CROW
PETER CATCHES
ELLIS CHIPS
EDGAR RED CLOUD
JAKE KILLS ENEMY
MORRIS WOUNDED
SEVERT YOUNG BEAR
EVERETTE CATCHES

Women of All Red Nations

Lorelei DeCora Means, 1974

The 1960s and 1970s were a time of social awakening in the United States for both American Indian women and men. Within the national civil rights movement, African American women and Chicanas were making their voices heard, as were Native American women. American Indian women were present in large numbers during the 1969 occupation of Alcatraz Island, during the 1972 occupation of the Washington DC office of the Bureau of Indian Affairs, and at Wounded Knee in 1973. In these and other protests, native women took on both traditional and activist roles: some cooked, some took care of children, and others marched, petitioned, occupied, and fought alongside their brothers to force the U.S. government to acknowledge its treaty obligations, to revoke federal Termination and relocation policies, and to open a new era of tribal self-determination and native rights.

Before and after the Wounded Knee occupation, American Indian women activists were not only part of the American Indian Movement (AIM) but also established their own organizations. In 1974 Lorelei DeCora Means, a Minneconjou Lakota, and Madonna Thunderhawk and Phyllis Young, both Hunkpapa Lakotas, were joined by other American Indian women to form a new group called Women of All Red Nations (WARN). Many of these native women had been active in AIM but also had developed an awareness of the distinctive gendered experiences of Indian men and women at the hands of the U.S. government. For instance, many native women were arrested, charged, and convicted — and some died — for their roles in the Red Power activist movement and because of their association with male activists. These women's sacrifices were matched by the fates suffered by large numbers of activist men, particularly AIM members, who were victims of police brutality and targets of government counterintelligence surveillance and infiltration campaigns, endured long prison terms, and in many cases, were killed as a result of their protest and resistance activities.

WARN members argued that the U.S. government's paternalist and colonialist handling of Indian affairs had different consequences for Indian women and men. These differences could be seen in both reservation and urban Indian communities. On reservations, Indian women and children bore the greater burden of poor nutrition, inadequate health care, and forced or deceptive sterilization programs; native women and children also faced higher levels of domestic violence resulting from poverty, joblessness, substance abuse, and hopelessness. As Madonna Thunderhawk explained, "Indian women have had to be strong because of what this colonialist system has done to our men. I mean, alcohol, suicides, car wrecks, the whole thing. And after Wounded Knee, while all that persecution of the men was going on, the women had to keep things going."

WARN'S response to these problems and abuses was to organize, to participate in protests (like Camp Yellow Thunder in South Dakota's Black Hills), to demand an end to police brutality, and to insist on full treaty and civil rights for American Indian people. Because of the more benign treatment afforded Indian women by federal officials, and because of federal officials' tendency to underestimate and misunderstand Indian women's power, many native women seized the opportunity to organize and to act for the betterment of their communities in ways that native men often could not. Thus in many ways WARN women represented the modern-day equivalent of a traditional women's society. By organizing native women, the WARN founders felt that they could fulfill their responsibilities to protect and ensure native rights for all. The following statement appeared in 1985.

We are *American Indian* women, in that order. We are oppressed, first and foremost, as American Indians, as peoples colonized by the United States of America, *not* as women. As Indians, we can never forget that. Our survival, the survival of every one of us — man, woman, and child — as *Indians*, depends on it. Decolonization is the agenda, the whole agenda, and until it is accomplished it is the *only* agenda that counts for American Indians. It will take every one of us — every single one of us — to get the job done. We haven't got the time, energy, or resources for anything else while our lands are being destroyed and our children are dying of avoidable diseases and malnutrition. So we tend to view those who come to us wanting to form alliances on the basis of "new" and "different" or "broader" or "more important" issues to be a little less than friends, especially since most of them come from the Euroamerican population which benefits most directly from our ongoing colonization.

The Longest Walk

Washington DC, July 1978

The last major national protest event of the Red Power movement began in the spring of 1978 in full view of Alcatraz Island, when a group of Native Americans set out for Washington DC on "The Longest Walk," a journey designed both to symbolize the forced removal of Indians from their homelands and to draw attention to a growing backlash in government and in the country against Indian treaty rights. There were several bills pending before Congress that harkened back to the old Termination policies of the 1950s, and Longest Walk marchers hoped to provide a dramatic protest backdrop to tribal lobbying efforts to keep Self-Determination the cornerstone of federal Indian policy.

The following account, published in the Mohawk newspaper *Akwesasne Notes* in the summer of 1978, describes several stops made by marchers on the Longest Walk. Here we see a description of reservation and urban Indians and of elders and native youth as they move full circle on a march through time and space from the early exhilarating days of Alcatraz activism to the spiritual and peaceful atmosphere of the Longest Walk.

They formed an impressive line. There were twenty-four people in all, young men and women, and older people. They were dressed in their traditional dress. It had been explained to us that some of the older people did not speak English. The occasion was historic — for the first time, a group of Navajo people had come to Onondaga to a Six Nations Council.

An older woman spoke and introduced herself. She spoke through an interpreter, a younger woman who spoke flawless English. She said that she was very happy to have been able to visit our country. Then she said that where she came from they were told that there were no Indians to the east of the Mississippi.

"I didn't even know there were any Indians at all here," she said. "But now I know." People laughed. The atmosphere was relaxed and friendly.

"We came here from The Longest Walk," one of the younger women said. "Our elders have come with us. My grandmother here," she said, pointing out one of the older women, "when she first joined the walk she saw that the people were running. So she ran too! In fact, we couldn't even catch up with her. She ran a couple of miles!" Everyone laughed. The older women laughed, too.

A young, powerful looking man in a huge cowboy hat stepped forward to speak. "We are called Navajo by the non-Indians," he said. "But we do not call ourselves Navajo. That name was given to us by the Spanish. We call ourselves Dine, which means 'the people.' That is who we are." The people gathered in the longhouse nodded.

We were camped in a park in Maryland. The place of the camp was a large field, and around the edges of the field were pitched tents and tee-pees, and a few army tents. The Maryland national guard was there, administering field kitchens. The water supply was in military water tanks which were mounted on small trailers. The national guard people ran the camp stoves and pretty much maintained a low profile.

It was one of those hot, sunny days, and the people were gathered in a great circle to discuss their problems. Vernon Bellecourt had called the assembly. "We want the people to gather around here," he said, "so that we can discuss our problems. We want the people to speak out, to tell us what is happening. That's what we are here for."

Various people were introduced, a pipe was passed among the people who had led and participated in much of the Walk. A few speeches were made. The people sat on the ground patiently, listening, watching.

We were gathered on a Friday night just outside of Washington, D.C., in Greenbelt Park. We were over near the Lakota camp. It was a hot night, and it was very late. Russell Means was speaking.

"We have talked to the people at the White House," he said, "and they tell us that President Carter is in Europe this week and that he won't get back until Wednesday or so. When he does get back, he'll have a lot of work to catch up on, and they tell us that he won't be able to see us."

A man standing nearby said, "When he gets to Germany, some people will demonstrate there. While he talks about human rights in the Soviet Union, they will tell him to go home and talk to the Longest Walk."

"Carter won't see us," Means continued, "but Mondale is going to meet with us after he's been briefed on Wednesday."

"Carter doesn't want to talk to us," someone else said. "He doesn't know anything about Indians anyway."

"I know it's against our usual ways," Russell added, "but they want a list of the names of the people who will be meeting with Mondale. They need that list fairly soon."

One of the Dine people stepped forward. "My grandmother wants to speak. I will translate."

An older woman stood. She said that she and her people have walked for months and that they came here for a meeting with Carter. She said she was in no hurry, and that she and her group would be willing to wait. She felt that the Indian delegations should meet with both Mondale and Carter at the same time, and suggested that they could stay here in the park until they were granted a meeting.

Quite a few people agreed, but it was clear that Means didn't expect to see Carter.

It was nearly 2:30 a.m., and there would be prayers at dawn.

The final leg of the Longest Walk came on a Saturday. We were a little late getting started. Someone ran through the camps announcing that there was to be a bus ride first, then a twelve-mile walk into Washington. The buses were about a mile from the furthest camp area.

As we walked toward the buses it became obvious that the trees hid from view a much larger camp than was generally visible. Down the long paths they came, people from the Northern Great Plains, the Pacific Northwest, the deserts, and the woodlands of the East. As we walked toward the park entrance, the trickle of people became a steady stream, then a river. It was obvious that there were a lot of people. We walked quietly. There were white people, and Black people. And Indians. All kinds of Indians.

A woman ahead asked, "What are we supposed to do this morning? What's first on the agenda?" A man walking with her looked up at the cloudless sky overhead, "The first thing," he said, "is that we take part in the Hottest Walk into the city. Then we're supposed to go to a park in the middle of town where there is a rally."

"And what about after the walk?" she asked. "What do you think will come of it? Even after we go there and we tell them about what we want, that we want our rights? What do you think will happen then?"

"The Longest Wait," he said.

The backlash that Longest Walk marchers were trying to speak against was a response to the gains of the Red Power movement, the legal successes of native rights attorneys, and the increasing political control over reservation decision making and resource rights by tribal governments. The end of Termination and the advent of Self-Determination marked a period of much change in Indian country, but old ways of thinking and entrenched rights were not easy to overcome. The following editorial exchange between Wilcomb E. Washburn, director of the Smithsonian Institution's Office of American Studies, and Joseph de La Cruz, president of the Quinault Tribal Council and head of the

National Tribal Chairmen's Association, which was published in the *New York Times* in the summer of 1978 at the end of the Longest Walk, reflects both the old and the new, the backlash and the backbone.

An Indian Media Play
Wilcomb E. Washburn
Director of the Smithsonian Institution's Office
of American Studies
July 20, 1978

Washington — The spectacle of the American Indian participating in "The Longest Walk" — a "spiritual journey" to protest certain "anti-Indian" bills introduced in Congress — illustrates once again the frightening ability of the news media to shape the presentation of issues by special interest groups and the perception of those issues by the public.

What is, in fact, the statement of a radical Indian minority is perceived by the reader or viewer as a general expression of all Indian people. It is conceded that most Indians are opposed to the bills. What is important is that the current demonstration attempts, in the form of a nonviolent, "spiritual walk" of dramatic character, to promote the cause of one element of the Indian people, those opposed to established tribal governments, against another, those elected to represent Indian people through such governments.

The catch words, so often lost in the media coverage, are "traditional and spiritual leaders." What is condemned by the walk leaders are the elected political leaders, the tribal governments whose existence (when they continue to survive) or revival (when they had been destroyed) was incorporated into the law of the land by the Indian Reorganization Act of 1934.

That law, in halting the destruction of tribal governments by which assimilation of individual Indians into the majority culture was to be achieved, required that the tribal governments function under Western democratic tradition, giving men and women an equal and individual say in the selection of tribal leaders.

Though the law saved tribal existence, the form that it established has given critics of tribal governments the opportunity to charge that tribal leaders, even though elected by a majority of the tribal members, are "frequently controlled or hindered by the Interior Department," according to the walk's "Statement to the People of the United States and World," to the point of "denial of even the slightest amount of real self-government."

The reorganization act is denounced in the same document because it allegedly "continues to destroy the traditional government of our people by pitting brother against brother." Hence, the thrust of the Longest Walk's effort is to unseal the regularly elected tribal leaders and replace them with "traditional" and "spiritual" leaders whose right to their presumed leadership will, if necessary, be enforced by American Indian Movement activists against the wishes of a majority.

In 1972, AIM leaders — who form the core of the leadership of the present walk — sought the same ends by the destruction of the Bureau of Indian Affairs headquarters in Washington. A good portion of the recent white "backlash" may be attributed to that demonstration. Walk leaders, on the other hand, attribute it to the concealed hand of greedy corporations seeking to exploit Indian lands.

The present walk has a carefully constructed spiritual, religious, educational, and nonviolent character, expressive of the increased sophistication of AIM leaders, particularly of Dennis Banks, who conceived the idea of the walk. Even a Japanese Buddhist group emphasizing world peace has joined the marchers.

Walk leaders have gone out of their way to blur their differences with established tribal leaders by emphasizing their shared opposition to the bills in Congress that would diminish the powers of Indian tribal governments. Messages of support or good wishes have been obtained from some elected tribal officials — even from the Oglala Tribal Chairman, Elijah Whirlwind Horse, at Pine Ridge, S.D., site of the attempt by AIM and Russell Means, a walk leader, to oust Richard Wilson from the tribal chairmanship in 1974.

The Federal Government has once more demonstrated that it is more concerned with the feelings of its enemies than of its friends. As in 1972, when Mr. Means and other AIM leaders were elevated to the status of statesmen dealing directly with the President and his top advisers, the Longest Walk leaders have obtained White House intervention to gain logistical support for their marches and, even more significantly, the use of the Mall for their demonstrations. To provide a focus so rich with visual symbolism (namely, a Plains tepee in the shadow of the Washington Monument) unwittingly honors not the Indian leaders elected by the tribes, but those who have sought unsuccessfully to depose them.

While asserting the needs for Indian people to control their own destiny, the radicals have undermined Indian sovereignty as it has been shaped and expanded in recent decades by the Supreme Court, and by the Executive and Legislative branches of government. That churches, well-wishers, and the Federal Government have allowed themselves to share in this assault demonstrates not only a failure of will, but an absence of intelligence.

On Knowing What Is Good for the American Indian
Joseph de La Cruz
President of the Quinault Tribal Council
and Head of the National Tribal Chairmen's Association
August 2, 1978

To the Editor:

In an obvious effort to discredit the "Longest Walk," which is the mildest form of Indian protest one could imagine, an article on the *New York Times* Op-Ed page on July 20 reached the ultimate in deception and misrepresentation. Wilcomb E. Washburn has tried to discredit the Indians' action by claiming it is a statement of a "radical Indian minority" which has come to Washington to "condemn . . . elected political leaders" in the tribal governments.

Mr. Washburn's thesis is fairly typical of attitudes by non-Indians who consider themselves experts on Indian affairs. Things have not really changed that much over the years. Most of the problems Indians find themselves faced with today result from Federal Indian policies made by non-Indians who are certain *they* know what is good for the Indians and don't bother to ask the Indians.

One perfect example is the fake concern shown for elected tribal leaders, who Washburn fears will be replaced by traditional and spiritual leaders. While he is totally wrong in attempting to define this as the purpose of the "Longest Walk," he seems incapable of understanding the destruction of Indian values accomplished by the 1934 Indian Reorganization Act, which he praises so highly.

That act was the written expression by the United States Government and those who knew "what was good for the Indians" on how the Indians should elect their leaders. Prior to that time, Indian tribes chose their leaders as they had for thousands of years, i.e., by consensus of the tribe.

The requirement in 1934 that Indians should elect their leaders the same as white men do was alien to most of the Indian people. Too often, the result was that only aggressive, educated Indians of mixed blood participated, were elected and took control of tribal governments. In some cases, these were the Indians who cooperated with and subordinated themselves to the United States Government. It was, and still is, an advanced stage of the kind of colonialism of which the Indian people have been primary victims.

To this day, many tribes have traditional leaders and traditional Indians who refuse to take part in the white man's election processes. The Hopi nation in Arizona is one perfect example. There the traditionalists have rejected the tribal leaders' efforts to displace the Navajos from disputed land areas immediately. They also refused to take part in elections which have supposedly decided the will of the Hopi tribe with respect to the Navajo-Hopi dispute.

On the other hand, some tribes have taken the approach of electing their traditional or spiritual leaders to the tribal council in elections that are conducted under the Indian Reorganization Act. As I understand it, this tactic is followed not necessarily to circumvent the elective process but simply to express the will of tribal members that their governments receive the guidance and leadership of spiritual or traditional elders.

For a white man such as Wilcomb Washburn to make the flat statement that those on the "Longest Walk" represent only a militant minority is itself the ultimate in white arrogance. He brings as much knowledge to that concept as he does to his statement that Pine Ridge, South Dakota, was the site of an attempt by the American Indian Movement and Russell Means to oust Richard Wilson as tribal chairman in 1974.

Although Washburn tries his damnedest to make it sound like an attempted coup, what really happened in 1974 was a tribal election in which Russell Means ran against the incumbent chairman, Richard Wilson. It is like describing Jimmy Carter's election in 1976 as a takeover of the Federal Government.

By playing on the general public's lack of knowledge of Indian issues and Indian affairs, Washburn is attempting to discredit a responsible and legitimate attempt by Indian people to air their grievances to the Federal Government. The Indians have found it difficult enough to get the press to cover the real issues with which they are concerned. Instead, some of the press coverage has treated the "Longest Walk" like a freak show. The Indians and the people of the United States deserve something better.

The Activist Legacy of Red Power

The 1980s and 1990s were decades of decreased but continuing activism and resistance in Indian country. The ongoing struggles to defend tribal treaty rights and the rights and dignity of native people focused on several themes: the protection and return of sacred Indian lands, the repatriation of native burial remains and sacred objects, the preservation of tribal sovereignty and treaty rights, and the objection to demeaning and commercial uses of Indian images, mascots, and cultures. Notable protest events of this era included the six-year-long occupation of the Black Hills in South Dakota at Camp Yellow Thunder, the demands by many tribes for the return of the remains of Indian ancestors and their sacred objects held in museums and universities around the country, the resistance by reservation communities against the siting of toxic waste dumps and dangerous industries on Indian land, the insistence on control over reservation resources including gaming rights, and the protests at high school, college, and professional sporting events against the use of Indian names and mascots.

The following three statements assessed the legacy of Red Power more than three decades after the first fish-ins marked the early stirrings of the movement. The first is by one of the founders of the American Indian Movement, Dennis Banks, who summarizes some of AIM's achievements and some of the challenges faced by AIM activists. The second statement is by AIM leader Russell Means, who reflects on the impact of AIM on reservations and in urban Indian communities. The third statement is by Janet McCloud, an activist from the earliest fish-in days, who speaks powerfully about personal costs and important accomplishments of AIM and the Red Power activists.

STATEMENT BY DENNIS BANKS

When AIM was founded on July 28, 1968, in Minneapolis, Minnesota, the living conditions we found ourselves in were deplorable. It wasn't that we didn't know there was racism in the cities. It was how racism forced us into squalid slum tenement buildings, closed doors to job opportunities, and fostered racist laws, jails, courts, and prisons. Beginning with our founding meeting, we immediately set out to bring about change in those institutions of public concern: housing, education, employment, welfare, and the courts.

Because we took to the streets and began demonstrating with signs, placards, and bullhorns, the media termed us militants, activists, and outsiders. Not once did they admit to the many wrongs we faced daily. Not once did the Minneapolis and St. Paul papers run editorials agreeing with our positions. But this negative reporting didn't stop our campaign to challenge the employment picture of Native People nor attack the slum housing conditions, the de-humanizing handling of Native People on welfare, the racist and discriminatory practices in the police department, sheriff's department, courts, and prison system. Fifty percent of the 1,000 inmates in Minnesota prisons were Native People, yet the ratio of Native People living in Minnesota was (like now) only one percent. It was shameful.

In 1971 we opened our first Native Peoples' survival school in Minneapolis. That same year we founded — with joint efforts of the black community — the Legal Rights Center. A welfare rights and reform committee was established, as well as a jobs and jobs-training task force. We began monitoring the police arrests through our AIM Patrol and assigned observers to the city, county, and state courts. We notified prison officials of our campaign and formed a Prison Watch to notify us of Native inmate traffic. We began to move and results began to emerge. AIM never let up. Never will.

Today, because of AIM, more than 20,000 Native People have received legal assistance through the Legal Rights Center. The job training turned into the Indian Industrialization Center, which has trained more than 5,000 Native People and has placed over 8,000 people into jobs still being held. Native People are employed by the courts and the police. The prisons are no longer disproportionately crowded with Native People. Yes, we still have many social problems like alcoholism, drug abuse, and gang violence. And like the 1960s, we as Native People must band together, as parents, grandparents, and teachers, to provide solutions to these problems and provide direction for the future. This I see is the most pressing issue of our time: the social destruction of our community. Family strength is giving way to street values, community gatherings are now either funerals or wakes, and parental guidance is being replaced by police counselors. Is this our future? No, it isn't. And I know you will join me as I say never to that way of life.

AIM has worked night and day to bring about much-needed change. In order to bring about meaningful change, we also have to educate and re-educate ourselves. That's why I call upon Native People to share their information with each other. I believe sharing is perhaps the last real action we have to help each other. When our children are becoming parents as children; when our children start roaming in gangs or packs; when our children challenge the very foundation of what being Indian is; then I believe we must not only share each other's cries for help but we must rush to defend that heritage that was handed down to us. Seven generations ago our ancestors believed in and thought about us. It is in these beliefs that we find our spiritual foundation. And that foundation must never be attacked.

An eagle is an eagle, still practicing the ways of its ancestors, long since gone. The beaver still makes its home along the streams and creeks of our land. The buffalo still teaches its young and the salmon still travels the thousands of miles to spawn its future generations. If we Native People are to survive as a cultural species, then we must follow the way of our ancestors. We must continue to sing the songs and have ceremonies to welcome each day. Like the eagle and the buffalo, we must never abandon our old ways. Those ways have been good to us and they will provide us with direction for our future generations. Like an eagle flying high, we are who we are. Still strong!

Our land struggle will always be going on, and we must always support those issues related to our lands. If, however, we cannot rise to the occasion of developing ourselves for the land, then perhaps we must back up and face the struggle of social behavior head-on. In the end that's what we must ultimately do. Face the Struggle and Accept the Challenge.

Once we do that, who cares what they call us?

STATEMENT BY RUSSELL MEANS

Our great-grandfathers knew all about sovereignty and self-determination, but our parents were forced to forget those things. There isn't much to brag about on the reservations and in the urban Indian ghettos, but just about every admirable quality that remains in today's Indian people is the result of the American Indian Movement's flint striking the white man's steel. In the 1970s and 1980s, we lit a fire across Indian country. We fought for changes in school curricula to eliminate racist lies, and we are winning. We fought for community control of police, and on a few reservations it's now a reality. We fought to instill pride in our songs and in our language, in our cultural wisdom, inspiring a small renaissance in the teaching of our languages. We fought for our dignity. Today, at least on our reservations, elders, headmen, and other leaders are treated with respect. A few urban Indian communities have finally begun to recognize the need to address the cultural education of their youths. Thanks to AIM, for the first time in this century, Indian people stand at the threshold of freedom and responsibility.

STATEMENT BY JANET MCCLOUD

The greatest beneficiaries of the American Indian Movement are the tribal council leaders who are always quick to seize the opportunities created by the Movement, and to claim unwarranted credit for the positive social changes won for Indian people.

The tribal leaders and others who denounce AIM justify their actions by pointing out the human weaknesses of individual AIM people, with never a glance at their own. . . . Indian people can disagree 'til doomsday about which defensive strategy is best, or whether we should even resist. If we continue to disagree on politics, policy, philosophy, and enter into destructive personality clashes, we will lose all. . . .

And who protects the Indian people now that the FBI has almost destroyed the American Indian Movement? Nobody. Do we see tribal leaders who claim the credit for AIM's labors and sacrifices rushing to protect and defend the Indian people against the onslaughts they face today? . . . Few acknowledge that real change only began to take place after the tremendous sacrifices of the young warriors of the American Indian Movement. The beneficiaries of the Movement live in new homes, drive new cars, live longer, have better health, are better educated, have well-paid jobs, etc., while the real warriors lie unrecognized in their graves or in prison cells.

The American Indian Movement supports the efforts of all tribal leaders and programs that genuinely promote the better health, education and welfare of the Indian people. Neither AIM nor any other organized resistance movement of Indian people begrudges any benefit their people receive; they rejoice at all improvements, this is what they fight for. But the warriors have never grabbed benefits for themselves, and the few who do were never true Movement people. That is how you tell the difference between leaders and opportunists.

We need our warriors, and where are they? In prisons, in hiding, pursued relentlessly by the FBI, or paroled to one county in one state, unable to travel, or forbidden to talk for or about their people, lest they be imprisoned again? How many Indian people will take the time to send a card or gift to warriors rotting in prisons? . . . It is time that Indian people, those who have received most from the American Indian Movement, took some time to count their blessings, to give credit where credit is due. Don't forget the warriors, we may never see their like again.

References and Further Reading

Banks, Dennis. 1994. Foreword to *Native American: A Portrait of the People*, ed. Duane Champagne. Detroit: Visible Ink.

Boxberger, Daniel. 1989. *To Fish in Common*. Lincoln: University of Nebraska Press.

Cohen, Fay G. 1996. *Treaties on Trial: The Continuing Controversy over Northwest Indian Fishing Rights*. Seattle: University of Washington Press, 1986.

Deloria, Vine, Jr. 1994. "Alcatraz, Activism, and Accommodation." *American Indian Culture and Research Journal* 18:25–32.

Fortunate Eagle, Adam. 1992. *Alcatraz! Alcatraz! The Indian Occupation of 1969–71*. San Francisco: Heyday.

Jaimes, M. Annette, and Theresa Halsey. 1992. "American Indian Women: At the Center of Indigenous Resistance in Contemporary North America." In *The State of Native North America: Genocide, Colonization, and Resistance*, ed. M. A. Jaimes. Boston: South End.

Jensen, Richard E., R. Eli Paul, and John E. Carter. 1992. *Eyewitness at Wounded Knee*. Lincoln: University of Nebraska Press.

Johnson, Troy. 1996. *The Occupation of Alcatraz Island: Indian Self-Determination and the Rise of Indian Activism*. Urbana: University of Illinois Press.

Johnson, Troy, Joane Nagel, and Duane Champagne. 1997. *American Indian Activism: Alcatraz to the Longest Walk*. Urbana: University of Illinois Press.

Kipp, Woody. 1994. "The Eagles I Fed Who Did Not Love Me." *American Indian Culture and Research Journal* 18:213–32.

Lauderdale, John Vance. 1996. *After Wounded Knee: Correspondence of Major and Surgeon John Vance Lauderdale while Serving with the Army Occupying the Pine Ridge Indian Reservation, 1890–1891*. East Lansing: Michigan State University Press.

Matthiessen, Peter. 1991. *In the Spirit of Crazy Horse*. New York: Viking.

Means, Russell, with Marvin J. Wolf. 1995. *Where White Men Fear to Tread: The Autobiography of Russell Means*. New York: St. Martin's.

Nagel, Joane. 1996. *American Indian Ethnic Renewal: Red Power and the Resurgence of Identity and Culture*. New York: Oxford University Press.

Smith, Paul Chaat, and Robert Allen Warrior. 1996. *Like a Hurricane: The Indian Movement from Alcatraz to Wounded Knee*. New York: Free Press.

Weyler, Rex. 1992. *Blood of the Land: The Government and Corporate War against First Nations*. Philadelphia: New Society.

2 Self-Determination and Tribal Sovereignty

Indian Self-Government

Felix S. Cohen, 1949

Acknowledgment of Native Americans' rights of self-government is not new. In fact, since the early days of the republic many in and out of government have urged that Indian people be allowed to govern themselves. Laws have been passed based on the premise that the U.S. government would eventually step aside and let Indians run their own affairs, and even when other laws conferred on the Department of the Interior certain powers over the Indians, they frequently stipulated that the powers were temporary and that they should be transferred to the Indians as soon as possible.

But until the 1970s, when the period of Self-Determination in federal Indian policy began, such designs were never realized, and the government's stranglehold over Indian affairs grew progressively tighter. Felix S. Cohen was a distinguished legal philosopher and battler for Indian rights and the author of the *Handbook of Federal Indian Law*, published in 1942 and updated in 1982. From 1933 to 1948 Cohen was an assistant solicitor in the Department of the Interior, where he rendered notable service on behalf of Native Americans. After leaving the government, he entered into private law practice and taught at City College of New York and at the Yale Law School. As a general counsel for the Association on American Indian Affairs, he continued, both as a lawyer and as an author, to champion Indian causes until his death in 1953 at the age of forty-six.

Many of Felix S. Cohen's writings on Indian affairs are still relevant today. This one, a persuasive commentary on the nature of self-government and its application in the federal government's relations with Indians, was published in *The American Indian* in 1949.

Not all who speak of self-government mean the same thing by the term. Therefore let me say at the outset that by self-government I mean that form of government in which decisions are made not by the people who are wisest, or ablest, or closest to some throne in Washington or in Heaven, but, rather by the people who are most directly affected by the decisions. I think that if we conceive of self-government in these matter-of-fact terms, we may avoid some confusion.

Let us admit that self-government includes graft, corruption, and the making of decisions by inexpert minds. Certainly these are features of self-government in white cities and counties, and so we ought not to be scared out of our wits if somebody jumps up in the middle of a discussion of Indian self-government and shouts "graft" or "corruption."

Self-government is not a new or radical idea. Rather, it is one of the oldest staple ingredients of the American way of life. Many Indians in this country enjoyed self-government long before European immigrants who came to these shores did. It took the white colonists north of the Rio Grande about 170 years to rid themselves of the traditional European pattern of the divine right of kings or, what we call today, the long arm of bureaucracy, and to substitute the less efficient but more satisfying Indian pattern of self-government. South of the Rio Grande the process took more than three centuries, and there are some who are still skeptical as to the completeness of the shift.

This is not the time and place to discuss the ways in which the Indian pattern of self-government undermined the patterns which the colonists first brought to this country, patterns of feudalism, landlordism and serf-dom, economic monopoly and special privilege, patterns of religious in-tolerance and nationalism and the divine right of kings. It was not only Franklin and Jefferson who went to school with Indian teachers, like the Iroquois statesman Canasatego, to learn the ways of federal union and democracy. It was no less the great political thinkers of Europe, in the years following the discovery of the New World, who undermined an-cient dogmas when they saw spread before them on the panorama of the Western Hemisphere new societies in which liberty, equality, and frater-nity were more perfectly realized than they were realized in contempo-rary Europe, societies in which government drew its just powers from the consent of the governed. To Vitoria, Grotius, Locke, Montaigne, Montesquieu, Voltaire, and Rousseau, Indian liberty and self-government provided a new polestar in political thinking. But, for the present, I want merely to emphasize that Indian self-government is not a new or radical policy but an ancient fact. It is not something friends of the Indians can confer upon the Indians. Nobody can grant self-government to anybody else. We all recall that when Alexander was ruler of most of the known civilized world, he once visited the philosopher Diogenes, who was mak-ing his home in an old bathtub. Diogenes was a rich man because he did not want anything that he did not have. He was a mighty man because he could master himself. Alexander admired Diogenes for these qualities, and standing before him said, "Oh, Diogenes, if there is anything that I can grant you, tell me and I will grant it." To which Diogenes replied, "You are standing in my sunlight. Get out of the way." The Federal Government which is, today, the dominant power of the civilized world cannot give self-government to an Indian community. All it can really do for self-government is to get out of the way. . . .

I recall very vividly in 1934 working on a study for the Indian Office of legal rights of Indian tribes which was to serve as a guide in the drafting of tribal constitutions under the Wheeler-Howard Act. I found that the laws and court decisions clearly recognized that Indian tribes have all the governmental rights of any state or municipality except insofar as those rights have been curtailed or qualified by Act of Congress or by treaty, and such qualifications are relatively minor, in fact. When, at last, my job was done and the Solicitor's opinion had been reviewed and approved by the proper authorities of the Interior Department and properly mimeographed, I learned to my dismay that all copies of the opinion in the Indian Office had been carefully hidden away in a cabinet and that when an Indian was found reading this opinion, the copy was forthwith taken from his hands and placed under lock and key. Incidentally, the Indian whose reading was thus interrupted had spent more years in school and college than the men who controlled the lock and key. The Indian Office was sure that the opinion, if released to the public, would be more disturbing. I suppose they were right. The opinion was disturbing to the Indian Office. Its suppression was equally disturbing to me. My despondency was somewhat relieved when I found that Chief Justice Marshall and Pope Paul III and Bartholomew de las Casas had all received the same treatment. It was of John Marshall's decision upholding the rights of self-government of the Cherokee Tribe that an old Indian fighter in the White House, President Jackson, said, "John Marshall has made his decision. Now let him enforce it." The sovereign State of Georgia paid no attention to the decision of the United States Supreme Court and the good missionary whom the Supreme Court had freed continued to languish in a Georgia prison. And what happened to John Marshall in 1832 was not novel. The same thing happened to Bartholomew de las Casas 300 years earlier when, as Archbishop of Chiapas, he endeavored to read to his flock of Spanish landowners the guarantees of Indian freedom signed by the Pope and by the King of Spain. He was not allowed to read these documents by the outraged landowners of his archdiocese. In fact, he was driven from his church. History has a strange way of repeating itself. I was relieved to find myself in such good company, and so, instead of resigning, I distributed copies of the opinion where I thought they would do the most good.

How can we explain the fact that despite all the respect and reverence shown to the principle of Indian self-government across four centuries, there is so little left today of the fact of Indian self-government? How can we explain this discrepancy between word and deed?

The simplest explanation, of course, and the one that is easiest for simple, unsophisticated Indians to understand is the explanation in terms of white man's hypocrisy.

I think we must go deeper into the wellsprings of human conduct and belief to understand what is happening in the field of Indian self-government and to relate facts to words. . . .

I recall that when we were helping Indians draft the constitutions and charters which were supposed to be the vehicles of self-government under the Wheeler-Howard Act, all of the Indian Bureau officials were very strongly in favor of self-government, and in favor of allowing all tribes to exercise to the full extent their inherent legal rights. There was only one difficulty. The people of the Education Division were in favor of self-government in forestry, credit, leasing, law and order, and every other field of social activity except education. Of course, education, they thought, was a highly technical matter in which tribal council politics should have no part. Education should be left to the experts, according to the experts, and the experts were to be found in the Education Division. Similarly, with the Forestry Division. They were all in favor of self-government with respect to education, credit, agricultural leases, law and order, and everything else except for forestry. Forestry, of course, involved matters of particular complexity and difficulty in which the experts ought to make the decisions, and the experts, of course, were to be found in the Forestry Division. So it was with the Credit Section, the Leasing Section, the Law and Order Division, and all the other divisions and subdivisions of the Indian Bureau. The result was that while every official was in favor of self-government generally, by the same token he was opposed to self-government in the particular field over which he had any jurisdiction. In that field he could see very clearly the advantages of the expert knowledge which he and his staff had accumulated, and the disadvantages of lay judgment influenced by so-called political considerations which would be involved in decisions of local councils.

Those of us in the Department who had been given a special responsibility for protecting Indian tribal self-government finally went to the Commissioner and pointed out that if we followed the traditional practice of yielding to each expert division on the matter with which it was concerned, there would be no Indian self-government. There was a long and bloody argument and eventually the Commissioner upheld the principle which is now written into most Indian tribal charters, that the Indians themselves, at some point or other, may dispense with supervisory controls over most of their various activities. Some of the charters include a special probationary period of five years or ten years, during which leases and contracts are subject to Departmental control. In many cases, particularly among the Oklahoma tribes, this period has terminated and the Indians are free, if they choose to do so, to make their own leases and contracts and various other economic decisions without Departmental control. That, at least, is what the charters and constitutions say.

Yet I must add that instances have been called to my attention where decisions and ordinances that were not supposed to be subject to review by superintendents or by the Commissioner of Indian Affairs have been rescinded or vetoed by these officials. Tribes without independent legal guidance frequently acquiesce in such infringements upon their constitutional and corporate powers. Thus many of the gains of the Roosevelt era are being chipped away. . . .

Let us hope that we will not have to wait and see, as Admiral Doenitz saw, what happens when self-government and minority rights are subordinated to expert government and the leadership principle. Let us be thankful that in this country we have, in laboratory proportions before us, in proportions so small that the individual effort of half a dozen of us can make a real difference, this perennial conflict between democratic self-government and the various modern forms of aristocracy, or government by experts. The issue we face is not the issue merely of whether Indians will regain their independence of spirit. Our interest in Indian self-government today is not the interest of sentimentalists or antiquarians. We have a vital concern with Indian self-government because the Indian is to America what the Jew was to the Russian Czars and Hitler's Germany. For us, the Indian tribe is the miners' canary, and when it flutters and droops we know that the poison gasses of intolerance threaten all other minorities in our land. And who of us is not a member of some minority?

The issue is not only an issue of Indian rights; it is the much larger one of whether American liberty can be preserved. If we fight only for our *own* liberty because it is our own, are we any better than the dog who fights for his bone? We must believe in liberty itself to defend it effectively. What is my own divides me from my fellow man. Liberty, which is the other side of the shield of tolerance, is a social affair that unites me with my fellow man. If we fight for civil liberties for our side, we show that we believe not in civil liberties but in our side. But when those of us who never were Indians and never expect to be Indians fight for the cause of Indian self-government, we are fighting for something that is not limited by the accidents of race and creed and birth; we are fighting for what Las Casas and Vitoria and Pope Paul III called the integrity or salvation of our own souls. We are fighting for what Jefferson called the basic rights of man. We are fighting for the last best hope of earth. And these are causes that should carry us through many defeats.

Indian Statement on Policy and Legislation

Washington DC, February 2, 1967

When the Democrats took over the White House in 1961, many observers of American Indian affairs hoped to see an end to the era of Termination and its assaults on and erosion of treaty rights, tribal sovereignty, Indian land claims, and reservation economies. The end of Termination policies was slow in coming, however. Although the Kennedy administration conducted inquiries into the negative effects of Republican Termination policies on Native American communities, and it did not undertake *new* Termination legislation, nothing much was done to reverse the course of federal Indian policy. In fact, a number of tribes were terminated during the John F. Kennedy and early Lyndon B. Johnson administrations.

Despite the Johnson administration's assurance that it would further Indian self-determination, action did not follow the words. In 1966 and 1967 Interior Department officials prepared a so-called omnibus bill of new economic legislation for presentation to Congress as an Indian Resources Development Act. While the bill was being drafted by department "experts," Commissioner of Indian Affairs Robert Bennett, himself an Oneida Indian, and various department officials met with Indian spokesmen at hearings around the nation, supposedly to learn what kind of legislation the tribes wanted. Although no hint was given the Indians that the bill was already being written in Washington, a tentative draft of it came into their hands during the course of the hearings.

Realization of the new deception, plus the fact that the draft did not reflect what the Indians considered to be their true needs and desires, angered them. Despite their protests, the Department of the Interior, still not trusting the competency of American Indians to know what was good for them and continuing to impose its own ideas on them, readied a final draft of the bill for Congress.

In February 1967 a large group of Indians, called together in Washington to give their approval to the bill, instead voiced their opposition to it. Although some of its provisions seemed acceptable, the bill included many proposals that stirred new fears and bitterness among the Indians. They missed most of all a commitment by the administration to repudiate the hated 1953 congressional termination resolution, which still hung threateningly over their tribes, and they were divided on how harshly to express their disapproval. A final, somewhat mild statement, sent by the group to President Johnson on February 2 and signed by the conference leaders, Norman Hollow, Earl Old Person, and Roger Jourdain, merely pointed out objections to certain portions of the bill and asked for more time for the tribes to consider the entire draft.

In the end Congress, recognizing the Indians' opposition to the measure, ignored it, and the so-called omnibus bill died ignominiously. In retrospect, Native Americans' study and disapproval of the bill, as reflected in their Washington conference's February 1967 statement to the president, were a significant step along the road of asserting control over policies that would affect them.

Following are excerpts from their statement.

Dear Mr. President:

Upon presentation of and analysis by the delegates of this legislation, certain major titles and provisions thereof were rigorously opposed and unanimously rejected upon the grounds that they are inimical to, and uncongruous with, the present needs, capabilities and conditions of the American Indians. Implementation of certain of the managerial techniques of the proposed legislation affecting mortgage, hypothecation and sale of Indian lands would render the Indian people immediately vulnerable to subversive economic forces, leading inevitably and inalterably to the prompt erosion and demise of the social and economic culture of the American Indian.

Enactment of this legislation by the Congress would constitute a breach of the trust comprehended under original Indian treaties, if not in word, then in the spirit of the same. . . .

For other citizens government exists to serve them — as a matter of right and not of favor. It is time that government consistently recognize that it is our servant and not our master. Many of our difficulties today, we feel, lie in the unresponsiveness of public officials to our social and economic needs, despite the fact that adequate legislation exists to further Indian progress in many fields. The last major progressive policy and legislation was adopted in 1934 — 33 years ago. Today, we need a revision and updating of that policy. That policy saved our lands, insured our rights of limited self-government, and opened the door to financial credit for Indians.

Today, we need a reaffirmation of our rights to continue to occupy the lands remaining to us. Our very existence as a people is dependent on our lands. The tax status of Indian lands is founded on agreement by the Indians and the United States. This immunity is recognition that the Indian people paid more than adequate consideration when they gave up valuable land in exchange for smaller, less valuable parcels — today occupied by some 300,000 to 500,000 Indians.

Today, we are faced with threats of termination. We ask you to seek the repudiation of the ideas behind Concurrent Resolution 108, adopted in 1953. . . .

Mr. President, we wish to cooperate. With your understanding and consideration we will succeed. . . .

Respectfully submitted,
Chairman, Norman Hollow
Co-chairman, Earl Old Person
Co-chairman, Roger Jourdain

The American Indian and
the Bureau of Indian Affairs

A Study, with Recommendations by Alvin M. Josephy Jr.

February 11, 1969

When the Democrats left office in 1969, the record of the preceding eight years showed a steadily intensifying Indian demand for self-determination, beginning with the Chicago "Declaration of Indian Purpose" of 1961 and coming from more and more elements of the Indian population. Save for some lip service, however, and a slight groping in the direction of permitting American Indians to have a greater participatory role in discussing and managing programs that were framed in Washington for them, the eight-year record also showed that both the Kennedy and Johnson administrations had remained, on the whole, indifferent to this trend. The one bright spot, for a time at least, had been the OEO antipoverty programs, but they were special. No important change had occurred in either policy or substance in the more vital relationship between the Bureau of Indian Affairs and the Indian people the agency was supposed to serve. An observer could conclude that the Democrats for eight years had continued the governmental attitudes about American Indians that they had inherited from the past: the assimilation of the Indians was still the ultimate national goal, and Indians were still judged not competent enough to know what was best for them.

In actuality, this is what had occurred in the 1961–69 period. The real rulers of Indian policy were not in the Department of the Interior but in the congressional committees on Interior and Insular Affairs and in the Bureau of the Budget. Both held a whip hand over the secretary of the interior and his Bureau of Indian Affairs in regard to direction, thrust, and appropriations for Indian policies and programs, and both had clung stubbornly to the non-Indians' traditional ideas of what was best for American Indians. By 1969 both were still deaf to the Indians' rising demand for control of their own affairs, and both had the power to prevent any meaningful response by the Department of the Interior to what Native Americans wanted. The result, in effect, was that the Bureau of Indian Affairs, the agency of government responsible for the Indians' welfare, was accountable not to the Indians whom it was supposed to serve and protect but to powerful bodies hostile to Indian self-determination, the congressional committees, and the Bureau of the Budget.

Thus many native people remembered with bitterness that termination of federal relations with the tribes had been the policy of the Eisenhower regime, the last Republican administration in office, and faced the prospect of the Nixon administration with considerable uncertainty, and even fear. On September 27, 1968, during his campaign for election, Nixon had promised the Indians that termination of tribal recognition would not be "a policy objective" of his administration and that in no case would termination be imposed without their consent. Indians had applauded that statement, but after the election they looked for a more concrete assertion from the president-elect, guaranteeing that the September promise had not been campaign oratory and spelling out for them in specific terms what the new administration's Indian policy would be.

The position of American Indians in U.S. society, in truth, had reached a point where decisive change could occur. In the view of many, the time for the realization of self-determination had arrived. A new administration, willing to assume the initiative in bringing new attitudes to Congress and the Bureau of the Budget, could respond to the Indians' demands for control and power over their own affairs while continuing to observe treaty obligations and protect the Indians' lands and resources.

On the eve of assuming office, the new administration recognized that at the very least it would have to make a clean break with the termination image it had inherited from the Republicans of the 1950s. But it was out of touch with the Indians of 1969. It took President Nixon many months to find an Indian commissioner of Indian affairs acceptable to the Republican party. It took him a year and a half to frame and announce his administration's Indian policy. In the meantime, Republican officials conscientiously acquainted themselves with Native Americans and their needs.

The following document was one of the first foundations upon which the new administration developed the Indian policy that it eventually proclaimed in July 1970. The document was written in January and February 1969 at the request of the president-elect and served as a briefing for him on the then-current status of Indian affairs and on events in federal-Indian relations during the Democratic administrations of the 1960s. Such a background, providing orientation as well as recommendations based on American Indians' own expressed desires and proposals for solutions to their needs, was considered necessary before the new administration could proceed to consider its own policy.

The first section of the report, taking note of American Indians' continued opposition to the termination policy and of their fears that the new Republican administration would revive it, recommends that the president re-enunciate his promise on termination given the Indians in September 1968. This was ultimately done, first by Vice President Spiro Agnew and Secretary of the Interior Walter Hickel to the National Congress of American Indians in October 1969 and finally by the president in his Message to Congress on Indian Affairs in July 1970.

The report's second section, titled "The Context of This Study," is basically an orientation lesson in history and points of view for non-Indians dealing with federal-Indian relations in 1969. The third section is a chronological recapitulation of studies and major developments in Indian affairs during the 1961–69 period, revealing the steady Indian demand for self-determination and the government's continued deafness to it. It concludes with the admonition that the time has come to make American Indian self-determination a reality but points out that certain governmental obstacles stand in the way. One of those obstacles, the responsibility of the Department of the Interior to interests that competed with the Indians, is dealt with in the fourth section, which proposes transferring the Bureau of Indian Affairs to the Executive Office of the President but suggests, also, several alternative solutions. The second obstacle, deficiencies in the structure of the Bureau of Indian Affairs that worked inherently to prevent Indian self-determination from becoming a reality, is examined in the fifth section, which also suggests how the bureau might be reorganized. The report's final section discusses specific Indian programs and recommends that they be initiated, planned, and carried out under Indian control and direction.

Following are excerpts from the various sections of the report.

I. A FIRST PRIORITY

It is the purpose of this study to provide an understanding of the shape and substance of present-day federal-Indian relationships and the ability of the Bureau of Indian Affairs to serve efficiently as a vehicle for the management of those relations, as well as to make recommendations for a course upon which to embark in 1969. But among the questions to be examined are where, if not in the Interior Department, functions of federal-Indian relationships should be placed; what, if any, restructuring should be considered within the Bureau of Indian Affairs; which programs and their administration require changes? Any proposed alteration from the status quo would obviously stir again the embers of the Indians' fear of termination. . . .

It is not necessary to argue the wrongs versus the motives of the termination period of 1953–58, or review the specifics of the human damage that occurred. Recognition that the policy should not again be enforced is today so widespread that Indians, as well as all non-Indians knowledgeable about Indian affairs, enthusiastically applauded the statement by President Nixon, addressed to the Indian people through the National Congress of American Indians, on September 27, 1968, during his campaign for election: "Termination of tribal recognition will not be a policy objective, and in no case will it be imposed without Indian consent."

This was a clear, reassuring statement, but now that the new administration has assumed office it requires, at the earliest convenient opportunity, reiteration to the Indian tribes and peoples. . . .

It is therefore recommended that the Adminstration, hopefully through the President himself, find and take advantage of an opportunity to address the Indian people, possibly through the National Congress of American Indians in Washington, re-enunciating the statement given the Indians on September 27, 1968, particularly as it refers to termination, and making clear that the new Administration has no intention of disrupting the Indian peoples by new directions in policy, but will carry out the promises made on September 27, 1968, and make them meaningful.

Such a statement will not only have great meaning for the American Indians and prepare the ground for productive federal-Indian relations in the years immediately ahead, but will receive the approving reaction of all alienated and dispossessed peoples as well as those in the United States and in other nations to whom the treatment of the American Indians is symbolic of the broadest attitudes of the Administration.

II. THE CONTEXT OF THIS STUDY

It has been said often enough, and with great truth, that expert knowledge of the cultures and histories, not alone of Indians generally, but of the many separate tribes, is needed to understand Indian needs, desires, actions, and responses, as well as to work intelligently and compassionately with Indians to help frame, administer, and service policies and programs for their benefit.

There is no doubt that many of the failures and frustrations that mark the course of federal-Indian relations, past and present, can be ascribed to deficiencies of knowledge about Indians among non-Indians who are involved in managing Indian affairs. Indians have long complained about officials who listen to them but don't seem to understand them, and many of the complaints and criticisms that Indians level at the Bureau of Indian Affairs result from actions and programs that were imposed by well-intentioned whites, but bear no relation to the realities of what a tribe, fashioned by a particular history and culture, needed, desired, or could accept and carry out with success.

The Peace Corps, which oriented its enrollees in the backgrounds and cultures of the peoples to whom they were being sent, might have taught the Bureau of Indian Affairs a lesson. But even today, little attention is paid to such instruction of Bureau personnel, and in its proper place in this study a recommendation will be made on that subject. In this section, however, it is appropriate to make several general observations as necessary prerequisites for a more vivid understanding of the implications of the findings and recommendations in the following portions of this study. In a sense they provide a basis and context for a realistic approach to federal-Indian relations in 1969 and to what, if anything, requires rethinking and change.

1) In the great mass of treaties, statutes, laws, and regulations that have been built up during the long course of federal-Indian relations, the non-Indian, to use an analogy, often becomes lost among the trees of Indian affairs and too rarely steps back far enough to see the forest whole. He forgets basic truths about Indians that must never be forgotten, if only because they are in the minds of the Indians with whom non-Indians are trying to work. It would appear unnecessary to restate such facts that the Indians were here for thousands of years; that this is their homeland; that they evolved their own distinctive cultures and did not share the points of view, attitudes, and thinking that came to the rest of the American population from Judeo-Christian and Western Civilization legacies; that although the Indians were conquered militarily (and are the only portion of the American population that reflects that experience), they are confirming a lesson of history, namely that no people has ever been coerced by another people into scuttling its own culture; and that although acculturation and assimilation do occur, they occur only on the individual's own terms. The awareness of such generalizations makes clear the implications of a further facet of Indian affairs that has continuing relevancy, and especially to this study, namely the Indians' position, and therefore their posture, vis-à-vis the government.

In matters that are of the most importance to them, the Indians, unlike all other Americans, do not yet enjoy self-government. They are still governed, not entirely unlike colonial subjects, by strangers whom they neither elected nor appointed and who are not accountable to them. As late as 1934 the rule of the "governor" was absolute; since then, tribal councils, like the legislatures of many modern colonies, have acquired authority over a broadening range of tribal affairs. But the "governor" is still present with the apparatus of management and the powers of direction, influence, finances, and veto to use when and where they really count. The practical meaning of this relationship of the American government to its Indian citizens in this extraordinarily late day and age was noted recently in a study titled "The Indian: The Forgotten American," published in the *Harvard Law Review* in June 1968. Its authors, Warren H. Cohen and Philip J. Mause, commented: "The BIA possesses final authority over most tribal actions as well as over many decisions made by Indians as individuals. BIA approval is required, for example, when a tribe enters into a contract, expends money, or amends its constitution. Although normal expectation in American society is that a private individual or group may do anything unless it is specifically prohibited by the government, it might be said that the normal expectation on the reservation is that the Indians may not do anything unless it is specifically permitted by the government."

The psychological implications of the Indians' status as compared with that of the rest of the American body politic loom with increasing significance in Indian affairs today, especially as larger numbers of young Indians become educated and motivated to seek the full measure of self-government enjoyed by all other Americans. To an extent, the full perspective of this "forest-view" of all Indians is obscured by dilemmas posed by the obligatory trust function of the government. But a banker, exercising a trust function for a non-Indian citizen, applies himself only to the substance of the trust and does not govern the life of his client or necessarily manage his other affairs. One task in Indian affairs is inevitably to narrow the trustee's domain to the substance of the trust (to be discussed later) and to remove his authority from other areas. The logic of attempting to achieve such a goal can, again, only be appreciated in full by viewing the "forest" whole, and not being enmeshed and inhibited among the trees.

2) To the incoming member of a new Administration the questions and problems of federal-Indian relations are of the here and now. Decisions concerning changes or the retention of the status quo will be made largely

within the context of today alone. But to the Indian, the context is an immensely broader one and possesses a vividness and influence that often leads to the frustration and failure of policies and programs when the non-Indian administrator fails to comprehend its relevancy. The context is history, the details and individual steps of which may be unknown to the contemporary non-Indian official, but are still intimate and potent in Indian thinking and responses.

To the Indian, 1969 is a continuation of an unbroken narrative of policies, programs, and promises, often abruptly changing, disorganizing, contradictory, and unrealistic, and of people, many of them still personally remembered, who gave promises and orders and who sometimes worked for good and sometimes for harm. In Washington discussions will occur today, and policies and programs will be considered according to the current situation. But the Indian's mind will also be on a legacy of pacification, army and missionary rule, punishments and repression, allotments, treaty sessions and sacred promises, laws and special rights acknowledged in return for land cessions, and orders given by the government in the 1920's, countermanded in the 1930's, countermanded again in the 1950's, and countermanded once more in the 1960's. Specifically, the Indian's response will be conditioned by the knowledge of a Mr. Smith or a Captain Jones who came to the reservation as the agent of a President in the mid-nineteenth century and told the tribal leaders something that their descendants have kept alive from generation to generation. He will color his reactions to a proposal with the evergreen memories of battles won or lost, of injuries and injustices, of land taken from his people by fraud, deceit, and corruption, of lost hunting, fishing, and water rights, and of zigzag policies of administrations that came to office, just like the new one, and then left. . . .

3) Despite the fear of termination and various programmatic and administrative shortcomings, some of which were quite serious and will be discussed in later sections, a number of profound and important improvements did occur in Indian affairs during the last eight years. One of them, fraught with significance for the future direction of Indian affairs, requires the most serious recognition.

Indians had long asserted, but usually to deaf ears, that the individual tribes knew better than the government what kinds of programs they needed and wanted, and that if they could play decisive roles in the planning of such programs, they could, with technical and financial assistance, demonstrate an ability to learn quickly to administer and execute them successfully.

This assertion was stated forcibly in a "Declaration of Indian Purpose" by some 420 Indian leaders of 67 tribes at a gathering in Chicago in June, 1961, but, although endorsed to some extent by Secretary Udall's Task Force the same year, received no serious recognition or encouragement from the Bureau of Indian Affairs. The Indians were deemed not to know what was best for them, and programs continued to be imposed on them. . . .

4) In the same vein, it must be noted that the non-Indian population of the United States, reacting to a multitude of winds of change abroad in the world in recent years, is beginning to turn away from a long-held view regarding the Indian's destiny — and therefore from what were long considered the proper policies and programs for him. From the time of Jamestown and Plymouth, the most benign attitude of the white man concerning Indians was, assimilate or die. Missionaries and agencies of government tried to rush Indians into becoming Christianized farmers, and from the administration of George Washington until the present day national policy, stated or implicit, has been directed toward the turning of the Indian into a white man, the alternative seeming to be only continued primitivism, economic stagnation, and ultimate obliteration by white society. All programs, actions, and attitudes of government have supported this policy which derived its mandate from the non-Indian population and its representatives in Congress.

At the same time, a minority opinion always existed that expressed the view that Indian progress and development, far from being assisted, was actually being crippled and delayed by the "either-or" choice, that Indians would resist attempts to force and hurry their assimilation, and that such attempts would not only fail to achieve their purpose but were morally wrong, since no people had the right to strip a culture from another people. Inevitably, the merits of the point of view of the latter group were obscured by superficial and erroneous arguments that they were more interested in seeing Indian cultures preserved than allowing the Indians to develop, and the minority was unable to bring about a meaningful dialogue that might have produced an impact on national policy, which throughout the Kennedy and Johnson administrations continued, in essence, to point toward the ultimate goal of Indian assimilation.

Of late, however, Indian articulateness, studies of Indian education, and changing attitudes among the American people concerning minority groups have combined to pose the acceptance of a different destiny for the American Indians, one in which they would be allowed to develop on their own terms and at their own chosen rate of speed — bi-culturally if they so desired — being assisted to create a viable economic life for their people, but not being pressured to give up any parts of their individual cultures which they wished to retain, and not being urged to take on any of the dominant society's traits which they did not want. The pros and cons of such a policy need not be argued here. But the strength, particularly among the Indians, of those who maintain that Indian self-determination is now the surest road to Indian progress and development, that it will see a new and electrifying rebirth of Indian initiative and vigor, and that its result will be the growth of viable and healthy Indian communities within the nation has grown to the point where the new administration must take note of the areas in which it may soon engender significant confrontations. . . .

The Indians' demand for self-determination will increase steadily, but there will be many ways to move soundly with it. Perhaps the best way, short of the enunciation of an Administration point of view on the subject, will be a clear and purposeful redefinition of the Bureau of Indian Affairs' functions, procedures, and limits of authority, together with a restructuring of the Bureau to accommodate to the changes. Though the changes would not be drastic, intentions and effects on the reservations would be altered, and a natural process tending toward increased self-determination would come into play. Any such change from the status quo would, of course, require the support of the Congress and the Bureau of the Budget and would demand that the Administration play a positive persuasive role with both bodies. . . .

III. STUDIES AND MAJOR DEVELOPMENTS IN THE LAST EIGHT YEARS

"During the last eight years," an Indian leader said recently, "Indian policies and programs have been studied to death. What we need is for someone to begin paying attention to some of the things that the Indians recommended in those studies."

There is no need in 1969 to repeat the experience of the Kennedy Administration of 1961 with another full-fledged, Task Force–type study of Indian affairs, complete with months of hearings and subordinate studies. . . .

A brief conclusion from the . . . record of what has, and has not, occurred during the last eight years illuminates the following:

1) Both the appropriations and functions of the Bureau of Indian Affairs have increased greatly, and many other Federal agencies, including the OEO, EDA, HAA, the Office of Education, and the Labor Department, now share the reservation scene with the BIA;

2) The BIA's greatest expansion has occurred in the fields of education, vocational training and placement, housing, and industrial and community development, and is evidence that a change in its orientation from the primacy of its trust function to that of development has become an established fact;

3) The obligations conferred by the trust function still require the wielding of authority over other matters by Bureau officials and result in many of the conflicts between the Bureau and the Indians, as well as much of the BIA's negativism and delays. Increasingly, the Indians are requesting the right to assume full responsibility for the management of their income and final authority over such matters as attorney contracts, tribal codes, and constitutional actions — while having their lands continue inviolate in trust status;

4) The principle of self-determination has been accepted and is already being applied in small ways on some reservations. The BIA has begun a trend of negotiating with tribes to permit them, through contracts, to provide some services; this too is encouraging the process of self-determination. But Indian participation and decision-making are still the exception and are being frustrated and denied too regularly by the Bureau's present organization;

5) At the same time, the BIA's structure still leads to a malaise within the Bureau as bad as eight years ago that positively holds back progress;

6) *The top priority is for a change in the administration of Indian affairs to accelerate Indian progress and achieve the maximum effective implementation of Indian policies and programs by utilizing, and not impeding, the Indians' development of self-determination.*

IV. POSITIONING INDIAN AFFAIRS
IN THE FEDERAL GOVERNMENT

This study now addresses itself to specific recommendations for a course upon which to embark in 1969, including:

The positioning of the administration of Indian affairs within the government;

The reorganization of the B I A's structure;

Programmatic approaches.

This section concerns the first of those items. . . .

This study recommends that a meaningful and determined reorganization of the administration of Indian affairs, together with the providing of an effective Administration thrust to go forward to the opportunities of tomorrow and not simply solve the problems of yesterday, can only be accomplished by moving the Bureau of Indian Affairs to the Executive Office of the Presidency, for the objectives of Indian affairs in 1969 require nothing less than the priority, mandate, and visibility which the President himself can give them. . . .

. . .

It is recommended, therefore, at the very least, that if the Bureau remains in the Department of the Interior, it should be placed under an Assistant Secretary for Indian and Territorial Affairs, who can give the proper attention to decision-making at the topmost level of the Department.

. . .

Wherever the present Bureau of Indian Affairs is positioned within the government, its structure must be thoroughly reorganized.

. . .

It is recommended, therefore, that the reorganization of the structure of the Bureau . . . include:

— the elimination of the Offices of the Assistant Commissioners for Community Services and Economic Development, together with all the staffs and Divisions of those Offices;

— the readjustment of the present Offices of the Assistant Commissioners for Administration, Engineering, and Program Coordination as guidance, coordinating, budgeting, administration, and management arms of the Bureau, reporting to the Commissioner;

— a separate structure for the Assistant Commissioner for Education, who would report to the Commissioner, but would retain his present staffs and Divisions, and would have direct line authority to all elements of the educational system, as well as coordinators with area and agency programs, tribes, and state and local school systems;

— the addition of regional coordinating desk officers, reporting to the Commissioner, but without line authority;

— the addition of an Office of Urban Indian Affairs, concerned with the problems of urban Indians and reporting to the Commissioner;

— the retention of area offices headed by Assistant Commissioners, but the elimination of all branches at the area level and the reorientation of the area office's function to that of providing guidance, advice, and assistance to reservations; and

— the focusing of primary operational attention on the reservations by placing all specialists, save those in education, on the reservation and giving the superintendent authority over them and their budgeting, and a direct line via the area Assistant Commissioner to the Office of the Commissioner.

. . .

In addition to Bureau reorganization, the following recommendations are also made:

— The National Council on Indian Opportunity, which has already proved its value, should be continued, with its present functions adequately funded;

— Training programs, and adequate orientation seminars in Indian (and tribal) history and cultures, should be set up and carried out systematically for Bureau personnel who work at every level of the Bureau;

— Superintendents, area heads, and the new Office concerned with urban Indian affairs should be directed to seek from the tribes and Indian communities the most effective methods by which information about government programs can be communicated to the individual Indians.

. . .

— Contracts with tribes must be accompanied by improved payment procedures, a continuity of planning and programming, the ending of unnecessary supervision and requirements, the provision of necessary working capital and equipment, and an agreement that tribes should receive a fair return, not be required to pay sub-standard wages, and be offered projects that will require them to develop their own staffs of skilled personnel.

. . .

— Attention should be given, and steps taken, to end the Bureau's deficiencies in the field of research and development; in the lack of meaningful and adequate data on Indians and Indian affairs; in the use of consultants and non-government experts; and in the modernization of its administrative, fiscal, record-keeping, and other management practices.

— Indian Affairs should be headed by an Indian, but he should possess all the qualities of dedication, determination, knowledge, and vigor that the leadership of the federal conduct of Indian affairs now requires. Indians should also be placed in as many policy- and decision-making positions within the Bureau as possible. Moreover, if the Bureau is kept within the Department of the Interior, the Secretary should have an Indian staff assistant primarily responsible for liaison with the new Assistant Secretary for Indian and Territorial Affairs, the BIA, and Indian affairs generally.

VI. PROGRAMMATIC RECOMMENDATIONS

It is certain that the worst problems afflicting American Indians will never be ended without programs that are adequately funded. It is accepted that the Indians do not have the funds themselves and that they do not have access to the sources of credit that are usually available to other Americans. But the actual funding of programs for Indians by the government has never approached the level required by the massive dimensions of the problems.

A few of the facts obscured by the promulgation of intentions in President Johnson's Message on Indian Affairs on March 6, 1968, underscore the point. The Message conveyed proposals for many new or expanded programs which, somehow, were to be financed by only a 10 percent increase in federal expenditures for Indians above the appropriations of the previous year. One of the proposals was for a 10 percent increase in funds for health programs, including a number of items that would make available to the Indians greater numbers of trained personnel to help cope with the many serious health problems on the reservations. Before the year was over, the exact opposite had come to pass, and the Public Health Service was pointing out that, under Section 201 of the Revenue and Expenditure Control Act of 1968, Public Law 90-364, the Division of Indian Health was facing a reduction of almost 1,000 employees, or one-sixth of its total staff, principally among nursing personnel and other patient care supportive staff in the field. A reduction in staff is now occurring on reservations and in Indian hospitals, not only nullifying the promise held out in President Johnson's Message, but bringing a new crisis to the Indians. (Corrective legislation, it hardly needs pointing out, is required at the earliest possible moment.)

Again, the inadequacy of funding a program to deal effectively with another pressing problem is evidenced in the field of Indian housing. The Presidential Task Force had reported to the White House that at least three-quarters of all Indian houses on reservations were below minimum standards of decency and that over a 10-year period roughly 100,000 units, "of which approximately 80,000 are new, would have to be provided for the housing needs of the Indian population." The President's response to the Task Force's assertion that this would require a 10-year program costing approximately $1 billion was to propose an increase of only 1,000 new Indian homes (for a total of 2,500) to be built under HUD programs in fiscal year '69.

The American taxpayer may wonder with increasing impatience why Indian problems are not solved, and why expenditures for those problems continue to mount each year. One demonstrable answer is that the expenditures have never been high enough to do much more than keep the problems going. In the years after the Indians' pacification, the appropriations barely met the minimum subsistence needs of the Indians. In more recent years, with an increasing Indian population and a growing complexity of reservation problems, the appropriations have risen, but consistently have stayed well below a level needed to carry out intentions. It may be impossible, because of higher priority needs elsewhere in the federal budget and the consequent requirement for economy in the Indian budget, to attempt to solve the Indians' problems once and for all with the same kind of massive appropriations that have characterized the most ambitious aid programs for some of the underdeveloped peoples overseas. But it should be emphasized that the Indians are Americans, and that until a similar approach is adopted for them, Indian programs will continue to limp along, and Indian development will proceed at an unsatisfactory pace. In addition, because of the rapid increase in the Indians' population, there is every prospect that their economic, educational, and health levels will drop steadily behind those of the rest of the population, and that each Administration will leave the Indians worse off, in relation to the rest of the American people, than it found them.

Adequate funding, therefore, should be a major concern of every Indian program. . . .

The planning and application of all economic development programs, long- and short-range, should reflect the Indians' own needs, desires, and cultural traits. By bringing the Indians into the planning and decision-making process, programs need not fail, as they have in the past. . . .

With minor exceptions, the Indians desire the federal government to continue to provide its trust protection for their lands, and the government must continue to give that protection. But it should be possible, by amending the Indian Reorganization Act and other pertinent statutes, to reduce the number of ancillary obligations and responsibilities of the trustee. In their drive for self-determination and self-government, tribes will press increasingly for the right to program their judgment funds, have authority over their budgets, and assume full responsibility for the management of their income, the making of contracts with attorneys, and the framing of tribal codes, resolutions, and constitutional actions. Without abandoning the trusteeship protection of lands, the government should be in a position to be able to transfer those other responsibilities, piece-meal or in full, to tribes deemed ready to assume them. For some tribes, that day may already have arrived, and the continued denial to them of rights they are able to exercise for themselves may be viewed as the most stultifying of all the obstacles that inhibit them on their road to development.

"We Speak as Indians"

American Indian Task Force,
Washington DC, November 1969

The 1960s were a period of much social upheaval and change in the United States. The civil rights movement had challenged the long-standing prevailing racial order that disadvantaged non-whites in economic, social, and political life, and both the U.S. government and its citizens were forced to begin examining their assumptions about justice and equality, particularly insofar as race was concerned. This atmosphere of self-reflection and a new willingness to consider difficult social issues such as poverty and racism opened the door to further discussion of Termination and its negative consequences for Indian communities.

Our Brother's Keeper was essentially a revelation of conditions and it contained no recommendations. Prior to its publication, Edgar Cahn won endorsement for the study's findings from a group of Indian leaders of various ages, interests, and tribal affiliations, and as an Indian Editorial Board they served as sponsors for the book when it was issued.

The next step, in the view of the Citizens' Advocate Center, was for American Indians to decide for themselves what, if anything, they wished to do with the report. With the center's assistance, the Indian Editorial Board was turned into a so-called American Indian Task Force and enlarged to forty-two members. The roster of the task force, comprising many of the best-known Indian leaders in the country, included the following persons:

Earl Old Person, Chairman, Blackfeet Tribe; President, National Congress of American Indians

Jess Six Killer, Cherokee; Executive Director, American Indians United

George Groundhog, Cherokee; Director, Original Cherokee Community Organization

Viola Hatch, Cheyenne-Arapaho; field worker, Oklahomans for Indian Opportunity

Dennis J. Banks, Chippewa; Director, American Indian Movement

Clyde Bellecourt, Chippewa; President, American Indian Movement

Ted Holappa, Chippewa; Executive Director, American Indian Cultural Center, Los Angeles

Simon Howard, Chippewa

Roger Jourdain, Chairman, Red Lake Chippewa; Regional Vice President, NCAI

Lucy Covington, Colville tribal councilwoman

H. Miles Brandon, Eskimo; member, Alaska Federation of Natives

Margaret Nick, Eskimo

D'Arcy McNickle, Flathead

Thomas Banyacya, Hopi

Douglas L. Sakiestewa, Hopi-Navajo

James Wahpepah, Chairman, Kickapoo Tribal Council; President, Oklahomans for Indian Opportunity

John Belindo, Kiowa-Navajo; Executive Director, NCAI

Mary Cornelius, Chairman, Little Shell Tribe of Turtle Mountain Chippewa

Monroe M. Weso, Menominee

Wendell Chino, Chairman, Mescalero Apache Tribal Council; former President, NCAI

Bernard Second, Mescalero Apache

Peterson Zah, Navajo

Peter MacDonald, Navajo; Executive Director, Office of Navajo Economic Opportunity

Dr. Taylor McKenzie, Navajo

Janet McCloud, Tulalip

Ernie Stevens, Oneida; Executive Director, Intertribal Council of California

Charles H. Lohah, Osage

Cipriano Manuel, Papago

Archie J. LaCoote, Passamaquoddy

Al Elgin, Pomo; Executive Director, Intertribal Friendship House, Oakland, California

William Pensoneau, Ponca; President, National Indian Youth Council

Martha Grass, Ponca

Seferino Tenerio, Pueblo

James Vidovich, Chairman, Pyramid Lake Paiutes

Kesley Edmo, Shoshone

E. Ray Briggs, Sioux

Johnson Holy Rock, Sioux

Cato Valandra, former chairman, Rosebud Sioux

Paul Bernal, Taos Pueblo

Rose Crow Flies High, Three Affiliated Tribes

Francis McKinley, Ute; member, Far West Laboratory for Educational Research

Angelo LaMere, Winnebago; member of Great Lakes Intertribal Council

In November 1969 members of the Indian Task Force met in Washington, pondered principally the book's major theme regarding the lack of governmental accountability to the Indians, and developed a new approach toward American Indian self-determination. On November 12 the Indians met in the White House with Vice President Spiro Agnew and various presidential assistants and presented a statement that incorporated their new idea. Two days later, at the Capitol, they read to members of Congress and the Washington press another statement expanding on Indian grievances and calling for a new day for the tribes. Excerpts from both statements, making clear what these diverse Indian leaders had agreed upon, follow.

The Task Force's Statement Presented to Vice President Spiro Agnew and White House Staff
November 10, 1969

We speak as Indians who care about what has happened to our people. We speak out because every individual must, and there must be some who are willing to start a process. We do not view ourselves as "chosen leaders" or an "Indian elite," though we come from various backgrounds and diverse tribes. But we do claim to be a cross-section of concerned nonestablishment Indians.

We came together initially to assist in providing information for the book *Our Brother's Keeper* and to state whether, within our own personal knowledge, it spoke the truth.

The national concern aroused by *Our Brother's Keeper* cannot be allowed to dissipate. One of the main points made by this book is that, unlike most Americans, the Indians have little or no forum for redress of grievances and wrongs committed against them. The Task Force believes that there must be a direct channel of communication so that Indian voices are not lost in the Bureau of Indian Affairs, the Department of Interior, the Bureau of the Budget, Congressional Committees, or other parts of the bureaucratic and political maze in which Indians are now trapped. We are, therefore, proposing a process which could provide a way in which Indians could speak directly to the government of the United States, both to seek a redress of grievances and to initiate and shape Indian policy. . . .

The Task Force proposes that a process of dialogue be initiated in all areas which shall coincide with the eleven area offices of the Bureau of Indian Affairs.

Each of these eleven areas is partially represented by individual members of the Task Force but it would be the responsibility of the entire Task Force, working with others, to expand in each area to insure that it included a broad spectrum of representation from numerous tribes, tribal chairmen, local organizations, individual spokesmen involved in issues, and representatives of urban Indians from cities within each area. Thus, the Task Force will establish separate and broadly representative Boards of Inquiry which would conduct hearings, receive grievances, and generate recommendations in the manner set forth below.

1. That a working meeting of the Task Force, with the National Council on Indian Opportunity, be convened to determine the best way to present the idea of conferences and hearings.

2. That further area conferences be held to explain the need to begin the hearing process with each area's reprsentatives to the Task Force and NCIO to discuss ways to expand the concept and lay groundwork for the hearings.

3. That there be hearings in each of the eleven areas — these hearings are to take testimony in open meetings from groups, tribes, and individuals about the needs and situations of the various people and to call for specific recommendations from the people. We urge federal agencies to attend the hearings as observers.

A. After the hearings, there will be continued input into the process through complaint and evaluation process by having a local center or person to take complaints in each local community. A "circuit rider" is to be hired by the local Board of Inquiry who will take the complaints and make recommendations about solutions.

B. Red ribbon "grand juries," composed entirely of Indians, should be convened in order to investigate and report upon deprivations of rights, charges of inaction or unresponsiveness by officials, lack of effectiveness of educational, health, and other services — and . . . where the facts appear to warrant it, the red ribbon "grand jury" shall not only come forward with findings of fact, but should also, by prior arrangement with the U.S. Attorney, present an "indictment" which the U.S. Attorney or (in the event of conflict of interest) a lawyer provided by the government shall be called upon to investigate such charges and represent Indians in such a manner as to protect their rights and make government programs genuinely responsive to the desires and needs of Indians.

4. The Boards of Inquiry in the eleven areas are to meet again to evaluate the first round of hearings, include the continuing complaints, consider the circuit rider's findings, and take recommendation from another round of testimony to deal particularly with proposals and recommendations.

5. From each of the hearings and Boards of Inquiry, there is to be a National Board of Inquiry, composed of three members from each of the eleven areas to meet and make national recommendations. These members are to be chosen by an elective process by Indians. Finally, the entire process will result in the creation of a permanent ongoing local watchdog on bureaucratic programs.

We make this proposal because as Indians, we choose to go beyond talking about process and dialogue and consultation and to try to think through what would be a process that would be honest and would give Indians a genuine opportunity to be heard, to seek a redress of grievances, and to take the initiative in shaping government policy.

We propose that the Task Force, supplemented by additional Indians from additional tribes and organizations, form a core of a group which would contract to implement this proposal. We believe that the time has come, not only for Indians to be consulted, but for them to design and implement a process of consultation whereby they can speak out their own grievances as they know them, articulate their problems, shape proposals, draft recommendations, circulate proposed legislative or administrative action for widespread discussion among Indian peoples. We believe that such functions should be performed by Indians — that there is no question here as to whether qualified Indians exist when this proposal has come from Indians — and we believe there is a clear statutory duty to contract this function to Indians under 36 Stat. L. 861. We submit that this is not only desirable — but that it would be a major symbolic break with the past practice where no Indians have been the ones paid to become Indian experts, while Indians served as volunteer educators for non-Indians.

We do not come here to blame this administration for the failures of the past — it is our hope that by implementing a listening process, that another group like this, in some future time, will not be needed because this administration failed to hear the Indian peoples.

Press Statement to Congress Made
by American Indian Task Force
November 12, 1969

I. We, the first Americans, come to the Congress of the United States that you give us the chance to try to solve what you call the Indian problem. You have had two hundred years and you have not succeeded by your standards. It is clear that you have not succeeded in ours.

On Monday, we asked the Vice President of the United States to set into motion a process which would insure that our people could secure redress of grievances and could shape the government programs that affect and control their lives. . . .

We have asked the Vice President of the United States for Indian boards of inquiries which would hold hearings throughout the areas where Indians live, for area conferences, for red ribbon grand juries, for circuit riders to take complaints and for a National Board of Inquiry to meet and make national recommendations based upon the complaints and recommendations received on the grass roots level.

And we ask you to help us see that the process we proposed to the Vice President somehow becomes a reality. We hope that he will be willing to do it on his own. But we ask you, as the representatives of the people of the United States, to serve as our representatives too — to help us see that assurances do not become empty promises. And, if necessary, to enact legislation which will create such a process where Indians can really shape government policy and control their own lives and destinies if that is not done by the Executive Branch.

II. We come to you with a sense of impending betrayal at a moment when we wish to seek redress of grievances to ask you to broaden our access to the courts to protect the rights guaranteed us by your treaties and statutes. And we find, with a sense of horror, and impending doom, that instead, the Congress of the United States is on the verge of passing an Amendment to the Economic Opportunity Act which would effectively diminish the slight access to the courts we have gained in recent years through the advent of the OEO Legal Service Program. And it is an even greater irony that we find this to be the case when a governor's veto in at least one state has already killed a legal service program for Indians. What right do the governors have to interfere with what goes on on the reservation? What right do state governors have to interfere with the solemn promises made to us by the federal government in statutes and treaties which can only be enforced by resort to the courts? What right do you, or any generation of Americans, have to rip up the solemn promises of the past — promises made to us both by the Constitution and by the President of a nation which still holds and enjoys the land received in exchange for those treaties? There are none among you who would suggest that rights — and above all the right to petition one's government — can have any meaning at all without lawyers and without access to the forum where the people traditionally petition their government.

III. We come to you today to ask that you set your own house in order. We say that until the congressional committees which control nearly all Indian legislation cease to be hostile to the interests of the Indian, then we have been deprived of one of the three branches of what we have been repeatedly told is our government as well as yours.

The present committees have pushed for termination, and have fostered on Congress seemingly neutral and technical legislation, under the guise of Indian expertise, which has taken away our land, our water rights, our mineral resources and handed them over to the white man.

You have been duped — as we have been duped. These committees have created a monstrous bureaucracy insensitive to Indians which trembles and cringes before them. The Indian suffers — and the nation pays the bill. Nothing will change so long as this unholy alliance exists between the B I A and these Congressional Committees.

On Monday we asked the Vice President to seek a new arrangement within the Executive Branch of Government — one which will by-pass those channels which are hostile and insensitive to our interests. We asked him to set in motion a process by which our voices could be heard on our needs within the Executive Branch of Government.

Today, we come to seek a new arrangement with the Congress. We have come to seek a change in the committees that deal in Indian affairs. We ask that the committees of Congress not be dominated by interests which are hostile to our own survival. We ask that these committees act as a watchdog on federal programs which are passed especially for our benefit but which do not in fact benefit us because of the way the B I A runs them. And, we ask that these committees insure that we get our fair share of general legislation. We do not get our fair share of these programs now. And we do not have any means to seek redress when the very programs that are passed to help us in fact are used as means to enslave and oppress us.

We come here today to remind you that you are not just the representatives of local districts or of states. You are members of the Congress of the United States. You have national obligations. We know you are highly conscious of your national obligations when you deliberate on such problems as the war in Viet Nam. We know that you have even taken those obligations seriously enough to go to Viet Nam in order to personally inform yourself on how the Executive carries out the commitments of the United States.

We ask that you do no less at home — for the United States has made older and more sacred national commitments to the people who have occupied these shores for twenty-five thousand years. The United States has made national commitments in the form of treaties, legislation and the Constitution, itself, to our peoples. We ask you to come to our homes — in the cities and on the reservations. We ask that you seek with equal vigilance to determine whether national commitments have been kept to us. Guided tours by bureaucrats will only serve to hamper you in your search for truth.

You, the Congress of the United States, are being asked to come to see how we really live and to try to understand the values, the culture and the way of life we are fighting to preserve — an American way of life. A way of life which we believe is built upon respect for differences, a tolerance of diversity.

We cannot come to Washington. We are not rich. And we cannot afford the high price of democracy.

In essence, we ask the restoration of what you claimed at the founding of your nation — the inalienable right to pursue happiness. We cannot fail worse than the experts and the bureaucrats. We do not lack for knowledge — and we are not ashamed to hire experts and technicians. But our people do not lack for leaders, for sensitivity, for talent and ability. We ask for the right to pursue our dream — and we ask for you to respect that dream. That is the American way. We claim our birthright.

Message to Congress on Indian Affairs

President Richard M. Nixon, July 8, 1970

The long-awaited enunciation of President Nixon's Indian policy came in a special Presidential Message to Congress on Indian Affairs on July 8, 1970.

In many respects it was a logical culmination of all that had occurred and all that had been recommended in Indian affairs during the preceding decade. But in the full context of Indian-white relations in the United States, it was historic in tone and intent. It was a firm rebuttal by a chief executive of the nation of the white man's conviction — countenanced officially for many generations — that American Indians were incompetent to control their own affairs. It proclaimed for the executive branch of the government the Indians' right to self-determination and urged the Congress to join in making it the nation's policy and the official yardstick by which to measure future federal-Indian relations. It was the strongest assertion yet made by any president against the twin evils of paternalism and termination. And in its many proposals for dealing with reservation life, tribal grievances, and Indian demands to continue as Indians and manage their own affairs themselves, it showed that a national administration had at last listened to the Indians and accepted *their* ideas of what they needed and wanted. It would no longer be "either-or" for the Indians (be either a white man or an Indian). Forced assimilation into the mainstream, the most benign aim of federal Indian policy since colonial days, would be abandoned by President Nixon.

The message, however, was no more than a statement of intent. It did not, by itself, bring about self-determination or any of the measures it proposed. It created no new conditions on the reservations, and it did not halt abruptly the paternalism of the Bureau of Indian Affairs. But it pointed federal policy in a new direction and demanded new thinking and attitudes from those in the federal agencies who dealt in Indian affairs.

The Indians' response to the president's message was guarded. Most of them were pleased with its theme of self-determination, but they were skeptical whether the administration would take action to implement the words. Actions did follow. Administration bills, prepared with the participation of the Indian members of the National Council on Indian Opportunity, were introduced into Congress to carry out the major provisions of the message. Again the Indians were wary. The tribes had had no hand in framing the measures, and history had taught them to be guarded about what Washington officials decided was best for them. Even the Indians who found they could support the bills adopted a "watch and wait" attitude to see with what degree of commitment the administration would bring its persuasive powers to bear on Congress in behalf of the measures.

Meanwhile, the National Council on Indian Opportunity conducted two series of meetings with Native Americans around the country to discuss the bills and allow the Indians to recommend revisions in them or suggest new measures. And late in November the Bureau of Indian Affairs announced dramatic changes, formulated with the help of its Indian task forces, in structure, procedures, and philosophy, designed to accelerate the attainment of Indian self-determination. The changes coincided almost exactly with demands that Indians had been making since 1961. They included the redelegation of decision-making authorities from the area offices to the reservation level; the change of name and job description of the reservation "superintendent" to "field administrator," reflecting the shift of the bureau as a whole from the management of Indian affairs to the servicing of Indian needs; the reassignment of bureau personnel and the institution of rotation policies that would encourage better federal-Indian relations; the formalizing of procedures by which tribes could take control, with federal funding, of their own affairs; and the establishment of evaluation and inspection programs. In sum, the bureau changes, coupled with the legislation stemming from the president's message, set the stage at last for the realization of self-determination, and there could be no turning back. By making contracts to administer themselves all the programs formerly run for them by the Bureau of Indian Affairs, the Zuñi of New Mexico earlier in 1970 had already become the first tribe to take control of their own affairs. Now the so-called Zuñi plan could be adopted for all or part of their programs by other tribes, and by early December 1970 the bureau had almost thirty requests by Indian groups in different parts of the country to take over control of some or all of their own affairs.

It was, of course, only a start. The president's message and the bureau changes were large and historic steps forward. But American Indians were still "the poorest of the poor." Social, ecomomic, health, housing, and educational problems still beset every reservation. Aggressive white interests, including planners of government projects, still threatened Indian land, water, and other resources. Dictatorial bureaucrats and paternalistic white "experts" still held the upper hand on many reservations. Injustices and discrimination had not suddenly disappeared. In short, Indian Americans still faced a long struggle to attain the freedoms and standards of living enjoyed by all other Americans.

It is important to note that at the time that President Nixon and his advisors were drafting this statement on Indian policy, his advisors were negotiating with Indians of All Tribes who had occupied Alcatraz Island the previous November. This "Message to Congress" reflects the slow evolution of federal Indian policy away from Termination and toward Self-Determination. Whether or not this statement of intent would be turned into concrete legislation, passed by both houses of Congress and signed by the president, remained to be seen. Those debates, like the drafting of this policy message, would take place during the next few years against a backdrop of growing activism and increasing native militancy. Would the activism influence the legislative process? Students of U.S. and international politics have often observed that the demands of moderates become more appealing to decision-makers in the face of more militant and radical actions and demands. Sociologist Herbert Haines calls this a "radical flank effect," where a movement's radical flank shifts the debate further and faster than moderates alone could achieve. Red Power represented a radical flank in the Indian rights movement that would help to turn these ideas into the official Self-Determination policies of the 1970s and beyond. Following is the text of President Nixon's Indian Affairs Message.

TO THE CONGRESS OF THE UNITED STATES:

The first Americans — the Indians — are the most deprived and most isolated minority group in our nation. On virtually every scale of measurement — employment, income, education, health — the condition of the Indian people ranks at the bottom.

This condition is the heritage of centuries of injustice. From the time of their first contact with European settlers, the American Indians have been oppressed and brutalized, deprived of their ancestral lands and denied the opportunity to control their own destiny. Even the Federal programs which are intended to meet their needs have frequently proven to be ineffective and demeaning.

But the story of the Indian in America is something more than the record of the white man's frequent aggression, broken agreements, intermittent remorse and prolonged failure. It is a record also of endurance, of survival, of adaptation and creativity in the face of overwhelming obstacles. It is a record of enormous contributions to this country — to its art and culture, to its strength and spirit, to its sense of history and its sense of purpose.

It is long past time that the Indian policies of the Federal government began to recognize and build upon the capacities and insights of the Indian people. Both as a matter of justice and as a matter of enlightened social policy, we must begin to act on the basis of what the Indians themselves have long been telling us. The time has come to break decisively with the past and to create the conditions for a new era in which the Indian future is determined by Indian acts and Indian decisions.

SELF-DETERMINATION WITHOUT TERMINATION

The first and most basic question that must be answered with respect to Indian policy concerns the historic and legal relationship between the Federal government and Indian communities. In the past, this relationship has oscillated between two equally harsh and unacceptable extremes.

On the one hand, it has — at various times during previous Administrations — been the stated policy objective of both the Executive and Legislative branches of the Federal government eventually to terminate the trusteeship relationship between the Federal government and the Indian people. As recently as August of 1953, in House Concurrent Resolution 108, the Congress declared that termination was the long-range goal of its Indian policies. This would mean that Indian tribes would eventually lose any special standing they had under Federal law; the tax exempt status of their lands would be discontinued; Federal responsibility for their economic and social well-being would be repudiated; and the tribes themselves would be effectively dismantled. Tribal property would be divided among individual members who would then be assimilated into the society at large.

This policy of forced termination is wrong, in my judgment, for a number of reasons. First, the premises on which it rests are wrong. Termination implies that the Federal government has taken on a trusteeship responsibility for Indian communities as an act of generosity toward a disadvantaged people and that it can therefore discontinue this responsibility on a unilateral basis whenever it sees fit. But the unique status of Indian tribes does not rest on any premise such as this. The special relationship between Indians and the Federal government is the result instead of solemn obligations which have been entered into by the United States Government. Down through the years, through written treaties and through formal and informal agreements, our government has made specific commitments to the Indian people. For their part, the Indians have often surrendered claims to vast tracts of land and have accepted life on government reservations. In exchange, the government has agreed to provide community services such as health, education and public safety, services which would presumably allow Indian communities to enjoy a standard of living comparable to that of other Americans.

This goal, of course, has never been achieved. But the special relationship between the Indian tribes and the Federal government which arises from these agreements continues to carry immense moral and legal force. To terminate this relationship would be no more appropriate than to terminate the citizenship rights of any other American.

The second reason for rejecting forced termination is that the practical results have been clearly harmful in the few instances in which termination actually has been tried. The removal of Federal trusteeship responsibility has produced considerable disorientation among the affected Indians and has left them unable to relate to a myriad of Federal, State and local assistance efforts. Their economic and social condition has often been worse after termination than it was before.

The third argument I would make against forced termination concerns the effect it has had upon the overwhelming majority of tribes which still enjoy a special relationship with the Federal government. The very threat that this relationship may someday be ended has created a great deal of apprehension among Indian groups and this apprehension, in turn, has had a blighting effect on tribal progress. Any step that might result in greater social, economic or political autonomy is regarded with suspicion by many Indians who fear that it will only bring them closer to the day when the Federal government will disavow its responsibility and cut them adrift.

In short, the fear of one extreme policy, forced termination, has often worked to produce the opposite extreme: excessive dependence on the Federal government. In many cases this dependence is so great that the Indian community is almost entirely run by outsiders who are responsible and responsive to Federal officials in Washington, D.C., rather than to the communities they are supposed to be serving. This is the second of the two harsh approaches which have long plagued our Indian policies. Of the Department of the Interior's programs directly serving Indians, for example, only 1.5 percent are presently under Indian control. Only 2.4 percent of HEW's Indian health programs are run by Indians. The result is a burgeoning Federal bureaucracy, programs which are far less effective than they ought to be, and an erosion of Indian initiative and morale.

I believe that both of these policy extremes are wrong. Federal termination errs in one direction, Federal paternalism errs in the other. Only by clearly rejecting both of these extremes can we achieve a policy which truly serves the best interests of the Indian people. Self-determination among the Indian people can and must be encouraged without the threat of eventual termination. In my view, in fact, that is the only way that self-determination can effectively be fostered.

This, then, must be the goal of any new national policy toward the Indian people: to strengthen the Indian's sense of autonomy without threatening his sense of community. We must assure the Indian that he can assume control of his own life without being separated involuntarily from the tribal group. And we must make it clear that Indians can become independent of Federal control without being cut off from Federal concern and Federal support. My specific recommendations to the Congress are designed to carry out this policy.

1. REJECTING TERMINATION

Because termination is morally and legally unacceptable, because it produces bad practical results, and because the mere threat of termination tends to discourage greater self-sufficiency among Indian groups, I am asking the Congress to pass a new Concurrent Resolution which would expressly renounce, repudiate and repeal the termination policy as expressed in House Concurrent Resolution 108 of the 83rd Congress. This resolution would explicitly affirm the integrity and right to continued existence of all Indian tribes and Alaska native governments, recognizing that cultural pluralism is a source of national strength. It would assure these groups that the United States Government would continue to carry out its treaty and trusteeship obligations to them as long as the groups themselves believed that such a policy was necessary or desirable. It would guarantee that whenever Indian groups decided to assume control or responsibility for government service programs, they could do so and still receive adequate Federal financial support. In short, such a resolution would reaffirm for the Legislative branch — as I hereby affirm for the Executive branch — that the historic relationship between the Federal government and the Indian communities cannot be abridged without the consent of the Indians.

2. THE RIGHT TO CONTROL AND
OPERATE FEDERAL PROGRAMS

Even as we reject the goal of forced termination, so must we reject the suffocating pattern of paternalism. But how can we best do this? In the past, we have often assumed that because the government is obliged to provide certain services for Indians, it therefore must administer those same services. And to get rid of Federal administration, by the same token, often meant getting rid of the whole Federal program. But there is no necessary reason for this assumption. Federal support programs for non-Indian communities — hospitals and schools are two ready examples — are ordinarily administered by local authorities. There is no reason why Indian communities should be deprived of the privilege of self-determination merely because they receive monetary support from the Federal government. Nor should they lose Federal money because they reject Federal control.

For years we have talked about encouraging Indians to exercise greater self-determination, but our progress has never been commensurate with our promises. Part of the reason for this situation has been the threat of termination. But another reason is the fact that when a decision is made as to whether a Federal program will be turned over to Indian administration, it is the Federal authorities and not the Indian people who finally make that decision.

This situation should be reversed. In my judgment, it should be up to the Indian tribe to determine whether it is willing and able to assume administrative responsibility for a service program which is presently administered by a Federal agency. To this end, I am proposing legislation which would empower a tribe or a group of tribes or any other Indian community to take over the control or operation of Federally funded and administered programs in the Department of the Interior and the Department of Health, Education and Welfare whenever the tribal council or comparable community governing group voted to do so.

Under this legislation, it would not be necessary for the Federal agency administering the program to approve the transfer of responsibility. It is my hope and expectation that most such transfers of power would still take place consensually as a result of negotiations between the local community and the Federal government. But in those cases in which an impasse arises between the two parties, the final determination should rest with the Indian community.

Under the proposed legislation, Indian control of Indian programs would always be a wholly voluntary matter. It would be possible for an Indian group to select that program or that specified portion of a program that it wants to run without assuming responsibility for other components. The "right of retrocession" would also be guaranteed; this means that if the local community elected to administer a program and then later decided to give it back to the Federal government, it would always be able to do so.

Appropriate technical assistance to help local organizations successfully operate these programs would be provided by the Federal government. No tribe would risk economic disadvantage from managing its own programs; under the proposed legislation, locally-administered programs would be funded on equal terms with similar services still administered by Federal authorities. The legislation I propose would include appropriate protections against any action which endangered the rights, the health, the safety or the welfare of individuals. It would also contain accountability procedures to guard against gross negligence or mismanagement of Federal funds.

This legislation would apply only to services which go directly from the Federal government to the Indian community; those services which are channeled through State or local governments could still be turned over to Indian control by mutual consent. To run the activities for which they have assumed control, the Indian groups could employ local people or outside experts. If they chose to hire Federal employees who had formerly administered these projects, those employees would still enjoy the privileges of Federal employee benefit programs — under special legislation which will also be submitted to the Congress.

Legislation which guarantees the right of Indians to contract for the control or operation of Federal programs would directly channel more money into Indian communities, since Indians themselves would be administering programs and drawing salaries which now often go to non-Indian administrators. The potential for Indian control is significant, for we are talking about programs which annually spend over $400 million in Federal funds. A policy which encourages Indian administration of these programs will help build greater pride and resourcefulness within the Indian community. At the same time, programs which are managed and operated by Indians are likely to be more effective in meeting Indian needs.

I speak with added confidence about these anticipated results because of the favorable experience of programs which have already been turned over to Indian control. Under the auspices of the Office of Economic Opportunity, Indian communities now run more than 60 community action agencies which are located on Federal reservations. OEO is planning to spend some $57 million in Fiscal Year 1971 through Indian-controlled grantees. For over four years, many OEO-funded programs have operated under the control of local Indian organizations and the results have been most heartening.

Two Indian tribes — the Salt River Tribe and the Zuñi Tribe — have recently extended this principle of local control to virtually all of the programs which the Bureau of Indian Affairs has traditionally administered for them. Many Federal officials, including the Agency Superintendent, have been replaced by elected tribal officers or tribal employees. The time has now come to build on these experiences and to extend local Indian control — at a rate and to the degree that the Indians themselves establish.

3. RESTORING THE SACRED LANDS NEAR BLUE LAKE

No government policy toward Indians can be fully effective unless there is a relationship of trust and confidence between the Federal government and the Indian people. Such a relationship cannot be completed overnight; it is inevitably the product of a long series of words and actions. But we can contribute significantly to such a relationship by responding to just grievances which are especially important to the Indian people.

One such grievance concerns the sacred Indian lands at and near Blue Lake in New Mexico. From the fourteenth century, the Taos Pueblo Indians used these areas for religious and tribal purposes. In 1906, however, the United States Government appropriated these lands for the creation of a national forest. According to a recent determination of the Indian Claims Commission, the government "took said lands from petitioner without compensation."

For 64 years, the Taos Pueblo has been trying to regain possession of this sacred lake and watershed area in order to preserve it in its natural condition and limit its non-Indian use. The Taos Indians consider such action essential to the protection and expression of their religious faith.

The restoration of the Blue Lake lands to the Taos Pueblo Indians is an issue of unique and critical importance to Indians throughout the country. I therefore take this opportunity wholeheartedly to endorse legislation which would restore 48,000 acres of sacred land to the Taos Pueblo people, with the statutory promise that they would be able to use these lands for traditional purposes and that except for such uses the lands would remain forever wild.

With the addiiton of some perfecting amendments, legislation now pending in the Congress would properly achieve this goal. That legislation (H.R. 471) should promptly be amended and enacted. Such action would stand as an important symbol of this government's responsiveness to the just grievances of the American Indians.

4. INDIAN EDUCATION

One of the saddest aspects of Indian life in the United States is the low quality of Indian education. Drop-out rates for Indians are twice the national average and the average educational level for all Indians under Federal supervision is less than six school years. Again, at least a part of the problem stems from the fact that the Federal government is trying to do for Indians what many Indians could do better for themselves.

The Federal government now has responsibility for some 221,000 Indian children of school age. While over 50,000 of these children attend schools which are operated directly by the Bureau of Indian Affairs, only 750 Indian children are enrolled in schools where the responsibility for education has been contracted by the BIA to Indian school boards. Fortunately, this condition is beginning to change. The Ramah Navajo Community of New Mexico and the Rough Rock and Black Water Schools in Arizona are notable examples of schools which have recently been brought under local Indian control. Several other communities are now negotiating for similar arrangements.

Consistent with our policy that the Indian community should have the right to take over the control and operation of federally funded programs, we believe every Indian community wishing to do so should be able to control its own Indian schools. This control would be exercised by school boards selected by Indians and functioning much like other school boards throughout the nation. To assure that this goal is achieved, I am asking the Vice President, acting in his role as Chairman of the National Council on Indian Opportunity, to establish a Special Education Subcommittee of that Council. The members of that Subcommittee should be Indian educators who are selected by the Council's Indian members. The Subcommittee will provide technical assistance to Indian communities wishing to establish school boards, will conduct a nationwide review of the educational status of all Indian schoolchildren in whatever schools they may be attending, and will evaluate and report annually on the status of Indian education, including the extent of local control. This Subcommittee will act as a transitional mechanism; its objective should not be self-perpetuation but the actual transfer of Indian education to Indian communities.

We must also take specific action to benefit Indian children in public schools. Some 141,000 Indian children presently attend general public schools near their homes. Fifty-two thousand of these are absorbed by local school districts without special Federal aid. But 89,000 Indian children attend public schools in such high concentrations that the State or local school districts involved are eligible for special Federal assistance under the Johnson-O'Malley Act. In Fiscal Year 1971, the Johnson-O'Malley program will be funded at a level of some $20 million.

This Johnson-O'Malley money is designed to help Indian students, but since funds go directly to the school districts, the Indians have little if any influence over the way in which the money is spent. I therefore propose that the Congress amend the Johnson-O'Malley Act so as to authorize the Secretary of the Interior to channel funds under this act directly to Indian tribes and communities. Such a provision would give Indians the ability to help shape the schools which their children attend and, in some instances, to set up new school systems of their own. At the same time, I am directing the Secretary of the Interior to make every effort to ensure that Johnson-O'Malley funds which are presently directed to public school districts are actually spent to improve the education of Indian children in these districts.

5. ECONOMIC DEVELOPMENT LEGISLATION

Economic deprivation is among the most serious of Indian problems. Unemployment among Indians is ten times the national average; the unemployment rate runs as high as 80 percent on some of the poorest reservations. Eighty percent of reservation Indians have an income which falls below the poverty line; the average annual income for such families is only $1,500. As I said in September of 1968, it is critically important that the Federal government support and encourage efforts which help Indians develop their own economic infrastructure. To that end, I am proposing the "Indian Financing Act of 1970."

This act would do two things:

1. It would broaden the existing Revolving Loan Fund, which loans

money for Indian economic development projects. I am asking that the authorization for this fund be increased from approximately $25 million to $75 million.

2. It would provide additional incentives in the form of loan guarantees, loan insurance and interest subsidies to encourage *private* lenders to loan more money for Indian economic projects. An aggregate amount of $200 million would be authorized for loan guarantee and loan insurance purposes.

I also urge that legislation be enacted which would permit any tribe which chooses to do so to enter into leases of its land for up to 99 years. Indian people now own over 50 million acres of land that is held in trust by the Federal government. In order to compete in attracting investment capital for commercial, industrial and recreational development of these lands, it is essential that the tribes be able to offer long-term leases. Long-term leasing is preferable to selling such property since it enables tribes to preserve the trust ownership of their reservation homelands. But existing law limits the length of time for which many tribes can enter into such leases. Moreover, when long-term leasing is allowed, it has been granted by Congress on a case-by-case basis, a policy which again reflects a deep-rooted pattern of paternalism. The twenty reservations which have already been given authority for long-term leasing have realized important benefits from that privilege and this opportunity should now be extended to all Indian tribes.

Economic planning is another area where our efforts can be significantly improved. The comprehensive economic development plans that have been created by both the Pima-Maricopa and the Zuñi Tribes provide outstanding examples of interagency cooperation in fostering Indian economic growth. The Zuñi Plan, for example, extends for at least five years and involves a total of $55 million from the Departments of Interior, Housing and Urban Development, and Health, Education and Welfare and from the Office of Economic Opportunity and the Economic Development Administration. I am directing the Secretary of the Interior to play an active role in coordinating additional projects of this kind.

6. MORE MONEY FOR INDIAN HEALTH

Despite significant improvements in the past decade and a half, the health of Indian people still lags 20 to 25 years behind that of the general population. The average age at death among Indians is 44 years, about one-third less than the national average. Infant mortality is nearly 50% higher for Indians and Alaska natives than for the population at large; the tuberculosis rate is eight times as high and the suicide rate is twice that of the general population. Many infectious diseases such as trachoma and dysentery that have all but disappeared among other Americans continue to afflict the Indian people.

This Administration is determined that the health status of the first Americans will be improved. In order to initiate expanded efforts in this area, I will request the allocation of an additional $10 million for Indian health programs for the current fiscal year. This strengthened Federal effort will enable us to address ourselves more effectively to those health problems which are particularly important to the Indian community. We understand, for example, that areas of greatest concern to Indians include the prevention and control of alcoholism, the promotion of mental health and the control of middle-ear disease. We hope that the ravages of middle-ear disease — a particularly acute disease among Indians — can be brought under control within five years.

These and other Indian health programs will be most effective if more Indians are involved in running them. Yet — almost unbelievably — we are presently able to identify in this country only 30 physicians and fewer than 400 nurses of Indian descent. To meet this situation, we will expand our efforts to train Indians for health careers.

7. HELPING URBAN INDIANS

Our new census will probably show that a larger proportion of America's Indians are living off the reservation than ever before in our history. Some authorities even estimate that more Indians are living in cities and towns than are remaining on the reservation. Of those American Indians who are now dwelling in urban areas, approximately three-fourths are living in poverty.

The Bureau of Indian Affairs is organized to serve the 462,000 reservation Indians. The BIA's responsibility does not extend to Indians who have left the reservation, but this point is not always clearly understood. As a result of this misconception, Indians living in urban areas have often lost out on the opportunity to participate in other programs designed for disadvantaged groups. As a first step toward helping the urban Indians, I am instructing appropriate officials to do all they can to ensure that this misunderstanding is corrected.

But misunderstandings are not the most important problem confronting urban Indians. The biggest barrier faced by those Federal, State and local programs which are trying to serve urban Indians is the difficulty of locating and identifying them. Lost in the anonymity of the city, often cut off from family and friends, many urban Indians are slow to establish new community ties. Many drift from neighborhood to neighborhood; many shuttle back and forth between reservations and urban areas. Language and cultural differences compound these problems. As a result, Federal, State and local programs which are designed to help such persons often miss this most deprived and least understood segment of the urban poverty population.

This Administration is already taking steps which will help remedy this situation. In a joint effort, the Office of Economic Opportunity and the Department of Health, Education and Welfare will expand support to a total of seven urban Indian centers in major cities which will act as links between existing Federal, State and local service programs and the urban Indians. The Departments of Labor, Housing and Urban Development, and Commerce have pledged to cooperate with such experimental urban centers and the Bureau of Indian Affairs has expressed its willingness to contract with these centers for the performance of relocation services which assist reservation Indians in their transition to urban employment.

These efforts represent an important beginning in recognizing and alleviating the severe problems faced by urban Indians. We hope to learn a great deal from these projects and to expand our efforts as rapidly as possible. I am directing the Office of Economic Opportunity to lead these efforts.

8. INDIAN TRUST COUNSEL AUTHORITY

The United States Government acts as a legal trustee for the land and water rights of American Indians. These rights are often of critical economic importance to the Indian people; frequently they are also the subject of extensive legal dispute. In many of these legal confrontations, the Federal government is faced with an inherent conflict of interest. The Secretary of the Interior and the Attorney General must at the same time advance *both* the *national* interest in the use of land and water rights *and* the *private* interests of Indians in land which the government holds as trustee.

Every trustee has a legal obligation to advance the interests of the beneficiaries of the trust without reservation and with the highest degree of diligence and skill. Under present conditions, it is often difficult for the Department of the Interior and the Department of Justice to fulfill this obligation. No self-respecting law firm would ever allow itself to represent two opposing clients in one dispute; yet the Federal government has frequently found itself in precisely that position. There is considerable evidence that the Indians are the losers when such situations arise. More than that, the credibility of the Federal government is damaged whenever it appears that such a conflict of interest exists.

In order to correct this situation, I am calling on the Congress to establish an Indian Trust Counsel Authority to assure independent legal representation for the Indians' natural resource rights. This Authority would be governed by a three-man board of directors, appointed by the President with the advice and consent of the Senate. At least two of the board members would be Indian. The chief legal officer of the Authority would be designated as the Indian Trust Counsel.

The Indian Trust Counsel Authority would be independent of the Departments of the Interior and Justice and would be expressly empowered to bring suit in the name of the United States in its trustee capacity. The United States would waive its sovereign immunity from suit in connection with litigation involving the Authority.

9. ASSISTANT SECRETARY FOR INDIAN AND TERRITORIAL AFFAIRS

To help guide the implementation of a new national policy concerning American Indians, I am recommending to the Congress the establishment of a new position in the Department of the Interior — Assistant Secretary for Indian and Territorial Affairs. At present, the Commissioner of Indian Affairs reports to the Secretary of the Interior through the Assistant Secretary for Public Land Management — an officer who has many responsibilities in the natural resources area which compete with his concern for Indians. A new Assistant Secretary for Indian and Territorial Affairs would have only one concern — the Indian and territorial people, their land, and their progress and well-being. Secretary Hickel and I both believe this new position represents an elevation of Indian affairs to their proper role within the Department of the Interior and we urge Congress to act favorably on this proposal.

Many of the new programs which are outlined in this message have grown out of this Administration's experience with other Indian projects that have been initiated or expanded during the last 17 months.

The Office of Economic Opportunity has been particularly active in the development of new and experimental efforts. O E O's Fiscal Year 1971 budget request for Indian-related activities is up 18 percent from 1969 spending. In the last year alone — to mention just two examples — O E O doubled its funds for Indian economic development and tripled its expenditures for alcoholism and recovery programs. In areas such as housing and home improvement, health care, emergency food, legal services and education, O E O programs have been significantly expanded. As I said in my recent speech on the economy, I hope that the Congress will support this valuable work by appropriating the full amount requested for the Economic Opportunity Act.

The Bureau of Indian Affairs has already begun to implement our policy of contracting with local Indians for the operation of government programs. As I have noted, the Salt River Tribe and the Zuñi Tribe have taken over the bulk of Federal services; other projects ranging from job training centers to high school counseling programs have been contracted out to Indian groups on an individual basis in many areas of the country.

Economic development has also been stepped up. Of 195 commercial and industrial enterprises which have been established in Indian areas with B I A assistance, 71 have come into operation within the last two years. These enterprises provide jobs for more than 6,000 Indians and are expected to employ substantially more when full capacity is reached. A number of these businesses are now owned by Indians and many others are managed by them. To further increase individual Indian ownership, the B I A has this month initiated the Indian Business Development Fund which provides equity capital to Indians who go into business in reservation areas.

Since late 1967, the Economic Development Administration has approved approximately $80 million in projects on Indian reservations, including nearly $60 million in public works projects. The impact of such activities can be tremendous; on the Gila River Reservation in Arizona, for example, economic development projects over the last three years have helped to lower the unemployment rate from 56 to 18 percent, increase the median family income by 150 percent and cut the welfare rate by 50 percent.

There has been additional progress on many other fronts since January of 1969. New "Indian Desks" have been created in each of the human resource departments of the Federal government to help coordinate and accelerate Indian programs. We have supported an increase in funding of $4 million for the Navajo Irrigation Project. Housing efforts have picked up substantially; a new Indian Police Academy has been set up; Indian education efforts have been expanded — including an increase of $848,000 in scholarships for Indian college students and the establishment of the Navajo Community College, the first college in America planned, developed and operated by and for Indians. Altogether, obligational authority for Indian programs run by the Federal Government has increased from a little over $598 million in Fiscal Year 1970 to almost $626 million in Fiscal Year 1971.

Finally, I would mention the impact on the Indian population of the series of welfare reform proposals I have sent to the Congress. Because of the high rate of unemployment and underemployment among Indians, there is probably no other group in the country that would be helped as directly and as substantially by programs such as the new Family Assistance Plan and the proposed Family Health Insurance Plan. It is estimated, for example, that more than half of all Indian families would be eligible for Family Assistance benefits and the enactment of this legislation is therefore of critical importance to the American Indian.

This Administration has broken a good deal of new ground with respect to Indian problems in the last 17 months. We have learned many things and as a result we have been able to formulate a new approach to Indian affairs. Throughout this entire process, we have regularly consulted the opinions of the Indian people, and their views have played a major role in the formulation of Federal policy.

As we move ahead in this important work, it is essential that the Indian people continue to lead the way by participating in policy development to the greatest possible degree. In order to facilitate such participation, I am asking the Indian members of the National Council on Indian Opportunity to sponsor field hearings throughout the nation in order to establish continuing dialogue between the Executive branch of government and the Indian population of our country. I have asked the Vice President to see that the first round of field hearings is completed before October.

The recommendations of this Administration represent an historic step forward in Indian policy. We are proposing to break sharply with past approaches to Indian problems. In place of a long series of piecemeal reforms, we suggest a new and coherent strategy. In place of policies which simply call for more spending, we suggest policies which call for wiser spending. In place of policies which oscillate between the deadly extremes of forced termination and constant paternalism, we suggest a policy in which the Federal government and the Indian community play complementary roles.

But most importantly, we have turned from the question of *whether* the Federal government has a responsibility to Indians to the question of *how* that responsibility can best be fulfilled. We have concluded that the Indians will get better programs and that public monies will be more effectively expended if the people who are most affected by these programs are responsible for operating them.

The Indians of America need Federal assistance — this much has long been clear. What has not always been clear, however, is that the Federal government needs Indian energies and Indian leadership if its assistance is to be effective in improving the conditions of Indian life. It is a new and balanced relationship between the United States Government and the first Americans that is at the heart of our approach to Indian problems. And that is why we now approach these problems with new confidence that they will successfully be overcome.

Indian Self-Determination
and Education Assistance Act

January 4, 1975

At the end of 1970 the first of a series of bills was enacted that rang out the death knell of Termination and harkened in the new era of Self-Determination. On December 15, 1970, Congress passed PL91-550, returning Blue Lake and forty-eight-thousand acres of land in New Mexico to the Taos Pueblos. This was followed by the Alaska Native Claims Settlement Act of 1971, which recognized the land rights of Alaska Natives and provided for mineral royalties payments, land payments, land transfers, and the return of contested land to tribes in Oregon and Arizona. Many scholars identify the 1973 Menominee Restoration Act as the final reversal of Termination policy. The Menominee tribe was terminated in 1954 and its fate confirmed the worst fears of anti-terminationists. The tribe's termination led to an economic collapse and a political crisis that was only resolved with its reinstatement as an officially recognized tribe nearly twenty years later. The unfortunate experiences of the Menominee people provided Self-Determination advocates with convincing evidence of the failure of Termination policy.

Perhaps the most influential piece of Self-Determination legislation bears that name: the 1975 Indian Self-Determination and Education Assistance Act. Passed on January 4, 1975, the Self-Determination Act marked a revolutionary break with the past. Indian tribes were released from the strict control and supervision of the Bureau of Indian Affairs under a contracting provision, and the door was opened for tribal governments to take charge of many reservation social, economic, and political activities and programs. The Self-Determination Act's emphasis on decentralizing Indian services worried many Indian officials and reformers because of its potential for a withdrawal of federal support for Indian programs. The extent to which the 1975 Self-Determination Act lived up to its name or was really a program of continued termination imbedded in the language of self-determination would ultimately depend on its implementation, on court decisions interpreting its provisions, and on legislation to come.

To provide maximum Indian participation in the government and education of the Indian people; to provide for the full participation of Indian tribes in programs and services conducted by the federal Government for Indians and to encourage the development of human resources of the Indian people; to establish a program of assistance to upgrade Indian education; to support the right of Indian citizens to control their own educational activities; and for other purposes.

CONGRESSIONAL FINDINGS

Sec. 2. (a) The Congress, after careful review of the federal Government's historical and special legal relationship with, and resulting responsibilities to, American Indian people, finds that —

(1) the prolonged Federal domination of Indian service programs has served to retard rather than enhance the progress of Indian people and their communities by depriving Indians of the full opportunity to develop leadership skills crucial to the realization of self-government, and has denied to the Indian people an effective voice in the planning and implementation of programs for the benefit of Indians which are responsive to the true needs of Indian communities; and

(2) the Indian people will never surrender their desire to control their relationships both among themselves and with non-Indian governments, organizations, and persons.

(b) The Congress further finds that —

(1) true self-determination in any society of people is dependent upon an educational process which will insure the development of qualified people to fulfill meaningful leadership roles;

(2) the federal responsibility for and assistance to education of Indian children has not effected the desired level of educational achievement or created the diverse opportunities and personal satisfaction which education can and should provide; and

(3) parental and community control of the educational process is of crucial importance to the Indian people.

DECLARATION OF POLICY

Sec. 3.

(a) The Congress hereby recognizes the obligation of the United States to respond to the strong expression of the Indian people for self-determination by assuring maximum Indian participation in the direction of educational as well as other federal services to Indian communities so as to render such services more responsive to the needs and desires of those communities.

(b) The Congress declares its commitment to the maintenance of the Federal Government's unique and continuing relationship with and responsibility to the Indian people through the establishment of a meaningful Indian self-determination policy which will permit an orderly transition from Federal domination of programs for and services to Indians to effective and meaningful participation by the Indian people in the planning, conduct, and administration of those programs and services.

(c) The Congress declares that a major national goal of the United States is to provide the quantity and quality of educational services and opportunities which will permit Indian children to compete and excel in the life areas of their choice, and to achieve the measure of self-determination essential to their social and economic well-being.

GRANTS TO INDIAN TRIBAL ORGANIZATIONS

Sec. 104.

(a) The Secretary of the Interior is authorized, upon the request of any Indian tribe . . . to contract with or make a grant or grants to any tribal organization for —

(1) the strengthening or improvement of tribal government . . . ;

(2) the planning, training, evaluation of other activities designed to improve the capacity of a tribal organization to enter into a contract;

(3) the acquisition of land in connection with items (1) and (2) above: Provided, That in the case of land within reservation boundaries or which adjoins on at least two sides lands held in trust by the United States for the tribe or for individual Indians, the Secretary of Interior may (upon request of the tribe) acquire such land in trust for the tribe; or

(4) the planning, designing, monitoring, and evaluating of federal programs serving the tribe.

(b) The Secretary of Health, Education, and Welfare may . . . make grants to any Indian tribe or tribal organization for —

(1) the development, construction, operation, provision, or maintenance of adequate health facilities or services including the training of personnel for such work, from funds appropriated to the Indian Health Service for Indian health services or Indian health facilities; or

(2) planning, training, evaluation, or other activities designed to improve the capacity of a tribal organization to enter into a contract.

Indian Child Welfare Act

November 8, 1978

On November 8, 1978, the Ninety-fifth Congress enacted one of the most sweeping statutes in the field of Indian law, the Indian Child Welfare Act (ICWA). Prior to the ICWA, cases involving Indian children were resolved within the general framework of Indian law principles governing civil jurisdiction, that is, when all contacts were within Indian country, tribal jurisdiction was exclusive, and when there were few reservation contacts, state courts possessed jurisdiction. The ICWA shifted control of decisions involving Indian children from state courts to Indian tribal courts. The underlying premise of this important change was that Indian tribes as sovereign governments have a vital interest in any decisions about whether Indian children should be separated from their families and tribal communities.

Passage of the ICWA was prompted by deep concern among Indians and child welfare professionals about the historical experience of American Indians and Alaska Natives with the country's child welfare system. Causes for this concern included the disproportionately large number of Indian children who were being removed from their families and the frequency with which they were placed in non-Indian foster and adoptive settings. At the time of passage of the ICWA, 25–35 percent of all Indian children were separated from their families and placed in non-Indian homes or other institutions.

The Indian Child Welfare Act recognized the importance of tribal life and tried to make certain that the cultural values of Indian tribes were not denied to orphaned Indian children. In this act, Congress codified the disparate court decisions that had begun to form the body of Indian child welfare law, provided jurisdictional safeguards for tribal governments, and established an order of preference for the adoption and placement of Indian children.

Congress did not rely simply on recent court decisions in Indian cases, nor simply on the emotions raised during the Self-Determination era. Rather, Congress looked to the Constitution of the United States and the 1831 *Cherokee Nation v. Georgia* U.S. Supreme Court decision for guidance. In the more than two hundred years of U.S.-Indian relations the federal government and local states had exercised much control over Indian affairs, including the placement of Indian children outside tribal communities and families. Despite this history, in the ICWA the Congress declared "that it is the policy of this Nation to protect the best interests of Indian children and to promote the stability and security of Indian tribes and families by the establishment of minimum Federal standards for the removal of Indian children from their families and the placement of such children in foster or adoptive homes which will reflect the unique values of Indian culture."

The ICWA established priorities to be followed in Indian child placement. These priorities favored the child's extended family, tribe, or other Indian families. This preference for native families applied to both children who were to be adopted as well as children in foster care. These priorities dramatically reversed decades of federal and state policy that had led to the loss of thousands of Indian children from their tribal communities. Many of these native children had found themselves disconnected from their tribal roots, cut off from their cultural heritage, and adrift from their Indian identity.

Because of the changes it brought about, the Indian Child Welfare Act was controversial and likely to be challenged in court. That court test came more than a decade later in the U.S. Supreme Court case *Mississippi Band of Choctaw Indians v. Holyfield*. The question facing native communities, Indian families and children, and legal observers was, would the ICWA's protection of Indian children stand up in court? In the *Holyfield* case an Indian mother had given birth to twin girls in an off-reservation hospital and had immediately relinquished custody of the children to a non-Indian adoptive couple. The adoption was granted to the non-Indian adoptive parents by the Mississippi state court. Shortly thereafter the Mississippi Choctaw tribe attempted to overturn the adoption under the provisions of the ICWA, arguing that the tribe had exclusive jurisdiction. Both the child's birth mother and natural father were members of the Mississippi Choctaw tribe and lived on the reservation. The U.S. Supreme Court's landmark ruling favored the tribe, stating that the tribe did indeed have exclusive jurisdiction over the twin girls and could decide on their adoption. The ICWA had survived its court test, and the rights of Indian communities to determine the fate of their children remained the law of the land.

To establish standards for the placement of Indian children in foster or adoptive homes, to prevent the breakup of Indian families, and for other purposes.

Sec. 2. recognizing the special relationship between the United States and the Indian tribes and their members and the Federal responsibility to Indian people, the Congress finds —

(1) that clause 3, section 8, article I of the United States Constitution provides that "The Congress shall have power. . . .To regulate Com-

merce . . . with Indian tribes" and, through this and other constitutional authority, Congress has plenary power over Indian affairs;

(2) that Congress, through statutes, treaties, and the general course of dealing with Indian tribes, has assumed the responsibility for the protection and preservation of Indian tribes and their resources;

(3) that there is no resource that is more vital to the continued existence and integrity of Indian tribes than their children and that the United States has a direct interest, as trustee, in protecting Indian children who are members of or are eligible for membership in an Indian tribe;

(4) that an alarmingly high percentage of Indian families are broken up by the removal, often unwarranted, of their children from them by nontribal public and private agencies and that an alarmingly high percentage of such children are placed in non-Indian foster and adoptive homes and institutions; and

(5) that the States, exercising their recognized jurisdiction over Indian child custody proceedings through administrative and judicial bodies, have often failed to recognize the essential tribal relations of Indian people and the cultural and social standards prevailing in Indian communities and families.

Sec. 3. The Congress hereby declares that it is the policy of this Nation to protect the best interests of Indian children and to promote the stability and security of Indian tribes and families by establishment of minimum Federal standards for the removal of Indian children from their families and the placement of such children in foster or adoptive homes which will reflect the unique values of Indian culture, and by providing for assistance to Indian tribes in the operation of child and family service programs.

TITLE I — CHILD CUSTODY PROCEEDINGS

Sec. 101. (a) An Indian tribe shall have jurisdiction exclusive as to any State over any child custody proceeding involving an Indian child who resides or is domiciled within the reservation of such tribe. . . . Where an indian child is a ward of a tribal court, the Indian tribe shall retain exclusive jurisdiction, notwithstanding the residence or domicile of the child. (b) In any State court proceeding for the foster care placement of, or termination of parental rights to, an Indian child not domiciled or residing within the reservation of the Indian child's tribe, the court, in the absence of good cause to the contrary, shall transfer such proceedings to the jurisdiction of the tribe. . . .

(c) In any State court proceeding for the foster care placement of, or termination of parental rights to, an Indian child, the Indian custodian of the child and the Indian child's tribe shall have a right to intervene at any point in the proceeding.

Despite the legal protections for tribes and families seeking to keep their children within the community, the economic and social problems on many reservations represented a challenge to providing a nurturing and safe environment for Indian children. The comments of Cecilia Fire Thunder, Oglala Sioux, made at an Indian Child Welfare Conference held at the University of California, Los Angeles, American Indian Studies Center on January 15, 1992, reflected the concerns and actions of Indian professionals and tribe members who were trying to improve the lives of their most precious native resources — Indian children.

Statement by Cecelia Fire Thunder
January 15, 1992

As an Indian child welfare advocate, I'm very concerned about the future for children. I try very hard in all the things that I do to get more people in my community, Indian people, to become empowered so at the community level we can become stronger and we can get better services for our children. Also, at the community level, we can begin to heal so that we can provide safer places for our children. At the community level, we need to heal and begin that long journey to recovery so our children will have a fighting chance for the next seven generations; that they'll be healthier and stronger. More importantly, we need to recognize that it's not enough to just feed them. Every one of us in each of our communities needs to assume that responsibility.

It's a very painful place to be. I cry a lot, I get mad a lot, I scream a lot. But once I get over crying and screaming, I put the thing that the great spirit gave me called a brain to work. I start analyzing and strategizing and making the necessary phone calls toward getting our people together. In my community, we are now working closer together because we're becoming a stronger unit for the welfare of our children which is affecting our tribal legislation at regional social service agencies and at the national level. Next year we need to work even harder.

Statement on Indian Policy

President Ronald Reagan, January 24, 1983

During the 1970s many of the policies and legislative initiatives of Termination were reversed. American Indian tribal sovereignty and rights to federal services were legally reaffirmed, placing more control than ever before in the hands of Indian communities. The urban relocation programs of the 1950s and 1960s, which were designed to move reservation residents into U.S. cities and assimilate them into local economies and cultures, were halted and in their place were initiated reservation area redevelopment and economic development projects. Funding was made available to urban Indian centers to meet the needs of the growing population of urban Indians, and bilingual education programs were developed for newly funded reservation educational projects. Self-Determination represented a renewal of federally affirmed American Indian rights.

As we have seen, the Indian Self-Determination and Education Assistance Act of 1975 represented watershed Self-Determination legislation in that it reduced the power of the Bureau of Indian Affairs to control tribal finances by permitting tribes themselves to contract for tribal services, and the Indian Child Welfare Act of 1978 protected native children from being adopted outside Indian communities. Both acts reflected a strong federal endorsement of tribal sovereignty. A variety of legislation passed in the 1970s reversed decades of slippage in other areas of tribal rights. Among these acts were the 1972 Indian Education Act (providing resources and control for tribal education programs), the Indian Financing Act of 1974 (establishing a revolving loan fund to facilitate reservation economic development), the Indian Health Care Improvement Act of 1976 (improving and extending the mission of the Indian Health Service), the Tribally Controlled Community College Assistance Act of 1978 (providing funds for the establishment of reservation-based two-year colleges), and the 1978 American Indian Religious Freedom Act (affirming constitutional protection for native religious and spiritual practices). As a further sign of federal commitment and concern about Indian issues, from 1975 to 1977 the American Indian Policy Review Commission traveled around the country collecting information about the conditions of Native Americans in cities and on reservations; the AIPRC's findings were published in a final report with several appended volumes on specific subjects such as urban Indians and federal, state, and tribal jurisdiction.

The flurry of administrative and legislative activity surrounding federal Self-

Determination policy continued during the 1970s, the same decade in which Red Power activism also flourished. The nation's attention was drawn to one protest event after another — from Alcatraz to the occupations of federal property and national park sites and the takeovers of national and regional offices of the Bureau of Indian Affairs in the early 1970s, to the reservation sieges of the middle years of the decade, to the nationwide caravans and marches throughout the decade. While Congress debated and voted on self-determination legislation, Indians protested and fought for recognition and reform.

The link between the activism and the legislation, both of which dominated the 1970s, should not be underestimated. It is difficult to imagine that congressional deliberations on Self-Determination bills occurred without knowledge of what was happening outside the halls of the Capitol building in the streets and around the country. Congress was certainly aware of the activism. For instance, while Indians of All Tribes occupied Alcatraz Island, on December 23, 1969, Congress passed House Joint Resolution 1042 directing President Richard Nixon "to initiate immediate negotiations with delegated representatives of . . . the Indian community with the objective of transferring unencumbered title in fee of Alcatraz Island . . . to any . . . designated organization of the American Indian Community." The extensive media coverage of such events as the occupation of Alcatraz Island; the Trail of Broken Treaties; the occupations of BIA headquarters; the sieges at Wounded Knee, at Moss Lake, and on the Menominee Reservation; the Longest Walk; and the dozens of other protests, marches, occupations, and demonstrations served as a backdrop against which federal Indian policy was judged and reformed.

The decline in the amount of Red Power activism dovetailed with the election of Ronald Reagan as president in 1980, and once again Indians feared a return of the old Termination thinking by a Republican administration that promised a smaller federal government and a shrinking federal budget. Thus there was much interest in Indian country when President Reagan released his Indian policy statement on January 24, 1983. The statement was reassuring, emphasizing "government-to-government" relations between the federal government and Indian tribes, calling for a repudiation of Termination policy, and stressing tribal self-government and "self-sufficiency."

The honeymoon between the Reagan administration and Native America did not last long. As the 1980s progressed, Reagan administration cuts in federal Indian programs began to increase fears of a new termination era — not so much as a result of explicit Termination policies but as a result of the underfunding of Self-Determination programs. A 1984 National Indian Youth Council poll of 1,050 American Indian leaders nationwide, including tribal chairmen, directors of Indian organizations and programs, elected Indian officials, and Indians in managerial positions in the Bureau of Indian Affairs and Indian Health Service, found 80 percent of respondents reported "strong disapproval" of President Reagan's performance on nine issues listed on the poll. Disapproval gave way to anger and indignation when, on June 10, 1988, while giving a talk to Soviet students at Moscow State University, the president commented that the American people may have "made a mistake" when they "humored" Indians by setting up reservations rather than assimilating them into U.S. society: "Maybe we should not have humored them in that, wanting to stay in that kind of primitive life style. Maybe we should have said: 'No, come join us. Be citizens along with the rest of us.'"

Despite the thinking of an individual president, the foundation for Self-Determination laid in the 1970s survived the Reagan years, and the late 1980s and 1990s saw a continued reaffirmation of Indian self-determination as tribal communities continued to build their political, legal, cultural, and economic institutions, and as Congress and the courts continued to strengthen the sovereignty of Indian nations with legislation such as the 1988 Indian Gaming Regulatory Act, the 1990 Native American Graves Protection and Repatriation Act, and the 1994 amendments to the 1978 American Indian Religious Freedom Act.

This administration believes that responsibilities and resources should be restored to the governments which are closest to the people served. This philosophy applies not only to State and local governments but also to federally recognized American Indian tribes.

When European colonial powers began to explore and colonize this land, they entered into treaties with sovereign Indian nations. Our new nation continued to make treaties and to deal with Indian tribes on a government-to-government basis. Throughout our history, despite periods of conflict and shifting national policies in Indian affairs, the government-to-government relationship between the United States and the Indian tribes has endured. The Constitution, treaties, laws, and court decisions have consistently recognized a unique political relationship between Indian tribes and the United States which this administration pledges to uphold.

In 1970 President Nixon announced a national policy of self-determination for Indian tribes. At the heart of the new policy was a commitment by the Federal Government to foster and encourage tribal self-government. That commitment was signed into law in 1975 as the Indian Self-Determination and Education Assistance Act.

The principle of self-government set forth in this act was a good starting point. However, since 1975 there has been more rhetoric than action. Instead of fostering and encouraging self-government, Federal policies have by and large inhibited the political and economic development of the tribes. Excessive regulation and self-perpetuating bureaucracy have stifled local decision making, thwarted Indian control of Indian resources, and promoted dependency rather than self-sufficiency.

This administration intends to reverse this trend by removing the obstacles to self-government and by creating a more favorable environment for the development of healthy reservation economies. Tribal governments, the Federal Government, and the private sector will all have a role. This administration will take a flexible approach which recognizes the diversity among tribes and the right of each tribe to set its own priorities and goals. Change will not happen overnight. Development will be charted by the tribes, not by the Federal Government.

This administration honors the commitment the nation made in 1970 and 1975 to strengthen tribal governments and lessen Federal control over tribal governmental affairs. This administration is determined to turn these goals into reality. Our policy is to reaffirm dealing with Indian tribes on a government-to-government basis and to pursue the policy of self-government for Indian tribes without threatening termination.

In support of our policy, we shall continue to fulfill Federal trust responsibility for the physical and financial resources we hold in trust for the tribes and their members. The fulfillment of this unique responsibility will be accomplished in accordance with the highest standards.

TRIBAL SELF-GOVERNMENT

Tribal governments, like State and local governments, are more aware of the needs and desires of their citizens than is the Federal Government and should, therefore, have the primary responsibility for meeting those needs. The only effective way for Indian reservations to develop is through tribal governments which are responsive and accountable to their members.

Early in this nation's dealings with Indian tribes, Federal employees began to perform Indian tribal government functions. Despite the Indian Self-Determination Act, major tribal government functions — enforcing tribal laws, developing and managing tribal resources, providing health and social services, educating children — are frequently still carried on by Federal employees. The Federal Government must move away from this surrogate role which undermines the concept of self-government.

It is important to the concept of self-government that tribes reduce their dependence on Federal funds by providing a greater percentage of the cost of their self-government. Some tribes are already moving in this direction. This administration pledges to assist tribes in strengthening their governments by removing the Federal impediments to tribal self-government and tribal resource development. Necessary Federal funds will continue to be available. This administration affirms the right of tribes to determine the best way to meet the needs of their members and to establish and run programs which best meet those needs.

For small tribes which have the greatest need to develop core governmental capacities, this administration has developed through the Assistant Secretary of the Interior for Indian Affairs, the Small Tribes Initiative. This program will provide financial support necessary to allow these tribes to develop basic tribal administrative and management capabilities.

In keeping with the government-to-government relationship, Indian tribes are defined by law as eligible entities and receive direct funding, if they wish, in five block grant programs administered by the Department of Health and Human Services. These and other blocks to the States consolidated dozens of categorical Federal domestic assistance programs to reduce fragmentation and overlap, eliminate excessive Federal regulation, and provide for more local control. This administration now proposes that Indian tribes be eligible for direct funding in the Title XX social services block, the block with the largest appropriation and the greatest flexibility in service delivery.

In addition, we are moving the White House liaison for federally recognized tribes from the Office of Public Liaison to the Office of Intergovernmental Affairs, which maintains liaison with State and local governments. In the past several administrations, tribes have been placed along with vital interest groups, such as veterans, businessmen, and religious leaders. In moving the tribal government contact within the White House Intergovernmental Affairs staff, this administration is underscoring its commitment to recognizing tribal governments on a government-to-government basis.

Further, we are recommending that Congress expand the authorized membership of the Advisory Commission on Intergovernmental Relations to include a representative of Indian tribal governments. In the interim, before congressional action, we are requesting that the Assistant Secretary for Indian Affairs join the commission as an observer. We also supported and signed into law the Indian Tribal Government Tax Status Act which provides tribal governments with essentially the same treatment under Federal tax laws as applies to other governments with regard to revenue raising and saving mechanisms.

In addition, this administration calls upon Congress to replace House Current Resolution 108 of the 83d Congress, the resolution which establishes the now discredited policy of terminating the Federal-tribal relationship. Congress has implicitly rejected the termination policy by enacting the Indian Self-Determination and Education Assistance Act of 1975. However, because the termination policy declared in H. Con. Res. 108 has not been expressly and formally repudiated by a concurrent resolution of Congress, it continues to create among the Indian people an apprehension that the United States may not in the future honor the unique relationship between the Indian people and the Federal Government. A lingering threat of termination has no place in this administration policy of self-government for Indian tribes, and I ask Congress to again express its support of self-government.

These actions are but the first steps in restoring control to tribal governments. Much more needs to be done. Without sound reservation economies, the concept of self-government has little meaning. In the past, despite good intentions, the Federal Government has been one of the major obstacles to economic progress. This administration intends to remove the impediments to economic development and to encourage cooperative efforts among the tribes, the federal Government, and the private sector in developing reservation economies.

DEVELOPMENT OF RESERVATION ECONOMIES

The economies of American Indian reservations are extremely depressed, with unemployment rates among the highest in the country. Indian leaders have told this administration that the development of reservation economies is their number one priority. Growing economies provide jobs, promote self-sufficiency, and provide revenue for essential services. Past attempts to stimulate growth have been fragmented and largely ineffective. As a result, involvement of private industry has been limited, with only infrequent success. Developing reservation economies offers a special challenge: devising investment procedures consistent with the trust status, removing legal barriers which restrict the types of contracts tribes can enter into, and reducing the numerous and complex regulations which hinder economic growth.

Tribes have had limited opportunities to invest in their own economies, because often there has been no established resource base for community investment and development. Many reservations lack a developed physical infrastructure, including utilities, transportation, and other public services. They also often lack the regulatory, adjudicatory, and enforcement mechanisms necessary to interact with the private sector for reservation economic development. Development on the reservation offers potential for tribes and individual entrepreneurs in manufacturing, agribusiness, and modern technology, as well as fishing, livestock, arts and crafts, and other traditional livelihoods.

Natural resources such as timber, fishing, and energy provide an avenue of development for many tribes. Tribal governments have the responsibility to determine the extent and the methods of developing the tribe's natural resources. The Federal Government's responsibility should not be used to hinder tribes from taking advantage of economic development opportunities.

With regard to energy resources, both the Indian tribes and the Nation stand to gain from the prudent development and management of the vast coal, oil, gas, uranium, and other resources found on Indian lands. As already demonstrated by a number of tribes, these resources can become the foundation for economic development on many reservations, while lessening our nation's dependence on imported oil. The Federal role is to encourage the production of energy resources in ways consistent with Indian values and priorities. To that end, we have strongly supported the use of creative agreements such as joint ventures and other non-lease agreements for the development of Indian mineral resources.

It is the free market which will supply the bulk of the capital investments required to develop tribal energy and other resources. A fundamental prerequisite to economic development is capital formation. The establishment of a financial structure that is part of the Indian reservation community is essential to the development of Indian capital formation.

Federal support will be made available to tribes to assist them in developing the necessary management capability and in attracting private capital. As a first step in that direction, we provided funds in the FY 1983 budget to provide seed money to tribes to attract private funding for economic development ventures on reservations. As more tribes develop their capital resource base and increase their managerial expertise, they will have an opportunity to realize the maximum return on their investments and will be able to share an increasing portion of the business risk.

It is the policy of this administration to encourage private involvement, both Indian and non-Indian, in tribal economic development. In some cases, tribes and the private sector have already taken innovative approaches which have overcome the legislative and regulatory impediments to economic progress.

Since tribal governments have the primary responsibility for meeting the basic needs of Indian communities, they must be allowed the chance to succeed. This administration, therefore, is establishing a Presidential Advisory Commission on Indian Reservation Economies. The Commission, composed of tribal and private sector leaders, is to identify obstacles to economic growth in the public and private sector at all levels; examine and recommend changes in Federal law, regulations, and procedures to remove such obstacles; identify actions State, local, and tribal governments could take to rectify identified problems; and recommend ways for the private sector, both Indian and non-Indian, to participate in the development and growth of reservation economies. It is also to be charged with the responsibility of advising the President on recommended actions required to create a positive environment for the development and growth of reservation economies.

Numerous Federal agencies can offer specialized assistance and expertise to the tribes not only in economic development, but also in housing, health, education, job training, and other areas which are an integral part of reservation economies. It is to the advantage of the tribes, and in the interest of the taxpayers, that the Federal role be fully reviewed and coordinated. Therefore, this administration directs the Cabinet Council on Human Resources to act as a mechanism to ensure that Federal activities are nonduplicative, cost-effective, and consistent with the goal of encouraging self-government with a minimum of Federal interference.

SUMMARY

This administration intends to restore tribal governments to their rightful place among the governments of this nation and to enable tribal governments, along with State and local governments, to resume control over their own affairs.

This administration has sought suggestions from Indian leaders in forming the policies which we have announced. We intend to continue this dialogue with the tribes as these policies are implemented.

The governmental land economic reforms proposed for the benefit of Indian tribes and their members cannot be achieved in a vacuum.

This nation's economic health — and that of the tribes — depends on adopting this administration's full economic recovery program. This program calls for eliminating excessive Federal spending and taxes, removing burdensome regulations, and establishing a sound monetary policy. A full economic recovery will unleash the potential strength of the private sector and ensure a vigorous economic climate for development which will benefit not only Indian people but all other Americans as well.

REAGAN ADMINISTRATION
INDIAN POLICY INITIATIVES

— Request that Congress repudiate House Concurrent Resolution 108 of the 83d Congress which called for termination of the Federal-tribal relationship. The administration wants this lingering threat of termination replaced by a resolution expressing its support of a government-to-government relationship.

— Ask Congress to expand the authorized membership of the Advisory Commission on Intergovernmental Relations to include a representative of Indian tribal governments. In the interim, request that the Assistant Secretary of the Interior for Indian Affairs join the ACIR as an observer.

— Move the White House liaison for federally recognized tribes from the Office of Public Liaison to the Office of Intergovernmental Affairs.

— Establish a Presidential Advisory Commission on Indian Reservation Economies to identify obstacles to economic growth and recommend changes at all levels, recommend ways to encourage private sector involvement, and advise the President what actions are needed to create a positive environment for the development and growth of reservation economies.

— Support direct funding to Indian tribes under the Title XX social services block grant to States.

— Sought and obtained funds for FY 1983 to implement the Small Tribes Initiative to provide financial support needed to allow small tribes to develop basic tribal administrative and management capabilities.

— Sought and obtained funds for F Y 1983 to provide seed money for tribes for economic development ventures on reservations.

— Supported and signed into law the Tribal Governmental Tax Status Act which will provide tribal governments with the same revenue raising and saving mechanisms available to other governments.

— Support the use of creative agreements such as joint ventures and other non-lease agreements for the development of Indian mineral resources.

— Direct the Cabinet Council on Human Resources to act as a review and coordination mechanism to ensure that Federal activities are non-duplicative, cost-effective, and consistent with the goal of encouraging tribal self-government with a minimum of Federal interference.

Statement of Ada E. Deer
before the Senate Committee
on Indian Affairs

July 15, 1993

The 1980s and 1990s were a period of consolidation and expansion of tribal sovereignty and self-determination. It was also a time for Indian women to take their places alongside their brothers in assuming positions of equality and leadership in Indian self-government and national policy. Native women such as Janet McCloud, LaDonna Harris, Winona LaDuke, Madonna Thunderhawk, LaNada Means, and Anna Mae Aquash were committed activists during and after the Red Power period of the 1960s and 1970s. It wasn't until the 1980s, however, that there was a large-scale entry of women into positions of prominence in Indian tribal and federal government. In 1987 Wilma Mankiller became the principal chief of the Cherokee Nation of Oklahoma, and in 1993 Ada Deer was sworn in as assistant secretary of Indian affairs. In spite of the contributions of these native women, there remained pockets of resistance to Indian women as equal participants in the tribal political process. For instance, although Shinnecock women could legally vote in U.S. and New York State elections following the Indian Citizenship Act of 1924, it would be seventy more years before these women were permitted to vote in tribal elections. By the late 1990s, however, Indian women were not only voting in tribal elections, they were often running tribal governments. By the end of the decade and the turn of the century, women had assumed the heads of tribal governments in forty-four Alaskan Native communities, and women governed seventy-seven Indian tribes and nations in the lower forty-eight states. In total, nearly one-fifth of Indian governments were headed by women.

In her July 15, 1993, statement before the U.S. Senate Committee on Indian Affairs, Ada Deer recounted a bit about her life and the path that led her to the highest office in the Federal Indian Service ever to be held by a woman. She spoke about the experience of her tribe, the Menominees of Wisconsin, before and after the tribe's termination in 1954 and about the successful struggle for tribal reinstatement in 1973 — a struggle in which she played a central role as the chairperson of the Menominee Restoration Committee. Finally, she outlined her plans for the Bureau of Indian Affairs.

Mr. Chairman, Mr. Vice-Chairman, and other distinguished members of the Senate Committee on Indian Affairs, my name is Ada Elizabeth Deer and I am proud to say I am an enrolled member of the Menominee Indian Tribe of Wisconsin. I would like to thank you for your time and courtesies shown me during our recent interviews and for the opportunity to appear before you today. I am honored that President Clinton and Secretary Babbitt have nominated me as the first woman to be Assistant Secretary for Indian Affairs. I embrace this administration's theme of change. I have dedicated my life to being an agent of change, as a Menominee, as a Social Worker, and as a human being.

Personally, you should know that forty years ago my tribe the Menominee was terminated; twenty years ago we were restored; and today I come before you as a true survivor of Indian policy.

I was born on the Menominee Indian Reservation in Wisconsin, a land of dense forests, a winding wild river, and streams and lakes that nourish the land, animals, and the people. I am an extension of this environment that has fostered my growth and enriched my vision. An appreciation and reverence for the land is fundamental to being Indian.

Our family of seven lived in a log cabin on the banks of the Wolf River. We had no running water or electricity. Yet, while all of the statistics said we were poor, I never felt poor in spirit. My mother, Constance Wood Deer, was the single greatest influence on my life. She instilled in me rich values which have shaped my lifetime commitment to service.

One of the most compelling times in my life, however, involved the termination and restoration of my tribe. Pardon my brief historical account, but an understanding of history is critical to understanding Indian policy.

The leaders of my tribe had signed the Wolf River Treaty of 1854 guaranteeing the Menominees 250,000 acres of land — and sovereignty over that land — forever. This was no gift. Under decisions from Chief Justice John Marshall through the current Supreme Court, the Menominees, like other tribes, owned their land and much more before the treaty era. We ceded most of our aboriginal land held by us for thousands of years, and in the treaties reserved — thus the term "reservation" — a small part of it. Our tribal leaders were sophisticated people. They insisted upon land, sovereignty, and federal trust protection from onrushing settlers. In that time of crisis, one of the greatest collisions of cultures in the history of the world, our leaders relied upon those promises. Of course, promise after promise has been broken. By the end of the treaty making, in 1871, tribes held 140 million acres. But the non-Indians marching West wanted more, and so the General Allotment Act of 1887 was passed. Indian land was opened for homesteading on a wholesale basis and by the 1930s the tribal land base had dwindled to 50 million acres.

The next assault on our land and sovereignty was the termination policy of the 1950s. Termination was a misguided and now-discredited experiment that targeted several tribes, including mine. This policy completely abrogated the federal trust relationship. State jurisdiction was imposed on tribal members and land. My tribe literally went from being prosperous to being Wisconsin's newest, smallest, and poorest county. Many terminated tribes saw their land sold off. My tribe land was held by a state-chartered tribal corporation. The termination act stripped us of our treaty-guaranteed exemption from taxation and our tribal leaders were forced to begin to sell off ancestral tribal land to pay the taxes.

By the 1960s, my people were in despair. Poverty had sunk to new depths and we faced the loss of our land, tribal identity, and culture. My own personal choice was clear. I had to leave law school, return to the reservation, and create a coalition of tribal leaders to reverse termination. The 1950s and 1960s were a low point for Indian people in our history on this continent.

At Menominee, we collectively discovered the kind of determination that human beings only find in times of impending destruction. Against all odds, we invented a new policy — restoration. Finally, after grueling work by more people than I could ever possibly thank, our coalition pushed the Menominee Restoration Act through Congress. This legislation is a vivid reminder of how great a government can be when it is large enough to admit and rectify mistakes. It is also indicative of my tribe's spirit, tenacity, and ability to hold other sovereign entities accountable.

We have regained a sacred vision. Our vision is bright and clear throughout all of our homelands, whether at First Salmon Ceremony in the Pacific Northwest, at a secret ritual deep in the Pueblo kiva, or at a Sun Dance in Sioux country.

My vision for the Bureau of Indian Affairs is to create a progressive federal/tribal partnership. First and foremost, the heart of Indian policy must be strong, effective tribal sovereignty. There is no reason for me or for any of you to be reluctant to support the permanency of tribal sovereignty any more than we would be reluctant to support the permanency of federal or state sovereignty. There are three kinds of sovereignty recognized in the United States Constitution — tribal, state, and federal. It is our moral obligation to ensure that these rights are supported vigorously. The role of the federal government should be to support and to implement tribally inspired solutions to tribally defined problems. The days of federal paternalism are over.

Although Indians now constitute 90 percent of the employees in the Bureau of Indian Affairs, we must remember that the Bureau was created by non-Indians. It has not been a pro-active Indian institution. I want to activate and to mobilize people in the Bureau so that they can be creative and forward-looking. I want the Indian values of sharing, caring, and respect incorporated into their day-to-day work. I want to help BIA be a full partner in the effort to fulfill the Indian agenda developed in Indian country. The best way we can do this is for the tribes to decide what needs to be done and for the tribes to do it on their own terms, with our enthusiastic and constructive support.

In this new Administration, if we work together, I am confident that we can eliminate the barriers of the past and work with the tribes to embrace the challenges of the 21st century.

In closing, know that I bring a strong sense of history, vision, maturity, and compassion to the tasks before me.

Thank you very much.

References and Further Reading

Cohen, Felix S. 1942. *Handbook of Federal Indian Law*. Washington DC: Government Printing Office.

———. 1982. *Felix S. Cohen's Handbook of Federal Indian Law*. Charlottesville VA: Michie.

Cornell, Stephen. 1988. *The Return of the Native: American Indian Political Resurgence*. New York: Oxford University Press.

Fixico, Donald. 1986. *Termination and Relocation: Federal Indian Policy, 1945–1960*. Albuquerque: University of New Mexico Press.

Getches, David H., Charles F. Wilkinson, and Robert A. Williams Jr. 1993. *Cases and Materials on Federal Indian Law*. St. Paul MN: West.

Green, Donald E., and Thomas V. Tonnesen. *American Indians: Social Justice and Public Policy*. Ethnicity and Public Policy Series, vol. 9. Madison: University of Wisconsin System Institute on Race and Ethnicity.

Haines, Herbert H. 1988. *Black Radicals and the Civil Rights Mainstream, 1954–1970*. Knoxville: University of Tennessee Press.

Jaimes, M. Annette, with Theresa Halsey. 1992. "American Indian Women: At the Center of Indigenous Resistance in Contemporary North America." In *The State of Native America: Genocide, Colonization, and Resistance*, ed. M. Annette Jaimes. Boston: South End.

Josephy, Alvin M., Jr. 1982. *Now That the Buffalo's Gone: A Study of Today's American Indians*. New York: Alfred A. Knopf.

Klein, Barry T. 1995. *Reference Encyclopedia of the American Indian*. West Nyack NY: Todd.

O'Brien, Sharon. 1989. *American Indian Tribal Governments*. Norman: University of Oklahoma Press.

Sandefur, Gary D., Ronald R. Rindfuss, and Barney Cohen. 1996. *Changing Numbers, Changing Needs: American Indian Demography and Public Health*. Washington DC: National Academy Press.

3 Economic Development and Land Claims

American Indian Capital Conference on Poverty

Statement Made for the Young People
by Melvin Thom, May 1964

In 1964 a momentous breakthrough occurred in Indian affairs. The Economic Opportunity Act, the major instrument of the Johnson administration's War on Poverty, included American Indians as beneficiaries of the act's programs. For the first time, Indians were asked to propose and work out the plans for programs they wished to have on their reservations. Once the proposals had been approved, funds were made available to Native Americans, who administered the programs themselves. At last Indians were permitted to take responsibility for the management of, and the handling of monies for, reservation programs, and on the whole they proved that they were, indeed, able to run their own affairs. Though this right was extended only to their management of Office of Economic Opportunity programs, the experience was not lost on the Indians. Almost at once it quickened their demand for similar rights over all government programs on the reservations, including those funded by the Bureau of Indian Affairs.

Up to the time of the Economic Opportunity Act, American Indians had not usually been included as beneficiaries of legislation intended for the general population. Although they had benefited under the provisions of the Area Redevelopment Act, passed in the early days of the Kennedy administration, it was an exception. Indians, most congressional representatives felt, were cared for by the appropriations for the Bureau of Indian Affairs, and when the Economic Opportunity Act was first framed, it seemed likely that Indians would be excluded from its provisions.

To convince official Washington that American Indians should be included in the act, a large American Indian Capital Conference on Poverty was convened in the capital May 9–12, 1964, when the legislation was still being written and debated. Several hundred Indians and as many non-Indians, gathered under the auspices of the Council on Indian Affairs, a federation of church groups and other Indian-interest organizations, visited congressional representatives and senators at the Capitol, held consultations with influential administration leaders, including Vice President Hubert Humphrey and Secretary of the Interior Stewart Udall, and won their point.

The conference was also notable because many young Indians, advocates of Red Power, showed up and for the first time demanded and gained the right to be heard by the older delegates. Near the close of the meeting their spokesman, Melvin Thom, a young Northern Paiute Indian from Walker River, Nevada, who was president of the National Indian Youth Council, stirred the conference with a statement "for the young people." Following are excerpts from his speech.

We are gathered here today to present the findings and recommendations of the poverty conditions which exist in our Indian homes. Poverty is nothing new to us. Many of us grew up in such conditions. We are joining in a concerted effort to remove the causes of poverty that destroy life among our people; this condition continues to eat away at our existence.

I would like to point out a little more about the basic Indian feeling toward the way he is being treated in regard to poverty. It is not easy to just sit down and make out a plan of action to remove poverty. It is not easy to even admit that we are poor. It is especially difficult for young people to say "We are poor — please help us." It is not easy to follow somebody always asking for help. The image of the American Indian is that of always asking. But the Indian youth fears this poverty and we have got to take a good look at what approach we are going to use to be rid of poverty.

The young people of the Indian tribes are going to be the ones to live with this, and sometime the Indian people are going to have to make a great effort — a concerted effort to remove poverty and the other conditions that have held the Indian people back from enjoying the comforts of life which we should be entitled to.

We as Indian youths know we cannot get away from the life which brought us here. To be an Indian is . . . life to us and the conditions under which we live and the lives of our parents and relatives are affected. We cannot relax until this condition is removed; our conscience will never be clear until we have put forth effort to improve our conditions and the conditions of those at home.

We must recognize and point out to others that we do want to live under better conditions, but we want to remember that we are Indians. We want to remain Indian people. We want this country to know that our Indian lands and homes are precious to us. We never want to see them taken away from us.

As Indian youths we say to you today that the Indian cannot be pushed into the mainstream of American life. Our recognition as Indian people and Indian tribes is very dear to us. We cannot work to destroy our lives as Indian people. This will never serve the needs of the Indian people or this country.

Many of our friends feel that the Indian's greatest dream is to be free from second-class citizenship. We as youths have been taught that this freedom from second-class citizenship should be our goal. Let it be heard from Indian youth today that we do not want to be freed from our special relationship with the Federal Government. We only want our relationship between Indian Tribes and the Government to be one of good working relationship. We do not want to destroy our culture, our life that brought us through the period in which the Indians were almost annihilated.

We do not want to be pushed into the mainstream of American life. The Indian youth fears this, and this fear should be investigated and re-moved. We want it to be understood by all those concerned with Indian welfare that no people can ever develop when there is fear and anxiety. There is fear among our Indian people today that our tribal relationship with the Federal Government will be terminated soon. This fear must be removed and life allowed to develop by free choices. The policy to push Indians into the mainstream of American life must be re-evaluated. We must have hope. We must have a goal. But that is not what the Indian people want. We will never be able to fully join in on that effort.

For any program or policy to work we must be involved at the grass-roots level. The responsibility to make decisions for ourselves must be placed in Indian hands. Any real help for Indian people must take cultural values into consideration. Programs set up to help people must fit into the cultural framework. . . .

We need to take a careful look at special programs. We need help for immediate plans and we also need to take into consideration the long-range policies and programs and where they are leading. What is needed at this time is a large national picture. The attitude that non-Indians, and some Indians, have is that someday the Indians are just going to disappear and that we should be working to make the Indians disappear is very wrong. We are not going to disappear. We have got to educate the American public and also our leaders that we are here to stay and that in staying here we have got to find a place for resolving our problems that will give us a life that has meaning for us and our Indian children and that there is a real hope that a complete life can be realized.

Indian tribes need greater political power to act. This country respects power and is based on the power system. If Indian communities and Indian tribes do not have political power we will never be able to hang on to what we have now. At the present time we have a right to own land — to exist as federal corporations — we have the self-building means to control this. There is a matter of putting that to work. We have a lot of communication to do. This communication has to come from the Indians themselves. We have got to get the message across. In the past our friends have taken it upon themselves to bring the message to the public and to the helping agencies. We have got to take a greater part in this role.

This conference is a good example of how we can work toward bringing our needs to the attention of the public and the helping agencies. The Indian youth should have an important role for he will be the one to be dealing with the benefits of the programs also. We must make an effort to achieve the goals of Indian people to act completely for themselves and a lot rests with the younger people. We have to stir up an interest among Indian youth that they have got to get together to make a concerted effort with our leading tribes and with the older Indian leadership.

We have to cooperate and learn to work together. The Indian youth have got to take this upon themselves because in many cases our older people do not have the means to communicate this message and too many of our young people have drifted off and gone into American cities and not served the Indians where they are needed. There is a great amount of work ahead for the Indians and their friends.

If the findings and recommendations of this conference can be realized we will have taken a big step in the way toward a better life for the Indian people. Maybe someday we will all look back and realize that at this conference the first big step was taken and how our future efforts were built on this work.

Return of Blue Lake to the Taos Pueblos

Public Law 91-550, December 15, 1970

The Indian students who occupied Alcatraz Island on November 20, 1969, and thus set into motion the Red Power movement had as their main objective the return of land to Indian people. Research has shown that the federal government, although feigning negotiations for the return of Alcatraz Island, never intended to do so. President Nixon did intend, however, to make good his promise made on September 27, 1968, in a message sent to the delegates of the National Congress of American Indians gathered in Omaha, Nebraska. The message began, "The sad plight of the American Indian is a stain on the honor of the American people." Nixon proposed a bold new plan for Indian self-determination that would transfer responsibility for tribal affairs from the federal government to Indian people. Nixon promised that if he were elected, "the right of self-determination of the Indian people will be respected and their participation in planning their own destiny will be encouraged." Taos Blue Lake would prove to be Nixon's first step in fulfilling this promise.

In 1906 the U.S. government appropriated the Taos Blue Lake area, a sacred site belonging to the Taos Pueblo Indians, and incorporated it into part of the Carson National Forest. In 1926 the Taos Indians, in reply to a compensation offer made by the U.S. government, waived the award, seeking return of Blue Lake instead. As a result, the Taos people got neither the compensation nor Blue Lake. On May 31, 1933, the Senate Indian Affairs Committee recommended that the Taos Indians be issued a permit to use Blue Lake for religious purposes. The permit was finally issued in 1940. On August 13, 1951, Taos Indians filed a suit before the Indian Claims Commission, seeking judicial support for the validity of title to the lake. On September 8, 1965, the Indian Claims Commission affirmed that the U.S. government had taken the area unjustly from its rightful owners, the Taos Pueblo Indians. On March 15, 1966, legislation was introduced to return Blue Lake to the Taos Indians; however, the bill died without action in the Senate Interior and Insular Affairs Subcommittee. On May 10, 1968, House Bill 3306 was introduced to restore the sacred area to the Taos Indians. While it passed the House of Representatives unanimously, it once again died in the Senate Interior and Insular Affairs Subcommittee.

In the politically charged climate brought about by the Alcatraz occupation, the Blue Lake bill was once again introduced in the Congress in 1969, and on December 15, 1970, the sacred Blue Lake was returned to the Taos Pueblo Indians. When signing the bill that returned the sacred lake to the Taos people, President Nixon stated, "this bill indicates a new direction in Indian affairs in this country, a new direction in which we will have the cooperation of both Democrats and Republicans, one in which there will be more of an attitude of cooperation rather than paternalism, one of self-determination rather than termination, one of mutual respect." In concluding remarks President Nixon stated, "I can't think of anything . . . that could make me more proud as president of the United States."

Be it enacted by the Senate and House of Representatives of the United States of America in Congress assembled, That section 4 of the Act of May 31, 1933 (48 Stat. 108), providing for the protection of the watershed within the Carson National Forest for the Pueblo de Taos Indians in New Mexico, be and hereby is amended to read as follows:

Sec. 4

(a) That, for the purpose of safeguarding the interests and welfare of the tribe of Indians known as the Pueblo de Taos of New Mexico, the following described lands and improvements thereon, upon which said Indians depend and have depended since time immemorial for water supply, forage for their domestic livestock, wood and timber for their personal use, and as the scene of certain religious ceremonials, are hereby declared to be held by the United States in trust for the Pueblo de Taos:

(b) The lands held in trust pursuant to this section shall be a part of the Pueblo de Taos Reservation, and shall be administered under the laws and regulations applicable to other trust Indian lands: Provided, That the Pueblo de Taos Indians shall use the lands for traditional purposes only, such as religious ceremonials, hunting and fishing, a source of water, forage for their domestic livestock, and wood, timber, and other natural resources for their personal use, all subject to such regulations for conservation purposes as the Secretary of the Interior may prescribe.

In his role as the Taos Pueblos' religious leader, Cacique (priest-chief) Juan de Jesus Romero responded to the return of Taos Blue Lake. With all the dignity of his ninety years and his spiritual position, he rose to speak. He revealed to his White House audience that his spiritual and religious devotions at Blue Lake and other tribal shrines included all of America and all Americans.

The life that I live belongs to the American people. . . . I have exercised within my Indian power and my spiritual way to do exactly what I have been told by the forefathers beyond my times. My responsibilities include all America and its people, and what we have in this good country of ours . . . in my prayers and in my daily talks in my spiritual ways. . . . In telling you the truth I go to Blue Lake with my little package of worship, with the thing that I have to give and offer to the spiritual way. . . . I know myself when I do this it will be included in all the walks, in all the lives of this country. . . . And this responsibility is [to] more than the material things . . . [It is] to protect the life and to protect what this America is, really beautiful, peace, honesty, truth, understanding, consideration.

Alaska Native Claims
Settlement Act

December 18, 1971

When Alaska became a state in 1959, the federal government granted the new state the right to select 102 million acres of land from the newly acquired "public domain." Selection was to be made within a twenty-five-year period. Indian title to land in Alaska, however, had not been settled, and Alaska Native villages protested state land selections by recording their own claims to land with the Bureau of Land Management. By 1964 Alaska Natives claimed more than 300 million acres, and the secretary of the interior, Stewart Udall, prohibited the state from selecting further land until the issue over Indian title was clarified.

Just as had happened to Taos Pueblo in New Mexico and on Alcatraz Island in California, Alaska Natives mobilized around land claims and issues such as education, health, and jobs. In Alaska they formed local and regional associations of villages. In 1965 and 1966 Alaska Natives created the Alaska Federation of Natives (AFN), a statewide organization empowered to pursue land claims on behalf of Alaska Natives and other community interests. The AFN led Alaska Natives to a congressional settlement in 1971 called the Alaska Native Claims Settlement Act (ANCSA), which set aside 44 million acres of land and awarded Alaska Natives an immediate $462 million cash settlement, and another $500 million in future payments for mineral rights. The act, however, extinguished Alaska Native title to nine-tenths of Alaska.

ANCSA marked the legislative beginning of the Self-Determination period. In their villages, the sixty thousand Native Alaskan people demanded title to 60 million acres of land following the discovery of oil on the North Slope in Alaska. On March 11, 1971, President Nixon announced that he "wanted to continue to be forthcoming on Indian affairs" and proposed ANCSA as a means of settling the dispute between the state and the Alaska Natives. The awarded land was to be divided among some 220 Native village corporations and 12 regional corporations established by the act to do business for profit. An additional regional corporation was established, comprising nonpermanent Native Alaskan residents. Alaska Natives were awarded shares in the newly created corporations.

Although the Alaska Federation of Natives approved the bill by a vote of 511 to 56, the act remains controversial among Alaska Natives, who fear that it will destroy their traditional lifestyle centered on hunting and fishing. While the act stimulated the economic development of the region, rights to millions of acres previously used for hunting and fishing were lost to Alaska Natives, and millions of acres ended up in national parks or forest reserves. Additionally, because the regional corporations seek to make a profit, they often pursue nontraditional subsistence activities such as mining and logging projects that destroy the traditional resources of their shareholders. A fear also exists that native people may one day lose their land to corporate bankruptcy or tax liability.

DECLARATION OF POLICY

Sec. 2. Congress finds and declares that —
(a) there is an immediate need for a fair and just settlement of all claims by Natives and Native groups of Alaska, based on aboriginal land claims;
(b) the settlement should be accomplished rapidly, with certainty, in conformity with the real economic and social needs of Natives, without litigation, with maximum participation by Natives in decisions affecting their rights and property, without establishing any permanent racially defined institutions, rights, privileges, or obligations, without creating a reservation system or lengthy wardship or trusteeship, and without adding to the categories of property and institutions enjoying special tax privileges or to the legislation establishing special relationships between the United States Government and the State of Alaska;
(c) no provision of this Act shall replace or diminish any right, privilege, or obligation of Natives as citizens of the United States or of Alaska, or relieve, replace, or diminish any obligation of the United States or of the State of Alaska to protect and promote the rights or welfare of Natives as citizens of the United States or of Alaska; the Secretary is authorized and directed, together with other appropriate agencies of the United States Government, to make a study of all Federal programs primarily designed to benefit Native people and to report back to the Congress with his recommendations for the future management and operation of these programs within three years of the date of enactment of this Act;

REGIONAL CORPORATIONS

Sec. 7.
(a) For purposes of this Act, the State of Alaska shall be divided by the Secretary within one year after the date of enactment of this Act into

twelve geographic regions, with each region composed as far as practicable of Natives having a common heritage and sharing common interests. In the absence of good cause shown to the contrary, such regions shall approximate the areas covered by the operations of the following existing Native associations;

(1) Arctic Slope Native Association (Barrow, Point Hope);
(2) Bering Straits Association (Seward Peninsula, Unalakleet, Saint Lawrence Island);
(3) Northwest Alaska Native Association (Kotzebue);
(4) Association of Village Council Presidents (southwest coast, all villages in the Bethel area, including all villages on the Lower Yukon River and the lower Kuskokwim River);
(5) Tanana Chiefs' Conference (Koyukuk, Middle and Upper Yukon Rivers, Upper Kuskokwim, Tanana River);
(6) Cook Inlet Association (Kenai, Tyonek, Eklutna, Iliamna);
(7) Bristol Bay Native Association (Dillingham, Upper Alaska Peninsula);
(8) Aleut league (Aleutian Islands, Pribilof Islands and that part of Alaska which is the Aleut League);
(9) Chugach Native Association (Cordova, Tatitlek, Port Graham, English Bay, Valdez, and Seward);
(10) Tlingit-Haida Central Council (southeastern Alaska, including Metlakatla);
(11) Kodiak Area Native Association (all villages on and around Kodiak Island); and
(12) Copper River Native Association (Copper Center, Glenn-Allen, Chitin, Mentasta).

Any dispute over the boundaries of a region or regions shall be resolved by a board of arbitrators consisting of one person selected by each of the Native associations involved, and an additional one or two persons, whichever is needed to make an odd number of arbitrators, such additional person or persons to be selected by the arbitrators selected by the Native associations involved.

(b) The Secretary may, on request made within one year of the date of enactment of this Act, by representative and responsible leaders of the Native associations listed in subsection (a), merge two or more of the twelve regions; Provided, That the twelve regions may not be reduced to less than seven, and there may be no fewer than seven Regional Corporations.

(c) If a majority of all eligible Natives eighteen years of age or older who are permanent residents of Alaska elect, pursuant to subsection 5(c), to be enrolled in a thirteenth region for Natives who are non-residents of Alaska, the Secretary shall establish such a region for the benefit of the Natives who elected to be enrolled therein, and they may establish a Regional Corporation pursuant to this Act.

(d) Five incorporators within each region, named by the Native association in the region, shall incorporate under the laws of Alaska a Regional Corporation to conduct business for profit, which shall be eligible for the benefits of this Act so long as it is organized and functions in accordance with this Act. The articles of incorporation shall include provisions necessary to carry out the terms of this Act.

Launching the Tribes
into a New Millennium

Council of Energy Resources Tribes, 1975

In 1973 tribal leaders, many of whom were strongly influenced by the activism of the 1960s, were awakened to the threat to tribal resources brought about by international events when O P E C, an international cartel of oil-producing states, imposed an oil embargo on most Western countries, thus creating an international energy crisis. This event did much to call attention to the strategic importance of Indian-owned energy resources. Indian lands, primarily in the western United States, contain over 200 billion tons of coal, 4.2 billion barrels of oil, and 17.5 trillion cubic feet of natural gas. Uranium also exists as an important mineral resource on some Indian reservations.

After the 1973 oil embargo, Indian leaders began to recognize that the mineral resources on Indian lands could be threatened by actions from abroad. In 1975 tribal leaders from twenty-five reservations containing energy resources agreed to establish the Council of Energy Resources Tribes (c e r t) to address these concerns. C E R T's primary function is to assist tribes in the development of their energy and mineral resources and to promote the welfare of member tribes through protection, conservation, control, and careful management of their oil, gas, shale, uranium, geothermal, and other energy resources. In 1976 c e r t members visited Washington D c and attempted to coordinate federal and private leasing policies of Indian lands. As a result, several long-term leases were renegotiated as Indian concern over the depletion of nonrenewable resources continued to grow. Today c e r t represents forty-nine tribes and monitors and negotiates resource contracts for the sale of oil, coal, gas, and minerals found on reservation lands.

C E R T represented the formation of what many non-Indians viewed as an Indian energy cartel, and its presence was met with rancor by many among the ranks of major multinational energy companies. Indian tribes were portrayed as greedy and profit-motivated. Reflecting this attitude by some in the energy business, a representative of one major company based in Denver said in 1980, "Those dumb Indians ought to be shot for not letting us dig on their lands. Everything, the national parks included, ought to be exploited." Peter MacDonald, Navajo tribal chairman and founding president of c e r t, provided his own analysis: "We were charged with capitalism in the first degree. . . . c e r t is not in the business of advocating rampant exploitation of the land . . . but it is more comfortable to think in terms of dichotomies. Us versus Them. Spiritual versus Material. Cultural Preservation versus Subsistence. Tribal Sovereignty versus Corporate America."

The Council of Energy Resource Tribes (CERT), a non-profit organization founded by twenty-five Tribal leaders in 1975, is composed of forty-nine federally recognized American Indian Tribes and four affiliate Canadian Indian Nations. The CERT member Tribes own significant energy resources — an estimated third of the United States low sulfur strippable coal; forty percent of its privately owned uranium; four percent of its oil and natural gas; and substantial quantities of oil shale and geothermal resources. CERT is governed by the elected leadership of its member Tribe representing nearly sixty percent of all American Indians living on or near reservations.

CERT and its member Tribes recognize that trained and experienced Indian people are essential to build healthy Tribal communities. Because of the longstanding shortage of Indian professionals, particularly in business, science and engineering, Tribes have often been forced to depend on outside assistance. CERT provides Tribes with managerial and technical resources to complement and strengthen Tribal expertise. CERT's integrated approach to resource management is a comprehensive strategy linking development of energy resources, achieving and maintaining environmental equity, building solid governmental infrastructures and creating a strong economic base.

In the past twenty years, the CERT Tribes have accomplished much — both individually and collectively. Crucial national legislation has been passed restructuring the federal role in Indian resource development. New relationships with industry have been forged. Coal leases have been renegotiated, oil and gas agreements have taken the form of joint ventures, and resource development agreements include provisions for appropriate Tribal employment, training and scholarship opportunities. Many of the nation's environmental laws have been amended to permit Tribes to assume the primary role in their administration of Tribal lands. Tribes now use sophisticated economic valuation criteria to assign value to their lands and resources. Tribal resource development today nets millions of dollars more for Tribes than ever before — funds which Tribes use to address governmental responsibilities such as building reservation infrastructures and providing health care, as well as to invest in the future.

The CERT member Tribes are determined to enter and thrive in the twenty-first century on their own terms. As sovereign nations, their vision of true self-determination has remained constant since CERT was founded and long before CERT's Tribal leadership has adopted a dynamic three-pronged approach to achieve this goal. First, Tribes must effectively govern within their own lands as well as play an important role in governing America. Second, Indian people must master the tools of modern technology to protect their cultural heritages. And third, Tribes must cultivate strong diversified economies while balancing environmental and cultural concerns with economic growth.

CERT remains dedicated to providing services and resources tailored to Tribes' needs as they strive to achieve their unique vision of the future.

United States v. Sioux Nation of Indians

Supreme Court of the United States

June 30, 1980

The Red Power quest for return of Indian lands was most vividly displayed in the struggle of the Lakota people to regain possession of the Sacred Black Hills (Paha Sapa). Although the court decision in favor of the Lakotas was handed down in 1980, the Lakotas had argued for more than a century that the United States had abrogated the Fort Laramie Treaty of April 29, 1868, and illegally laid claim to the Black Hills. The Fort Laramie Treaty contained a provision that promised that the Black Hills would be "set apart for the absolute and undisturbed use and occupation of the Indians herein named [the Lakota people]."

The violation of the 1868 treaty was the result of pressure from gold-seekers and land-hungry westerners that began as soon as the treaty was ratified. The discovery of gold in the Black Hills based on reports from Lieutenant Colonel George Armstrong Custer was widely reported in newspapers across the country in the 1870s. In addition, the land's suitability for grazing and cultivation created a demand for opening of the Black Hills to settlement. In 1876 presidential commissioner George Manypenny negotiated an illegal agreement with 10 percent of the Lakota chiefs for surrender of the Black Hills. The principal provisions were that the Lakotas would relinquish their rights to the Black Hills, their rights to hunt in unceded territories, in exchange for subsistence rations for as long as they would be needed to ensure the survival of the Lakota people. Manypenny ignored the provision in the Fort Laramie Treaty requiring approval by 75 percent of the adult male population. Aware of this requirement, Congress enacted the 1876 agreement and took the sacred Paha Sapa into U.S. possession. Since that time the Lakotas have regarded the agreement as a breach of the U.S. government's promise to set aside the Black Hills in perpetuity for the Lakota people.

In 1980 the tortuous journey through the Indian Claims Commission, lower courts, appellate courts, courts of appeals, and finally Congress ended. The U.S. Supreme court offered one of the largest Indian claims judgments when it awarded the Lakota people $17.5 million plus interest, a total slightly in excess of $106 million.

To this day the Lakotas refuse to touch the money awarded — now more than $400 million. Instead, they hold true to the demand, which they made more than a century ago and reaffirmed during the Red Power era, for return of their land. The Cheyenne River Sioux tribal council stated: "The welfare of ourselves and our descendants will not be promoted by accepting an award of money for our claim to the Black Hills of South Dakota. We hereby reject any award of money for the Black Hills . . . and do not abandon our claim to the lands taken by the Act of 1876." Severt Young Bear, a young Lakota activist, explains: "because land is sacred to me . . . [The whites] are trying to change our value system. To be a traditional person is to believe in our own culture, is to believe in yourself as a Lakota person; then you cannot sell the land."

Mr. Justice Blackmun delivered the opinion of the Court.

This case concerns the Black Hills of South Dakota, the Great Sioux Reservation, and a colorful, and in many respects tragic, chapter in the history of the Nation's West.

. . . For over a century now the Sioux Nation has claimed that the United States unlawfully abrogated the Fort Laramie Treaty of April 29, 1868, 15 Stat. 635, in Art. II of which the United States pledged that the Great Sioux Reservation, including the Black Hills, would be "set apart for the absolute and undisturbed use and occupation of the Indians herein named." The Fort Laramie Treaty was concluded at the culmination of the Powder River War of 1866–1867, a series of military engagements in which the Sioux tribes, led by their great chief, Red Cloud, fought to protect the integrity of earlier-recognized treaty lands from the incursion of white settlers.

The Fort Laramie Treaty included several agreements central to the issues presented in this case. First, it established the Great Sioux Reservation, a tract of land [comprising most of South Dakota west of the Missouri River] in addition to certain reservations already existing east of the Missouri. The United States "solemnly agree[d]" that no unauthorized persons "shall ever be permitted to pass over, settle upon, or reside in [this] territory." . . . Fourth, Art. XII of the treaty provided:

No treaty for the cession of any portion or part of the reservation herein described which may be held in common shall be of any validity or force as against the said Indians, unless executed and signed by at least three fourths of all the adult male Indians, occupying or interested in the same.

In sum, we conclude that the legal analysis and factual findings of the Court of Claims fully support its conclusion that the terms of the 1877 Act did not effect "a mere change in the form of investment of Indian tribal property." The 1877 Act effected a taking of tribal property, property which had been set aside for the exclusive occupation of the Sioux by the Fort Laramie Treaty of 1868. That taking implied an obligation on the part of the Government to make just compensation to the Sioux Nation, and that obligation, including an award of interest, must now, at last, be paid.

The judgment of the Court of Claims affirmed.

It is so ordered.

Mr. Justice Rehnquist, dissenting.

Nuclear Waste Policy Act

January 7, 1983

Public Law 97–425 requires that the president of the United States or the secretary of the interior notify the governing body of any affected Indian tribe on whose reservation a repository for the disposal of high-level radioactive waste or a spent nuclear fuel repository is proposed to be located. The law further discloses findings stating that radioactive waste creates "potential risks and requires safe and environmentally acceptable methods of disposal." The law then sets forth guidelines for the recommendation of candidate sites for the disposal of these dangerous materials.

Although Public Law 97–425 addressed the disposal of high-level radio-active waste and spent nuclear fuel, the control of hazardous waste on American Indian lands goes far beyond those issues. It includes uranium mining, coal strip-mining, railroads, electric generating plants, high-power transmission lines, mercury contamination, dangerous emissions discharge, hydroelectric exploration, toxic-waste dumping, and acid rain contamination. As lawmakers noted, "In 1975 100% of all federally produced uranium came from Indian reservations. That same year there were 380 uranium leases on Indian lands. . . . In 1976, four out of the ten largest coal strip-mines in the country were on Indian lands. . . . The Hanford nuclear reservation is well within the treaty area of the Yakima Indian Nation [in the state of Washington]. The nuclear site contains 570 square miles of land, and a significant portion of it is contaminated with radiation. In August 1973, over 115,000 gallons of liquid high-level radioactive waste seeped into the ground from a leaking storage tank."

In 1987 American Indian activists began to focus on this problem of on-reservation hazardous waste disposal. A study of twenty-five reservations found that nearly twelve hundred generators or power sites on or near these Indian lands were considered potentially acute health and environmental problems. Six of the reservations had sites that were considered to represent serious dangers to public health.

Despite the concerns of the American Indian people, the contamination has not stopped. Over the past four decades, studies show that a network of 280 facilities at some twenty weapons-making sites have produced massive quantities of highly radioactive waste. This includes waste resulting from the production of plutonium for nuclear weapons and reprocessing spent fuel from naval reactors. Because these facilities were contracted by the federal government and protected from regulation due to national security concerns, much of this dangerous material was stored or buried in ways that resulted in threats to human life. Billions of gallons of radioactive waste from bomb-grade material have been dumped directly into soil and groundwater. Millions more gallons of concentrated waste have been stored in tanks, many of which have leaked.

TITLE I — DISPOSAL AND STORAGE OF HIGH-LEVEL RADIOACTIVE WASTE, SPENT NUCLEAR FUEL, AND LOW-LEVEL RADIOACTIVE WASTE

STATE AND AFFECTED INDIAN TRIBE PARTICIPATION IN DEVELOPMENT OF PROPOSED REPOSITORIES FOR DEFENSE WASTE

Sec 101.

(a) Notification to States and Affected Indian Tribes. — Notwithstanding the provisions of section 8, upon any decision by the Secretary or the President to develop a repository for the disposal of high-level radioactive waste or spent nuclear fuel resulting exclusively from atomic energy defense activities, research and development activities of the Secretary, or both, and before proceeding with any site-specific investigations with respect to such repository, the Secretary shall notify the Governor and legislature of the State in which such repository is proposed to be located, or the governing body of the affected Indian tribe on whose reservation such repository is proposed to be located, as the case may be, of such decision.

(b) Participation of States and Affected Indian Tribes. — Following the receipt of any notification under subsection (a), the State or Indian tribe involved shall be entitled, with respect to the proposed repository involved, to rights of participation and consultation identical to those provided in sections 115 through 118, except that any financial assistance authorized to be provided to such State or affected Indian tribe under section 116(c) or 118(b) shall be made from amounts appropriated to the Secretary for purposes of carrying out this section.

Sec. 111.

(a) Findings. — The Congress finds that —

(1) radioactive waste creates potential risks and requires safe and environmentally acceptable methods of disposal;

(2) a national problem has been created by the accumulation of (A) spent nuclear fuel from nuclear reactors; and (B) radioactive waste from (i) reprocessing of spent nuclear fuel; (ii) activities related to medical research, diagnosis, and treatment; and (iii) other sources;

(3) Federal efforts during the past 30 years to devise a permanent solution to the problems of civilian radioactive waste disposal have not been adequate;

(4) while the Federal Government has the responsibility to provide for the permanent disposal of high-level radioactive waste and such spent nuclear fuel as may be disposed of in order to protect the public health and safety and the environment, the costs of such disposal should be the responsibility of the generators and owners of such waste and spent fuel;

(5) the generators and owners of high-level radioactive waste and spent nuclear fuel have the primary responsibility to provide for, and the responsibility to pay the costs of, the interim storage of such waste and spent fuel until such waste and spent fuel is accepted by the Secretary of Energy in accordance with the provisions of this Act;

(6) State and public participation in the planning and development of repositories is essential in order to promote public confidence in the safety of disposal of such waste and spent fuel;

(7) high-level radioactive waste and spent nuclear fuel have become major subjects of public concern, and appropriate precautions must be taken to ensure that such waste and spent fuel do not adversely affect the public health and safety and the environment for this or future generations.

Grace Thorpe, a Sac and Fox Indian and daughter of the late Jim Thorpe, is one of the leading national activists organizing to stop the environmental pollution of Indian reservations. Thorpe gives credit to the American Indian occupation of Alcatraz Island in 1969 as the catalyst for modern-day activism. In 1996 she stated that the Alcatraz occupation was the most important event in the Indian movement to date. The following statement is from her article entitled "No Nuclear Waste on Indian Land."

No Nuclear Waste on Indian Land
Grace F. Thorpe, No-Ten-O-Quah
(Wind Woman)

Our time is limited on earth. The creator above has lent the land to us for our life time. The creator has lent the water to us. The creator has lent the air to us just for our life time. These are gifts to us from the creator, for our use, for our survival for this limited time that we are on this earth.

The land was given to us to grow our food, the animals were given to us to eat. The water was given to us to drink and keep ourselves clean. The air was given to us to breathe. We should respect these gifts and not pollute them.

We are here only for a short period of time. We are here to protect the land, to improve the land for the other people that will follow us. This is our responsibility in return for using the creator's gifts to us.

The land will provide us with materials to make clothes to keep warm, the trees were given to us to make homes and to shade us in the hot summer and to provide fuel in the cold winters. In return we have to protect those gifts of the land, the sea and the air.

We cannot shirk our responsibilities for protecting the land, for protecting the waters and for protecting the air.

Nuclear waste is the most lethal poison known in the history of mankind.

What kind of people are we Americans that permit the production of materials that cannot be safely disposed of? Is making money the only criteria for success, is our health and our safety and the future generations of our people against deformities to be ignored? The nuclear industry must be stopped from producing its toxic waste until a safe method of disposal has been found.

We, the Indian people, must set an example for the rest of the nation. We, the Indian people must tell the polluters in no uncertain terms that we will not tolerate nuclear waste on our lands *no matter how much money the nuclear industry offers us. We, the Indian people, know that once nuclear waste is put in the ground that the land cannot be used again for one hundred thousand years or more.*

Other Indian voices of protest have been raised as well. Jane Yazzi, a Navajo, expressed her concern for the future of her people and stated:

When Waste Tech wanted to build an incinerator and dump on our land, they said they would give us thousands of dollars and a nice two-story house. But I thought about the land and how we rely on it — that this dump would poison the water and the land. It's not just temporary, my children and grandchildren will have to live on this land forever. Don't listen to these thieves that want our land; we need to protect Mother Earth.

The words of Russell Means, a Lakota Indian and American Indian activist, reflected similar concerns:

Right now, today, we who are living on the Pine Ridge Reservation are living on what white society has designated a "National Sacrifice Area." What this means is that we have a lot of uranium deposits here, and white culture (not us) needs this uranium as energy production material. The cheapest, most efficient way for industry to extract and deal with the processing of this uranium is to dump the waste by-products right here at the digging sites. Right here where we live. This waste is radioactive and will make the entire region uninhabitable forever. This is considered by industry, and by the white society that created this industry, to be an "acceptable" price to pay for energy resource development. Along the way they also plan to drain the water table under this part of South Dakota as part of the industrial process, so the region becomes doubly uninhabitable. The same sort of thing is happening down in the land of the Navajo and Hopi, up in the land of the Northern Cheyenne and Crow, and elsewhere. Thirty percent of the coal in the West and half of the uranium deposits in the United States have been found to lie under reservation land, so there is no way this can be called a minor issue.

We are resisting being turned into a National Sacrifice Area. We are resisting being turned into a national sacrifice people. The costs of this industrial process are not acceptable to us. It is genocide to dig uranium here and drain the water table — no more, no less.

California et al. v. Cabazon Band of Mission Indians et al.

Supreme Court of the United States, February 25, 1987

The decades since activist calls for self-determination have seen increased demands for, and assertions of, tribal sovereignty. A momentous step forward occurred on February 25, 1987, when the U.S. Supreme Court held that California could not regulate bingo and gambling on the Cabazon and Morongo Indian reservations. Despite state claims to the contrary, the court ruled that neither Public Law 280, granting the State of California criminal jurisdiction over offenses committed in Indian country and within the state, nor the 1970 Organized Crime Control Act, which made certain violations of state gambling laws federal offenses, was applicable within the reservations.

In 1987 the Cabazon and Morongo Bands of Mission Indians, both federally recognized Indian tribes, conducted bingo games on their reservations pursuant to an ordinance approved by the secretary of the interior. The Cabazon Band also opened a card club at which poker and other card games were played. The games were open to the public and had become a major source of employment for tribal members and the sole source of income for the Cabazon tribe. The State of California insisted that the profits from the gaming be used only for charitable purposes and that prizes awarded not exceed $250 per game. The tribes sued, seeking a judgment stating that neither Riverside County (in which the reservations are located) nor the State of California had authority to apply its ordinances inside the reservation. The state argued that high-stakes unregulated gaming would attract organized crime and was a misdemeanor in California.

The Supreme Court in its ruling held that "although state laws may be applied to tribal Indians on their reservations if Congress has expressly consented, Congress has not done so here either by Public Law 280 or by the Organized Crime Control Act of 1970." Indian tribes, as sovereign nations, are therefore not bound by state laws limiting gambling. The door was now open for Indian tribes throughout the nation to challenge state controls on reservation gaming. This would ultimately lead to the passing of the 1988 Gaming Regulatory Act, which codified the rights of tribes to establish gaming and outlined the process by which they could do so.

For tribes like the Cabazon, gaming has meant economic independence and the highest level of prosperity since the European invasion. Cabazon tribal chairman John James stated that "before gaming, unemployment here was at 50%. There was no running water, electricity or paved roads, and only three tribal families were living on the reservation. Unemployment is now zero, homes are being built and most of the tribe's seventy members have returned to enjoy free medical care, a daycare center and free college education. Our standard of living is up 400%."

"They never cared when we had nothing," said John Welmas, a Cabazon tribal member and the director of food and beverages for the Indio Casino. "Now that we have something, they want to stick their noses in it. I guess sovereignty is good only if you're standing on the side of the road selling blankets."

SYLLABUS:

Appellee Indian Tribes (Cabazon and Morongo Bands of Mission Indians) occupy reservations in Riverside County, Cal. Each Band, pursuant to its federally approved ordinance, conducts on its reservation bingo games that are open to the public. The Cabazon Band also operates a card club for playing draw poker and other card games. The gambling games are open to the public and are played predominantly by non-Indians coming onto the reservations. California sought to apply to the Tribes its statute governing the operation of bingo games. Riverside County also sought to apply its ordinance regulating bingo, as well as its ordinance prohibiting the playing of draw poker and other games. The Tribes instituted an action for declaratory relief in Federal District Court, which entered summary judgment for the Tribes, holding that neither the State nor the county had any authority to enforce its gambling laws within the reservations. The Court of Appeals affirmed.

Held:

1. Although state laws may be applied to tribal Indians on their reservations if Congress has expressly consented, Congress has not done so here either by Pub. L. 280 or by the Organized Crime Control Act of 1970 (OCCA).Pp. 207–214.

(a) In Pub. L. 280, the primary concern of which was combating lawlessness on reservations, California was granted broad criminal jurisdiction over offenses committed by or against Indians within all Indian country within the State but more limited, nonregulatory civil jurisdiction. When a State seeks to enforce a law within an Indian reservation under the authority of Pub. L. 280, it must be determined whether the state law is criminal in nature and thus fully applicable to the reservation, or civil in nature and applicable only as it may be relevant to private civil litigation in state court. There is a fair basis for the Court of Appeals conclusion that California's statute, which permits bingo games to be conducted only by certain types of organizations under certain restrictions, is not a "criminal/prohibitory" statute falling within Pub. L. 280's grant of criminal jurisdiction, but instead is a "civil/regulatory" statute not authorized by Pub. L. 280 to be enforced on Indian reservations. That an otherwise regulatory law is enforceable (as here) by criminal law within Pub. L. 280's meaning. Pp. 207–212.

(b) Enforcement of OCCA, which makes certain violations of state and local gambling laws violations of federal criminal law, is an exercise of federal rather than state authority. There is nothing in OCCA indicating that the States are to have any part in enforcing the federal laws or are authorized to make arrests on Indian reservations that in the absence of OCCA they could not effect. California may not make arrests on reservations and thus, through OCCA, enforce its gambling laws against Indian tribes.

Indian Gaming Regulatory Act

October 18, 1988

The heightened emphasis on tribal self-determination and tribal sovereignty during the 1970s and 1980s opened the door for an increasing number of tribes to explore alternative, local strategies of economic development. Many Indian communities turned to gaming as a means of revitalizing reservation economies. Large-scale, high-stake gaming operations began to appear on tribal lands in the late 1970s. In the 1980s gaming skyrocketed, leading to the 1987 *California v. Cabazon Band of Mission Indians* court challenge to Indian gaming described previously. After the courts affirmed native gaming rights, Indian gambling continued to grow. By 1989 it was estimated that there were more than one hundred gaming operations on Indian land, and by the early 1990s some estimates placed aggregate reservation gaming revenues in the billion-dollar range.

Many Native Americans saw gambling as a source of revenue consistent with the private-enterprise model emphasized by the federal government. Gaming income coupled with increased tribal employment could make a substantial improvement in the tribes' social and economic circumstances. States, however, objected and claimed that tribal gaming activities involved non-Indian customers and were inconsistent with state regulations. Concerns were also voiced that Indian gaming would invite infiltration by organized crime. While the Justice Department made this argument, the House Interior Committee disputed their contentions:

House Interior and Insular Affairs Committee
Hearings on H.R. 1920 and H.R. 2404
November 14, 1985

The reasons for the growth in gambling on Indian land are readily apparent. The Indian tribal governments see an opportunity for income that can make a substantial improvement in the tribe's conditions. The lack of any State or Federal regulation results in a competitive advantage over gambling regulated by the States. These advantages include no State imposed limits on the size of pots or prizes, no restrictions by the State on days or hours of operations, no costs for licenses or compliance with State requirements, and no State taxes on tribal gambling operations (statement of Marian Blank Horn, Principal Deputy Solicitor of the Department of the Interior).

On the issue of organized crime, the Committee has not found any conclusive evidence that such infiltration has occurred. The Justice Department, in its testimony on the bill, stated that, while it did not claim that Indian gambling operations were presently "mobbed up," there was still a potential for such infiltration by organized crime especially after such operations have become successful and have established their credentials and legitimacy.

The conclusion that organized crime has not infiltrated Indian gaming operations is also reflected in the findings of the 9th Circuit Court of Appeals decision in *Cabazon Band of Mission Indians and Morongo Band v. Riverside* (Feb. 26, 1986) which stated that, "in spite of the State's concerns about intrusion by organized crime in California, 'There is no evidence whatsoever that organized crime exists on these reservations.'"

The proliferation of tribal gaming operations was also encouraged by President Reagan's Indian Policy Statement which encouraged the tribes to reduce their dependence on Federal funds by providing a greater percentage of the cost of their self-government and which pledged to assist tribal governments by removing impediments to tribal self-government. This policy also encouraged private sector involvement and innovative approaches to overcome the legislative and regulatory impediments to economic progress. To comply with this policy and Federal law, the Department of the Interior has approved tribal ordinances and laws providing for tribal regulation of gaming activities on Indian lands and testified during Committee hearings that, "We wish to permit continuation of Indian bingo as a matter of federal policy, but recognized that it had to be regulated effectively to avoid the potential law enforcement problems."

The tribes had support from the executive branch of the federal government as well. President Ronald Reagan argued in favor of tribal gaming rights in his 1980 Statement on Indian Policy (see part 2). Nonetheless, because of the growing dispute between Indian tribes and states and the attempted individual state regulation of gaming, in 1988 Congress took up the issue. As a result, Congress passed the Indian Gaming Regulatory Act (IGRA) in October of that year.

Indian Gaming Regulatory Act
October 17, 1988

The Congress finds that —

(1) numerous Indian tribes have become engaged in or have licensed gaming activities on Indian lands as a means of generating tribal governmental revenue;

(2) Federal courts have held that section 81 of this title requires Secretarial review of management contracts dealing with Indian gaming, but does not provide standards for approval of such contracts;

(3) existing Federal law does not provide clear standards or regulations for the conduct of gaming on Indian lands;

(4) a principal goal of Federal Indian policy is to promote tribal economic development, tribal self-sufficiency, and strong tribal government; and

(5) Indian tribes have the exclusive right to regulate gaming activity on Indian lands if the gaming activity is not specifically prohibited by Federal law and is conducted within a State which does not, as a matter of criminal law and public policy, prohibit such gaming activity.

DECLARATION OF POLICY

The purpose of this chapter is —

(1) to provide a statutory basis for the operation of gaming by Indian tribes as a means of promoting tribal economic development, self-sufficiency, and strong tribal governments;

(2) to provide a statutory basis for the regulation of gaming by an Indian tribe adequate to shield it from organized crime and other corrupting influences, to ensure that the Indian tribe is the primary beneficiary of the gaming operation, and to assure that gaming is conducted fairly and honestly by both the operator and players; and

(3) to declare that the establishment of independent Federal regulatory authority for gaming on Indian lands, the establishment of Federal standards for gaming on Indian lands, and the establishment of a National Indian Gaming Commission are necessary to meet congressional concerns regarding gaming and to protect such gaming as a means of generating tribal revenue.

As might be expected, the passage of I G R A has not set well with the individual states, always jealous of states' rights. State governments continued to criticize Indian gaming as they saw Indian tribes revitalized and in possession of revenues over which states had no access or control. States charged that organized crime had infiltrated Indian gaming facilities and that tribes offered access to -gaming machines that were not legal under IGRA. As a result, during the 1990s numerous court cases were filed and awaited final U.S. Supreme Court decision. In the meantime, numerous bills were proposed before Congress to allow for some state control and inspection of Indian gaming enterprises. Tribes, on the other hand, pointed out that any state infringement was a direct assault on tribal sovereignty. Indian leaders moved to have the U.S. Senate Committee on Indian Affairs withdraw proposed gaming legislation that undermined tribal sovereignty.

Tribal Leaders Want Gaming Bill Withdrawn
American Indian Report
August 1994

Indian leaders want the Senate Committee on Indian Affairs to withdraw its proposed gaming bill saying that it undermines tribal sovereignty.

Leaders of the Senate committee introduced the bill in June after a year of negotiations between states and Indian tribes failed to yield a consensus on acceptable legislation.

A group representing the National Gaming Association and the National Congress of American Indians approved a resolution last month saying the bill is fundamentally flawed and should be withdrawn.

The resolution said the bill "would result in unprecedented usurpation of tribal sovereignty."

The Senate introduced the bill to help resolve legal and political disputes between tribes and states over who controls high-stakes gambling in Indian Country.

But instead of resolving the dispute, the proposed legislation has only intensified it.

The Senate proposal would overhaul the 1988 Indian Gaming Regulatory Act and give the federal government more control over tribal casinos.

Tribes say that federal oversight of their gaming operations would infringe on their rights as sovereign nations.

States fear that the legislation would deny them control over tribes who want to set up casinos off the reservation.

References and Further Reading

Ambler, Marjane. 1990. *Breaking the Iron Bonds: Indian Control of Energy Development*. Lawrence: University Press of Kansas.

American Indian Report. 1994. "Tribal Leaders Want Gaming Bill Withdrawn." *American Indian Report* 10:1–2.

Bolt, Christine. 1987. *American Indian Policy and American Reform*. Boston: Allen & Unwin.

Congressional Research Service. 1989. "Gambling on Indian Reservations." Washington DC: CRS Issue Brief, January 2.

Cornell, Stephen, and Joseph P. Kalt. 1992. *What Can Tribes Do? Strategies and Institutions in American Indian Economic Development*. American Indian Manual and Handbook Series, no. 4. Los Angeles: American Indian Studies Center.

Deloria, Vine, Jr. 1985. *American Indian Policy in the Twentieth Century*. Norman: University of Oklahoma Press.

Deloria, Vine, Jr., and Clifford Lytle. 1984. *The Nations Within*. New York: Pantheon.

El Nasser, Haya. 1993. "Critics Want Reservation Gaming Curbs." *USA Today*, May 20:A1.

Getches, David H., Charles F. Wilkinson, and Robert A. Williams Jr. 1993. *Cases and Materials on Federal Indian Law*. St. Paul MN: West.

Gordon, R. C., and Frank Waters. 1991. *The Taos Indians and the Battle for Blue Lake*. Sante Fe NM: Red Crane.

Lazarus, Edward. 1991. *Black Hills White Justice: The Sioux Nation Versus the United States: 1775 to the Present*. New York: Harper Collins.

Matthiessen, Peter. 1983. *In The Spirit of Crazy Horse*. New York: Viking.

Means, Russell. 1995. *Where White Men Fear To Tread*. New York: St. Martin's.

Prucha, Francis Paul. 1994. *American Indian Treaties: The History of a Political Anomaly*. Berkeley: University of California Press.

Thorpe, Grace. 1997. "No Nuclear Waste On Indian Land." Personal communication. July 25.

Washburn, Wilcomb E. 1971. *Red Man's Land / White Man's Law*. New York: Charles Scribner's Sons.

Yazzie, Jane. 1992. "Indigenous Economics: Toward a Natural World Order" *Akwe:kon* 9.

4 Education

Rough Rock Demonstration School and Rough Rock Community School

1965–

By the early 1960s, the federal government began to recognize that its national policy for educating American Indian children was a monumental failure. As a result, the Office of Economic Opportunity and the Bureau of Indian Affairs (BIA) discussed the idea of establishing a school that would help the Navajo people maintain and preserve their traditional culture and heritage while providing a quality education at the same time. The Rough Rock Demonstration School was founded in 1965 in an attempt to fulfill this need.

Located on Navajo Nation territory in Arizona, the school sits at the base of the majestic Black Mesa and has gone through many changes. During the early years, the school was funded by the BIA. In 1978, under the provisions of the 1975 Indian Self-Determination and Education Assistance Act, Rough Rock school became a contract school under tribal control. Since Rough Rock was no longer a "demonstration" school, the name was changed to the Rough Rock Community School. The school is accredited by the North Central Association of Colleges and Schools. Teachers are required to be certified with a degree in education, and preference in hiring is given to qualified Navajo tribal members or other Native American educators. While yearly enrollment varies, Rough Rock Community School maintains an enrollment of approximately four hundred students attending kindergarten through the twelfth grade. Continuing education and GED programs are offered as well. The philosophy and wisdom of the Rough Rock School Board and Navajo Nation are best captured in their mission statement.

Celebrating 30 Years of Navajo Education
Rough Rock School Board
Tse ch izhi Diné Bi olta

MISSION/PURPOSE AND VISION STATEMENTS OF ROUGH ROCK COMMUNITY SCHOOL

It is the PURPOSE of this school to educate, enlighten, motivate, challenge, and assist in the proper, cultural rearing of our Navajo children so they can be self-respecting, respectful of others, speak and practice their language and culture, and be totally functional in the Anglo society.

The OBJECTIVE this school and the community as a whole has is to teach and instill our sacred Navajo Language and way of life into each of our Navajo children who attends school here. NOT only is it an objective, but it is a very important RESPONSIBILITY.

Teaching our sacred Navajo Language is only one aspect of this responsibility. Teaching our children the significance of WHERE they have come from, WHY they are here on this Earth, WHAT they are made up of and represent, and where this LIFE leads to, is the foundation and integral aspect of the Navajo teaching process; this is what this school is responsible for in assisting us parents while we teach our children. Therefore, our sacred Navajo culture, philosophies, and language have to be the foundation of this institution and must be integrated into all aspects of Leadership, Administration, and Education. This entails integration into decision making standards, planning, and a code of regulations that all reflect the Navajo Way.

Our sacred Navajo Philosophy teaches us to set high standards for ourselves and to challenge ourselves. Therefore, we should set high ACADEMIC and MORAL standards for our children, so that they can be challenged mentally, emotionally, and spiritually, thus developing their AMBITION, MOTIVATION, and the tools needed in the quest to live the SIAHNAAGHI way of life. These life and career enhances need to be applied to the Navajo and English curriculum. It is the objective of this school to educate, train, and discipline our children to the degree that they can be competitive in the Anglo society, whether they choose college or vocational school, yet, knowing and practicing their sacred uniqueness as Navajo individuals.

It is also the responsibility of this school, the community, and the Tribe, to utilize one another's wisdom and knowledge, to cooperatively dream, plan, and implement those concepts that will fulfill the objectives and responsibilities set forth. Since the Navajo way is the foundation of this institution, the concept of Ke needs to be followed and adhered to, because it is the foundation of the proper teaching of respect, compassion, and a sacred disciplining mechanism, all of which are an extension of the larger Navajo holistic way of life.

This is what we believe are the PURPOSES, OBJECTIVES, and RESPONSIBILITY of this institution.

Navajo Community College
Diné College

1968–

The tribal leadership of the 1960s did not find schools, whether public or gov-ernment-operated, to be responsive to the Indian communities' needs for local control and Native American–relevant curriculum. As a result of this growing dissatisfaction, the Navajo Community College at Many Farms, Arizona, was founded in 1968 and opened its doors to students on January 21, 1969. The college was the first tribally established and Indian-controlled community col-lege in the United States and represented an experiment in the field of Ameri-can Indian education.

In October 1969 the Office of Economic Opportunity (OEO) announced con-tinued support for Navajo Community College. The OEO stated that "it is sup-porting this unique attempt to prove that a college can be responsive to the educational and economic needs of a rural community." On December 15, 1971, Public Law 92-189, the Navajo Community College Act, was passed into law and authorized Congress to appropriate $5.5 million to "ensure that the Navajo Indians and other qualified applicants have educational opportunities which are suited to their unique needs and interests."

Navajo Community College Act
December 15, 1971

PURPOSE

Sec. 2. It is the purpose of this Act to assist the Navajo Tribe of Indians in providing education to the members of the tribe and other qualified applicants through a community college, established by that tribe, known as the Navajo Community College.

GRANTS

Sec 3. The Secretary of Interior is authorized to make grants to the Navajo Tribe of Indians to assist the tribe in the construction, mainte-nance, and operation of the Navajo Community College. Such college

Indian students at Pacific Automotive Center in Oakland, California, 1971. American Indians were relocated to urban areas as part of a government attempt to detribalize Indian people and gain title to additional Indian lands. © Ilka Hartmann, 1999.

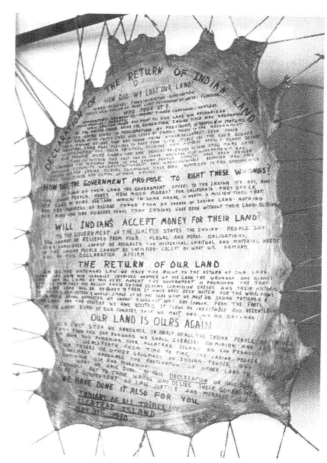

Declaration of the Return of Indian Land, written by members of Indians of All Tribes who occupied Alcatraz Island in November 1969. © Ilka Hartmann, 1999.

The Long Walk for Survival, a walk against hunger, nuclear
weapons and energy, and the draft, began on Alcatraz Island, 1980.
© Ilka Hartmann, 1999.

The Sacred Pole of the Omaha Nation was repatriated in August 1989.
© Ilka Hartmann, 1999.

Return to spiritual and cultural traditions. Paiute handgame players at
the Bear Dance in Janesville, California, 1984. © Ilka Hartmann, 1999.

Spiritual and cultural renewal. Larry Daylight, Shawnee, teaching his son Clayton Tecumseh how to play an Indian flute. © Ilka Hartmann, 1999.

shall be designed and operated by the Navajo Tribe to insure that the Navajo Indians and other qualified applicants have educational opportunities which are suited to their unique needs and interests.

AUTHORIZATION OF APPROPRIATIONS

Sec. 4. For the purpose of making grants under this Act, there are hereby authorized to be appropriated not to exceed $5,500,000 for construction, plus or minus such amounts, if any, as may be justified by reason of ordinary fluctuations from 1971 construction costs as indicated by engineering cost indexes applicable to the types of construction involved, and an annual sum of operation and maintenance of the college that does not exceed the average amount of the per capita contribution made by the Federal Government to the education of Indian students at federally operated institutions of the same type.

In 1997 the name of the Navajo Community College was officially changed to Diné College to reflect the change of the institution to a four-year college. Today, under the direction of a ten-member Board of Regents confirmed by the Government Services Committee of the Navajo Nation, Diné College has the responsibility to serve residents of the twenty-six-thousand-square-mile Navajo Nation, which spans portions of the states of Arizona, New Mexico, and Utah. As a postsecondary educational institution, Diné College awards degrees and technical certificates in areas important to the economic and social development of the Navajo Nation, including teacher's education and instruction in the Navajo language. Diné College seeks to encourage Navajo youth to become contributing members of the Navajo Nation and the larger society.

Diné College
Mission Statement

Diné College (formerly Navajo Community College) was established to meet the educational needs of the Navajo people. As the only academic postsecondary institution chartered by the Navajo Nation Council, the College offers two-year programs according to the needs of the Navajo Nation. The mission of the College is to:

Strengthen Personal Foundations for Responsible Learning and Living Consistent with Sa'ah Naagháí Bik'eh Hózhóón.
The college provides instruction and prepares students to have personal motivation and determination to clearly define and begin to develop their educational goals according to the protective and ethical values in SNBH.

Prepare Students for Careers and Further Studies.
The College prepares students for entry into the job market, provides courses that develop and upgrade college-level skills, and offers academically challenging and transferable college-level courses.

Promote and Perpetuate Navajo Language and Culture.
One unique function of Diné College is to promote, nurture, and enrich the language and culture of the Navajo people, in ways based on Sa'ah Naagháí Bik'eh Hózhóón.

Provide Community Services and Research.
The College provides educational programs, research, leadership, and consulting services to address community needs.

ACTIVITIES TO IMPLEMENT THE MISSION

- Two-year transfer programs
- Vocational Education
- Diné Studies
- Developmental Studies
- Research projects and consultant services
- On-site outreach programs
- Articulate programs with other institutions
- Diné Teacher Education Program

Diné College is a multi-campus institution. All campuses focus on the offering of educational programs, which prepare the student for transfer to four-year colleges/universities and for entry into employment. Developmental studies are offered at all sites for students who need further preparation for college-level studies. Courses in Navajo language, history, and culture are also available at all DC campuses.

The distinctiveness of each campus program derives from the needs of the community it serves together with the special characteristics of its faculty. Tsaile Campus is unique within the DC system in serving a large residential student population, as well as commuting students, and is the administrative center for the institution. Shiprock Campus has developed strengths in scientific research programs involving faculty and students. The Community Campus provides professional academic advising and educational opportunities including career counseling, assisting with [the] financial aid process, and preparing students for further studies.

MESSAGE FROM THE COLLEGE'S PRESIDENT

Yá 'á t'é é h, shi dine'é. (Welcome, my people, my relatives and my children.) As you seek to enter the doorway of education — let me encourage you to attend the institution of higher education of the Navajo Nation — **Navajo Community College. Navajo Community College** is definitely the place to be if you envision an education rich in Navajo culture, language, history and traditional teachings that integrate meaning and purpose into the western academic education.

As President, my vision for NCC is that "together we can develop Navajo Community College into a nationally recognized and respected institution that is the pride of the Navajo Nation. Our Curriculum and services will integrate the traditional values of the Diné language and culture with contemporary educational mandates. Our graduates will be prepared to approach any situation with competence and confidence, grounded in the philosophy of Sa'ah Naagháí Bik'eh Hózhóón."

The Navajo people should have joy and pride in attending "their College" on the Navajo Nation. At NCC, you receive the best in educational programs — knowledge of Navajo culture, history, language, values and principles — the development of a foundation so strong it will strengthen your determination to transfer to a more advanced educational institution and pursue your life in many different areas. We can help you gain the confidence and competence to succeed in a contemporary educational setting through the teachings of our ancestors.

Indian Education:
A National Tragedy and Challenge

1969 Report of the U.S. Senate Committee on Labor
and Public Welfare, Made by Its Special Subcommittee
on Indian Education

Historically, the federal government has assumed the responsibility for the education of Indian youths. Through the years the Bureau of Indian Affairs developed its own educational system, which has included both day and boarding schools, principally on, or adjacent to, reservations. As one of the only school systems run by the United States (another is administered by the Department of Defense for dependents of military personnel overseas), it might be expected to be a model of excellence. Instead, both Indians and non-Indians have attacked it for years as a national scandal — ill-equipped and maladministered, unresponsive to Indian backgrounds and needs, and positively injurious to the mental health and future of its students.

During the 1960s increasing attention was paid to the deficiencies of American Indian education. With good cause, Indian self-determinists began to demand that tribes take full control of the BIA schools that their children attended. For one thing, they felt acutely the harmful effects of a white school system, which, in trying to turn Indian children into whites as fast as possible, taught them nothing about their own Indian heritage and culture, shamed them for their Indianness, and left them stranded, without pride or self-assurance, neither white nor Indian.

Before he left office, President Johnson recommended that the BIA encourage the formation of Indian school boards for all federal schools, but by 1969 little progress had been made in that direction, principally because of opposition by the Bureau of the Budget. Indians, supported by a growing number of professional educators, had meanwhile intensified their criticism, going beyond the idea of merely establishing Indian school boards to a position in which they viewed Indian control of the education of their youths as a necessary basis for Indian management and control of all their own affairs.

Much ammunition was provided to critics of the existing system by the publication, in the fall of 1969, of the final report of a Special Senate Subcommittee on Indian Education. Under the chairmanship first of Senator Robert Kennedy and then, after his death, of his brother, Senator Edward Kennedy, the subcommittee had conducted a long and thorough examination of the subject.

As might have been expected, the BIA, which was the principal target of the report, paid little attention to it, and nothing immediately resulted from its publication. But the facts, succinctly surveyed in the following summary that preceded the body of the report, provided powerful arguments for Indians who were fighting for control of their schools.

For more than two years the members of this subcommittee have been gauging how well American Indians are educated. We have traveled to all parts of the country; we have visited Indians in their homes and in their schools; we have listened to Indians, to Government officials, and to experts; and we have looked closely into every aspect of the educational opportunities this Nation offers its Indian citizens.

Our work fills 4,077 pages in seven volumes of hearings and 450 pages in five volumes of committee prints. This report is the distillate of this work.

We are shocked at what we discovered.

Others before us were shocked. They recommended and made changes. Others after us will likely be shocked, too — despite our recommendations and efforts at reform. For there is so much to do — wrongs to right, omissions to fill, untruths to correct — that our own recommendations, concerned as they are with education alone, need supplementation across the whole board of Indian life.

We have developed page after page of statistics. These cold figures mark a stain on our national conscience, a stain which has spread slowly for hundreds of years. They tell a story, to be sure. But they cannot tell the whole story. They cannot, for example, tell of the despair, the frustration, the hopelessness, the poignancy, of children who want to learn but are not taught; of adults who try to read but have no one to teach them; of families which want to stay together but are forced apart; or of 9-year-old children who want neighborhood schools but are sent thousands of miles away to remote and alien boarding schools.

We have seen what these conditions do to Indian children and Indian families. The sights are not pleasant.

We have concluded that our national policies for educating American Indians are a failure of major proportions. They have not offered Indian children — either in years past or today — an educational opportunity anywhere near equal to that offered the great bulk of American children. Past generations of lawmakers and administrators have failed the American Indian. Our own generation thus faces a challenge — we can continue the unacceptable policies and programs of the past or we can recognize our failures, renew our commitments, and reinvest our efforts with new energy.

It is this latter course that the subcommittee chooses. We have made 60 separate recommendations. If they are all carried into force and effect, then we believe that all American Indians, children and adults, will have the unfettered opportunity to grow to their full potential. Decent education has been denied Indians in the past, and they have fallen far short of matching their promise with performance. But this need not always be so. Creative, imaginative, and above all, relevant educational experiences can blot the stain on our national conscience. This is the challenge the subcommittee believes faces our own generation.

This Nation's 600,000 American Indians are a diverse ethnic group. They live in all 50 States and speak some 300 separate languages. Four hundred thousand Indians live on reservations, and 200,000 live off reservations. The tribes have different customs and mores, and different wants and needs. The urban Indian has a world different from that of the rural Indian.

Indian children attend Federal, public, private, and mission schools. In the early days of this republic, what little formal education there was available to Indians was under the control of the church. Gradually, however, as the Nation expanded westward and Indian nations were conquered, the treaties between the conquering United States and the defeated Indian nations provided for the establishment of schools for Indian children. In 1842, for example, there were 37 Indian schools run by the U.S. Government. This number had increased to 106 in 1881, and to 226 in 1968.

This pattern of Federal responsibility for Indian education has been slowly changing. In 1968, for example, the education of Indian children in California, Idaho, Michigan, Minnesota, Nebraska, Oregon, Texas, Washington, and Wisconsin was the total responsibility of the State and not the Federal Government.

In 1968 there were 152,088 Indian children between the ages of 6 and 18. 142,630 attended one type of school or another. Most of these — 61.3 percent — attended public, non-Federal schools with non-Indian children. Another 32.7 percent were enrolled in Federal schools, and 6.0 percent attended mission and other schools. Some 6,616 school-age Indian children were not in school at all. The Bureau of Indian Affairs in the Department of the Interior, the Federal agency charged with managing

Indian affairs for the United States, was unable to determine the educational status of some 2,842 Indian children.

The Bureau of Indian Affairs operates 77 boarding schools and 147 day schools. There are 35,309 school-age Indian children in these boarding schools, and 16,139 in the day schools. Nearly 9,000 of the boarding-school children are under 9 years old.

In its investigation of "any and all matters pertaining to the education of Indian children" (S. Res. 165, August 31, 1967), the subcommittee thus was compelled to examine not only the Federal schools, but the State and local public schools and the mission schools as well.

What concerned us most deeply, as we carried out our mandate, was the low quality of virtually every aspect of the schooling available to Indian children. The school buildings themselves; the course materials and books; the attitude of teachers and administrative personnel; the accessibility of school buildings — all these are of shocking quality.

A few of the statistics we developed:

Forty thousand Navajo Indians, nearly a third of the entire tribe, are functional illiterates in English;

The average educational level for all Indians under Federal supervision is 5 school years;

More than one out of every five Indian men have less than 5 years of schooling;

Dropout rates for Indians are twice the national average;

In New Mexico, some Indian high school students walk 2 miles to the bus every day and then ride 50 miles to school;

The average age of top level BIA education administrators is 58 years;

In 1953 the BIA began a crash program to improve education for Navajo children. Between then and 1967, supervisory positions in BIA headquarters increased 113 percent; supervisory positions in BIA schools increased 144 percent; administrative and clerical positions in the BIA schools increased 94 percent. Yet, teaching positions increased only 20 percent;

In one school in Oklahoma the student body is 100 percent Indian; yet it is controlled by a three-man, non-Indian school board.

Only 18 percent of the students in Federal Indian schools go on to college; the national average is 50 percent;

Only 3 percent of Indian students who enroll in college graduate; the national average is 32 percent;

The BIA spends only $18 per year per child on textbooks and supplies, compared to a national average of $40;

Only one of every 100 Indian college graduates will receive a master's degree; and

Despite a Presidential directive 2 years ago, only one of the 226 BIA schools is governed by an elective school board.

These are only a few of the statistics which tell the story of how poor the quality of education is that American Indians have available to them. Running all through this report are many others, which are some measure of the depth of the tragedy. There are, too, specific examples of visits we made to various facilities in the Indian education system. These are too lengthy to summarize; however, the subcommittee believes that their cumulative effect is chilling.

We reacted to our findings by making a long series of specific recommendations. These recommendations embrace legislative changes; administrative changes; policy changes; structural changes — all of which are geared to making Indian education programs into models of excellence, not of bureaucratic calcification.

We have recommended that the Nation adopt as national policy a commitment to achieving educational excellence for American Indians. We have recommended that the Nation adopt as national goals a series of specific objectives relating to educational opportunities for American Indians. Taken together, this policy and these goals are a framework for a program of action. Clearly, this action program needs legislative and executive support if it is to meet its promise. Most of all, however, it needs dedicated and imaginative management by those Federal officials, and State and local officials as well, who have the principal responsibilities for educating American Indians.

We have recommended that there be convened a White House Conference on American Indian Affairs. We have recommended — although not unanimously — that there be established a Senate Select Committee on the Human Needs of American Indians. We have recommended the enactment of a comprehensive Indian Education statute, to replace the fragmented and inadequate education legislation now extant. We have recommended that the funds available for Indian education programs be markedly increased.

One theme running through all our recommendations is increased Indian participation and control of their own education programs. For far too long, the Nation has paid only token heed to the notion that Indians should have a strong voice in their own destiny. We have made a number of recommendations to correct this historic, anomalous paternalism. We have, for example, recommended that the Commissioner of the BIA be raised to the level of Assistant Secretary of the Department of Interior; that there be established a National Indian Board of Indian Education with authority to set standards and criteria for the Federal Indian schools; that local Indian boards of education be established for Indian school districts; and that Indian parental and community involvement be increased. These reforms, taken together, can — at last — make education of American Indians relevant to the lives of American Indians.

We have recommended programs to meet special, unmet needs in the Indian education field. Culturally-sensitive curriculum materials, for example, are seriously lacking; so are bi-lingual education efforts. Little educational material is available to Indians concerning nutrition and alcoholism. We have developed proposals in all these fields, and made strong recommendations to rectify their presently unacceptable status.

The subcommittee spent much time and devoted considerable effort to the "organization problem," a problem of long and high concern to those seeking reform of our policies toward American Indians. It is, in fact, two problems bound up as one — the internal organization of the Bureau of Indian Affairs, and the location of the Bureau within the Federal establishment. We made no final recommendation on this most serious issue. Instead, because we believe it critically important that the Indians themselves express their voices on this matter, we have suggested that it be put high on the agenda of the White House Conference on American Indian Affairs. Because, as we conceive it, this White House Conference will be organized by the Indians themselves, with the support of the National Council on Indian Opportunity, it is entirely appropriate that this organization problem be left for the conference.

In this report, we have compared the size and scope of the effort we believe must be mounted to the Marshall Plan which revitalized postwar Europe. We believe that we have, as a Nation, as great a moral and legal obligation to our Indian citizens today as we did after World War II to our European allies and adversaries.

The scope of this subcommittee's work was limited by its authorizing resolution to education. But as we traveled, and listened, and saw, we learned that education cannot be isolated from the other aspects of Indian life. These aspects, too, have much room for improvement. This lies in part behind the recommendation for a Senate Select Committee on the Human Needs of American Indians. Economic development, job training, legal representation in water rights and oil lease matters — these are only a few of the correlative problems sorely in need of attention.

In conclusion, it is sufficient to restate our basic finding: that our Nation's policies and programs for educating American Indians are a national tragedy. They present us with a national challenge of no small proportions. We believe that this report recommends the proper steps to meet this challenge. But we know that it will not be met without strong leadership and dedicated work. We believe that with this leadership for the Congress and the executive branch of the Government, the Nation can and will meet this challenge.

Big Rock School

Alcatraz Island

December, 1969

On December 11, 1969, the Big Rock School was opened in what had been the movie theater/meeting hall in the prison's main cell block. Twelve students were initially enrolled. The school enrollment fluctuated as the island population changed over time; however, Article 16 of the Island Regulations stated that "all children must attend school during the week."

The courses and curriculum at Big Rock School reflected the concerns of the Indian activists — Indian people needed to be educated in both non-Indian and Indian subjects. In addition to standard texts utilized in the California public school system, such as reading and math texts, a substantial amount of sophisticated tutorial material was donated to the school. The school began with grades one through six, and a Project Head Start program was set up in the former guards' quarters. A pre-primary education program was also established. The subject material itself included reading, writing, arithmetic, geography, health, and science studies. There were also native studies, which included Native American history and culture. Specific tribal information for each student was provided by the parents and others familiar with the material.

Teachers were drawn from the ranks of the Indian occupiers of Alcatraz Island. They included Indian teachers with traditional degrees in disciplines such as English and the social sciences, supported by Indian people who taught arts, crafts, and cultural heritage. Although not studying standard texts, students were instructed in native traditional skills such as beadwork, leatherwork, woodcarving, costume decoration, and sculpture. Dance and music instruction was provided by two Comanche teachers while two Tlingit Indians taught interested students how to carve miniature totem poles.

Peter Blue Cloud provides insight into these classrooms: "There was a gentle feeling of calm in the room where the young girls sat beading and making things from hides. Older girls and women taught, by showing, these ancient crafts. Voices here were very quiet. Young boys came to this room to watch, and soon they too were making headbands, or pouches. There is a very good feeling in working with the hands, your mind free to wonder and to dream."

The legacy of Big Rock School, just as the legacy of the occupation of Alca-

Unidentified woman walking toward Big Rock School,
which was on the ground floor of the Ira Hayes Building.
© Ilka Hartmann, 1999.

traz Island, lives on today. Following the forced removal of the remaining Indian occupiers from Alcatraz on June 11, 1971, the American Indian Charter
School of Oakland, California, was opened using the philosophy and much of
the material from the Big Rock School. That school remains in operation today.

Deganawide-Quetzalcoatl University (D-QU)

1971–

By 1970 Indian students were tired of going into college classrooms where American Indian history was recited by non-Indian professors who still taught that the "tawny savages" had been defeated and eliminated as a people in 1890. Young Indian activists, many of whom were involved in the Alcatraz occupation, began to demand courses that were relevant to Indian people. In northern California, Dr. Jack Forbes wrote to the federal government's General Services Administration and requested information on a 647-acre site located between Winters and Davis, California, as a possible location for an Indian university. In July 1970 founding members of the D-QU board of trustees met with the Yolo Native American Association to discuss the feasibility of the project, and a concept of a pan-Indian university was subsequently approved. As a result of the meeting, an ad hoc committee of Indians and Chicanos prepared a preliminary proposal for the establishment of Deganawide-Quetzalcoatl University.

Acquisition of the land for D-QU involved several twists and turns. On October 29, 1970, Senator George Murphy's office issued a press release stating that the proposed D-QU site in Davis would be given to the University of California for primate research and rice farming. The proposal by the University of California for use of the former Strategic Air Command military base had been incomplete, however, and D-QU had submitted the only legally complete request for the site. With a feeling of betrayal prompted by the October 29 press release, forty young American Indian activists occupied the site on November 3, 1970. "The land is ours" was the cry accompanying a claim to one square mile of the California Central Valley. The occupiers, including Grace Thorpe and other former Alcatraz occupiers, climbed over the site's fence and lay claim to the land.

The occupation was successful: on April 2, 1971, the federal government formally turned over the title to the 647-acre site to the trustees of D-QU. The Indians and Chicanos held a powwow and victory celebration. The university was funded through the Ford Foundation and federal grants totaling three hundred thousand dollars and opened for classes on July 7, 1971. Grace Thorpe taught a course entitled "Seminar in Surplus Land" that instructed students in "securing surplus land for education and health purposes."

The White House felt that the establishment of D-QU fulfilled the demands of the Alcatraz occupiers for an Indian university. In a letter from Bradley

Patterson, special assistant to President Richard Nixon, to Robert Coop, San Francisco regional director of Health, Education, and Welfare, Patterson stated, "I would think that the comparison between Alcatraz and D-Q would start occurring to people in the Bay Area." Jack Forbes, the Powhatan and Lenape Indian who made the initial request for the D-QU site, wrote of this politically charged period of activism: "These events took place in an atmosphere of increased activity on the part of urban and grassroots groups across the country. The Alcatraz occupation helped to instill a lot of confidence in ordinary Indian people, students, youth in general, old people, and traditionalists, who could use direct action to remedy old problems."

D-Q University
Mission Statement

The mission of D-Q University is to provide quality educational programs, community services, and other learning activities for the public that it serves. The curriculum will include a variety of academic courses that have as their base the cultures, history, languages, and sciences of tribal peoples. The curriculum will also include technical and enrichment courses to promote the intellectual growth and physical well-being of its students and the development of individual skills that prepare students for continuing education and employment. The university also recognizes the importance of community involvement, valuing diversity and inclusion, environmental awareness, [and] open access for all who have the desire and ability to learn.

Tribally Controlled
Community College Assistance Act
October 17, 1978

Although young Indian activists were in the forefront of the call for culturally relevant educational institutions, they were no longer alone. Studies conducted by the federal government that surveyed Indian educational progress indicated that many Indian youths felt culturally alienated in mainstream public and private college institutions. The limited number of Indian students graduating from high school and college inspired Congress to consider legislation to allow tribal communities to exercise full autonomy with regard to education on their reservations, and on October 17, 1978, Congress passed Public Law 95-471, the Tribally Controlled Community Colleges Act. The act provided for grants to tribally controlled community colleges, including Alaska Native village or village corporations, as designated by the secretary of the interior. Building on the experience of the Navajo tribally controlled college, this investment in Indian self-determination in higher education has now developed into a pan-Indian educational movement with twenty-nine tribally controlled colleges located throughout Indian country.

Most tribal colleges are physically and culturally unique, offering curricula based on the needs of their tribal youth. The colleges vary in size, facilities, course offerings, and degrees and certificates offered. Most tribal colleges place extraordinary emphasis on student retention and success. In Indian country, academic success, physical well-being, and personal esteem are inseparable. What happens at home and in the community eventually appears in the classroom. With this in mind, unique personal academic perspectives are therefore promoted throughout the campuses.

In addition to the more traditional academic courses, the tribal colleges offer a wide range of vocational courses in response to specific tribal economic needs. The colleges also provide academic programs that prepare students to transfer to four-year colleges, such as Sinte Gleska College located on the Rosebud Sioux Reservation in South Dakota.

It is important to emphasize that the success of tribal colleges rests on an Indian cultural foundation. Equally important is the recognition that the future of Indian tribes rests on the education of their tribal youth. Ron McNeil, Hunkpapa Lakota president of the American Indian College Fund, stated: "As a descendant of Sitting Bull and as an educator, I am committed to doing all I can to lighten the burden of poverty by supporting those grassroots institutions that are bringing about change. I believe the growing band of 29 American Indian colleges are absolutely crucial to the survival and growth of our Native American communities. In spite of the harsh statistics, there is great wisdom and courage in Indian country. Their survival is so important that I cannot just sit by. I must act and ask you to act, too. . . . The most important thing tribal colleges offer to Indian communities is hope. They are bringing new life to the reservations in the form of education and training."

DEFINITIONS

(1) "Indian" means a person who is a member of an Indian tribe and is eligible to receive services from the Secretary of the Interior;

(2) "Indian tribe" means any Indian tribe, band, nation, or other organized group or community, including any Alaskan Native village or regional or village corporation as defined in or established pursuant to the Alaskan Native Claims Settlement Act, which is recognized as eligible for the special programs and services provided by the United States to Indians because of their status as Indians;

(3) "Secretary," unless otherwise designated, means Secretary of the Interior;

(4) "tribally controlled community college" means an institution of higher education which is formally sanctioned, or chartered, by the governing body of an Indian tribe or tribes, except that no more than one such institution shall be recognized with respect to any such tribe;

(5) "institution of higher education" means an institution of higher education as defined by section 1201 (a) of the Higher Education Act of 1965, except that clause (2) of such section shall not be applicable;

(6) "national Indian organization" means an organization which the Secretary finds is nationally based, represents a substantial Indian constituency, and has expertise in the field of Indian education; and

(7) "full-time equivalent Indian student" means the number of Indians enrolled full-time, and the full-time equivalent of the number of Indians enrolled part-time (determined on the basis of the quotient of the sum of the credit hours of all part-time students divided by twelve) in each tribally controlled community college, calculated on the basis of registrations at the conclusion of the sixth week of an academic term.

TITLE I — TRIBALLY CONTROLLED COMMUNITY COLLEGES

PURPOSE

Sec. 101. It is the purpose of this title to provide grants for the operation and improvement of tribally controlled community colleges to insure continued and expanded educational opportunities for Indian students.

GRANTS AUTHORIZED

(a) The Secretary is authorized to make grants pursuant to this title to tribally controlled community colleges to aid in the post-secondary education of Indian students.

(b) Grants made pursuant to this title shall go into the general operating funds of the institution to defray the expense of activities related to education programs for Indian students. Funds provided pursuant to this title shall not be used in connection with religious worship or sectarian instruction.

Native American Languages Act

October 30, 1990

Recognizing that language retention is inherently and intrinsically connected with tribal survival and self-determination, Congress enacted the Native American Languages Act on October 30, 1990, as Title I of Public Law 101-477 that reauthorized the Tribally Controlled Community College Assistance Act of 1978.

The Native American Languages Act was designed to preserve, protect, and promote the practice and development of Indian languages. The act has been extremely important to Indian people given the government's historic efforts, especially in the nineteenth century, to eradicate Indian languages. This was particularly true in the government boarding schools where Native American children were punished for speaking their tribal languages. K. Tsianina Lomawaima, the daughter of a former Oklahoma Chilocco Indian Boarding School student, wrote that "discipline [at the boarding school] was strict and the children's time completely scheduled. They were not allowed to speak their native languages or practice native singing, dancing, or religion. . . . Boarding schools were designed to eradicate Indian ethnicity and tribal affiliation. . . . At best, school staff ignored tribal identity; at worst, they punished students harshly for speaking native languages or practicing native religions."

Although it represented a dramatic reaffirmation of the native content in Indian education, the Native American Languages Act has not arrested the decline in native language use or native language instruction. A 1994 study conducted by the Bureau of Indian Affairs estimated that more than half of all Indian languages are now extinct. Approximately 155 Indian languages remain in existence, although some are spoken by only a few individuals. Of this large number of languages spoken in the United States today fewer than one-fifth (13 percent) are being taught to Indian children.

FINDINGS

Sec. 102. The Congress finds that —

(1) the status of the cultures and languages of Native Americans is unique and the United States has the responsibility to act together with Native Americans to ensure the survival of these unique cultures and languages;

DECLARATION OF POLICY

Sec. 104. It is the policy of the United States to —

(1) preserve, protect, and promote the rights and freedom of Native Americans to use, practice, and develop Native American languages;

(2) allow exceptions to teacher certification requirements for Federal programs, and programs funded in whole or in part by the Federal Government, for instruction in Native American languages when such teacher certification requirements hinder the employment of qualified teachers who teach in Native American languages, and to encourage State and territorial governments to make similar exceptions;

(3) encourage and support the use of Native American languages as a medium of instruction in order to encourage and support —

(A) Native American language survival,

(B) educational opportunity,

(C) increased student success and performance,

(D) increased student awareness and knowledge of their culture and history, and

(E) increased student community pride;

(4) encourage State and local education programs to work with Native American parents, educators, Indian tribes, and other Native American governing bodies in the implementation of programs to put this policy into effect;

(5) recognize the right of Indian tribes and other Native American governing bodies to use Native American languages as a medium of instruction in all schools funded by the Secretary of the Interior;

(6) fully recognize the inherent right of Indian tribes and other Native American governing bodies, States, territories, and possessions of the United States to take action on, and give official status to, their Native American languages for the purpose of conducting their own business;

(7) support the granting of comparable proficiency achieved through course work in Native American language the same academic credit as comparable proficiency achieved through course work in a foreign language, with recognition of such Native American language proficiency by institutions of higher education as fulfilling foreign language entrance or degree requirements; and

(8) encourage all institutions of elementary, secondary, and higher edu-

cation, where appropriate, to include Native American languages in the curriculum in the same manner as foreign languages and to grant proficiency in Native American languages the same full academic credit as proficiency in foreign languages.

American Indian Tribal Colleges
and Universities
October 21, 1996

On October 21, 1996, President Clinton reaffirmed the federal government's commitment to educating Indian people by signing an executive order authorizing a White House Initiative on Tribal Colleges and Universities within the Department of Education to continue the support and development of tribal colleges into the twenty-first century.

John Echohawk, a Pawnee Indian and the executive director of the Native American Rights Fund, summed up the importance of education to Indian people and Indian tribes today in an article in *Children Today*:

> The importance of education for Native youth and their Tribes has taken on new dimensions in this modern era of Indian self-determination, in which Indian Tribes have taken their rightful place among the councils of governments in this country. Tribal governments are becoming increasingly sophisticated and are involved in a growing range of governmental functions, including taxation and environmental regulation.
>
> To properly carry out these responsibilities and programs, tribal governments need trained, educated Indian people who can perform the Tribal jobs and do them in ways that respect and integrate Tribal tradition and culture. College educated Indians have increasingly filled those jobs for Tribal governments, but more college educated youths are needed as the challenges grow. . . . There was a time when people thought that Indians could not be educated or did not want to be educated. As more and more Indians graduate from college today, that myth is destroyed.

Executive Order
October 21, 1996
Tribal Colleges and Universities

By the authority vested in me as President by the Constitution and laws of the United States of America, in reaffirmation of the special relationship of the Federal Government to American Indians and Alaska natives, and, for the purposes of helping to: (a) ensure that tribal colleges and universities are more fully recognized as accredited institutions, have access to the opportunities afforded other institutions, and have Federal resources committed to them on a continuing basis; (b) establish a mechanism that will increase accessibility of Federal resources for tribal colleges and universities in tribal communities; (c) promote access to high-quality educational opportunity for economically disadvantaged students; (d) promote the preservation and the revitalization of American Indian and Alaska Native languages and cultural traditions; (e) explore innovative approaches to better link tribal colleges with early childhood, elementary, and secondary education programs; and (f) support the National Education Goals, it is hereby ordered as follows:

There shall be established in the Department of Education the White House Initiative on Tribal Colleges and Universities ("Initiative"). The Initiative shall be authorized to:

(a) provide the staff support for the board;

(b) assist the Secretary in the role of liaison between the executive branch and tribal colleges;

(c) serve the Secretary in carrying out the Secretary's responsibilities under this order; and

(d) utilize the services, personnel, information, and facilities of other Federal, State, tribal, and local agencies with their consent, and with or without reimbursement, consistent with applicable law. To the extent permitted by law and regulations, each Federal agency shall cooperate in providing resources, including personnel detailed to the Initiative, to meet the objectives of the order.

SEC. 4. DEPARTMENT AND AGENCY PARTICIPATION.

Each participating executive department and agency (hereinafter collectively referred to as "agency"), as determined by the Secretary, shall appoint a senior official, who is full-time officer of the Federal Government and who is responsible for management or program administration, to serve as liaison to the White House Initiative. The official shall report directly to the agency head, or agency representative, on agency activity under this order and serve as liaison to the White House Initiative. To the extent permitted by law and regulation, each agency shall provide appropriate information in readily available formats requested by the White House Initiative staff pursuant to this order.

SEC. 5. FIVE-YEAR FEDERAL PLAN.

(a) Content. Each agency shall, in collaboration with tribal colleges, develop and document a Five-Year Plan of the agency's efforts to fulfill the purpose of this order. These Five-Year Plans shall include annual performance indicators and appropriate measurable objectives for the agency. The Plans shall address among other relevant issues:

(1) barriers impeding the access of tribal colleges to funding opportunities and to participation in Federal programs and ways to eliminate the barriers;

(2) technical assistance and information that will be made available to tribal colleges regarding the program activities of the agency and the preparation of applications for proposals for grants, cooperative agreements, or contracts; and

(3) an annual goal for agency funds to be awarded to tribally controlled colleges and universities in:

(A) grants, cooperative agreements, contracts, and procurement;

(B) related excess property-type acquisitions under various authorities such as section 923 of the Federal Agriculture Improvement and Reform Act of 1996 and the federal Property and Administrative Services Act of 1949;

(C) the transfer of excess and surplus Federal computer equipment under Executive Order 12999.

In developing the Five-Year Plans required by this order, agencies shall strive to include tribal colleges in all aspects and activities related to the attainment of the participation goals described in Executive Order 12928, "Promoting Procurement with Small Businesses Owned and Controlled by Socially and Economically Disadvantaged Individuals, Historically Black Colleges and Universities, and Minority Institutions." The Plans may also emphasize access to high-quality educational opportunity for economically disadvantaged Indian students; the preservation and revitalization of American Indian and Alaska Native languages and cultural traditions; innovative approaches to better link tribal colleges with early childhood, elementary, and secondary education programs; and the National Education Goals.

References and Further Reading

American Council on Education. 1994. "Minorities in Higher Education." *Tenth Annual Status Report*. Washington DC.

Blue Cloud, Peter. 1972. *Alcatraz Is Not an Island*. Berkeley: Wingbow.

Carnegie Foundation for the Advancement of Teaching. 1989. *Tribal Colleges: Shaping the Future of Native America*. Princeton: Princeton University Press.

Champagne, Duane. 1994. *The Native North American Almanac*. Detroit: Gale Research.

Coleman, Michael C. 1993. *American Indian Children at School: 1850–1930*. Jackson: University of Mississippi Press.

Echohawk, John. "The Importance of Education." *Children Today* 23: 30–32.

Forbes, Jack D. 1984. *Native Americans and Nixon: Presidential Politics and Minority Self-Determination*. Native American Politics Series, no. 2. Los Angeles: American Indian Studies Center.

Fuchs, Estelle, and Robert J. Havighurst. 1972. *To Live on This Earth: American Indian Education*. New York: Doubleday.

Johnson, Troy. 1996. *The Occupation of Alcatraz Island: Indian Self-Determination and the Rise of Indian Activism*. Urbana: University of Illinois Press.

Lomawaima, K. Tsianina. 1994. *They Called It Prairie Light: The Story of Chilocco Indian School*. Lincoln: University of Nebraska Press.

Mihesuah, Devon A. 1993. *Cultivating the Rosebuds: The Education of Women at the Cherokee Female Seminary, 1851–1909*. Urbana: University of Illinois Press.

Patterson, Bradley. 1971. "Letter to Robert Coop (19 April)." Richard M. Nixon Presidential Materials Project, Alexandria VA: White House Central Files, Subject Files, IN (1/1/71–5/31/71).

Prucha, Francis Paul. 1984. *The Great Father: The United States Government and the American Indians*. Lincoln: University of Nebraska Press.

Reyhner, John. 1994. *Teaching American Indian Students*. Norman: University of Oklahoma Press.

Senese, Guy B. 1991. *Self-Determination and the Social Education of Native Americans*. New York: Praeger.

Slapin, Beverly, and Doris Seale. 1988. *Books without Bias: Through Indian Eyes*. Berkeley: Oyate.

Szasz, Margaret. 1974. *Education and the American Indian: The Road to Self-Determination, 1928–1973*. Albuquerque: University of New Mexico Press.

———. 1988. *Indian Education in the American Colonies: 1607–1783*. Albuquerque: University of New Mexico Press.

5 Spiritual and Cultural Renewal

American Indian Religious Freedom Act

U.S. Congress Joint Resolution 102, August 11, 1978

The 1960s and 1970s were not only a time of protests and demonstrations against violations of treaty rights and a time of demands for equal civil rights for Indian people. The activist period was also a time of renewed spirituality for many young Native Americans. Many Indian protesters had been raised in cities, away from reservation traditions. One consequence of Red Power was that many Indians reaffirmed a connection with their tribal and spiritual roots. In this atmosphere of spiritual renewal, the abuses of the past were increasingly apparent and resented. Protesters and Indian leaders on reservations and in urban Indian communities demanded native cultural and religious rights — to wear long hair, to practice Indian religions in schools and prisons, to receive the same guarantees and enforcement of religious freedom as other Americans.

As a result of these demands and in light of past abuses, on August 11, 1978, the U.S. Congress passed Joint Resolution 102, generally referred to as the American Indian Religious Freedom Act, in order to protect American Indians' "inherent right of freedom to believe, express, and exercise the[ir] traditional religions" and to provide "access to sites, use and possession of sacred objects, and the freedom to worship through ceremonials and traditional rights." These protections promised a sharp break with the past. It was hoped that no longer would the beliefs of native peoples be denigrated and denied. No longer would native people be kept from practicing their spiritual traditions. No longer would Indian children and adults be forced to follow non-native religions in an effort to "civilize" them.

The American Indian Religious Freedom Act turned out to be only a first step in a long and uneven road toward protection of Indian spiritual and religious practices, but all journeys begin with a single step.

Whereas the freedom of religion for all people is an inherent right, fundamental to the democratic structure of the United States and is guaranteed by the First Amendment of the United States Constitution;

Whereas the United States has traditionally rejected the concept of a government denying individuals the right to practice their religion and, as a result, has benefited from a rich variety of religious heritages in this country;

Whereas the religious practices of the American Indian (as well as Native

Alaskan and Hawaiian) are an integral part of their culture, tradition, and heritage, such practices forming the basis of Indian identity and value systems;

Whereas the traditional American Indian religions, as an integral part of Indian life, are indispensable and irreplaceable;

Whereas the lack of a clear, comprehensive, and consistent Federal policy has often resulted in the abridgement of religious freedom for traditional American Indians;

Whereas such religious infringements result from the lack of knowledge or the insensitive and inflexible enforcement of Federal policies and regulations premised on a variety of laws;

Whereas such laws were designed for such worthwhile purposes as conservation and preservation of natural species and resources but were never intended to relate to Indian religious practices and, therefore, were passed without consideration of their effect on traditional American Indian religions;

Whereas such laws and policies often deny American Indians access to sacred sites required in their religions, including cemeteries;

Whereas such laws at times prohibit the use and possession of sacred objects necessary to the exercise of religious rites and ceremonies;

Whereas traditional American Indian ceremonies have been intruded upon, interfered with, and in a few instances banned: Now, therefore, be it

Resolved by the Senate and House of Representatives of the United States of America in Congress assembled, That henceforth it shall be the policy of the United States to protect and preserve for American Indians their inherent right of freedom to believe, express, and exercise the traditional religions of the American Indian, Eskimo, Aleut, and Native Hawaiian, including but not limited to access to sites, use and possession of sacred objects, and the freedom to worship through ceremonials and traditional rites.

Archaeological Resources Protection Act

October 31, 1979

A year after the passage of the 1978 American Indian Religious Freedom Act, Congress passed a law designed to help stop another long-standing abuse of native spiritual and cultural life — the looting of Indian graves and historical Indian sites. Although it would be another decade before the Congress and the U.S. natural history museums would come to terms with the issue of Native American burial remains and sacred objects on display in museums, the 1979 Archaeological Resources Protection Act marked the beginning of that process. While the 1979 act did not regulate the display or sale of Indian remains and objects already in the possession of individuals or museums, it did require a permit to excavate Indian sites. That such permits were issued by a "federal land manager," and not under the direct control of Indian authorities, rendered the Archeological Resources Protection Act relatively ineffective. It was, however, an important step toward shifting the moral ground upon which museums and their collections stood, a step on the path of revolutionary cultural change that would eventually be achieved by the repatriation movement.

To protect archaeological resources on public lands and Indian lands, and for other purposes. Be it enacted by the Senate and House of Representatives of the United States of America in Congress assembled,

FINDINGS AND PURPOSE

Sec. 2.
(a) The Congress finds that —
(1) archaeological resources on public lands and Indian lands are an accessible and irreplaceable part of the Nations's heritage;
(2) these resources are increasingly endangered because of their commercial attractiveness;
(3) existing Federal laws do not provide adequate protection to prevent the loss and destruction of these archaeological resources and sites resulting from uncontrolled excavations and pillage; and
(4) there is a wealth of archaeological information which has been legally obtained by private individuals for noncommercial purposes

and which could voluntarily be made available to professional ar-
chaeologists and institutions.

(b)   The purpose of this Act is to secure, for the present and the future
benefit of the American people, the protection of archaeological
resources and sites which are on public lands and Indian lands,
and to foster increased cooperation and exchange of information
between governmental authorities, the professional archaeological
community, and private individuals having collections of archaeological resources and data which were obtained before the date of
the enactment of this Act.

DEFINITIONS

Sec. 3. As used in this Act —

(1) The term "archaeological resource" means any material remains of
past human life or activities which are of archaeological interest, as determined under uniform regulations promulgated pursuant to this Act.
Such regulations containing such determination shall include, but not be
limited to: pottery, basketry, bottles, weapons, weapon projectiles, tools,
structures or portions of structures, pit houses, rock paintings, rock carv-
ings, intaglios, graves, human skeletal remains, or any portion or piece of
any of the foregoing items. Non-fossilized and fossilized paleontological
specimens, or any portion or piece thereof, shall not be considered archaeological resources, under the regulations under this paragraph, unless
found in an archaeological context. No item shall be treated as an archaeological resource under regulations under this paragraph unless such
item is at least 100 years of age.

PROHIBITED ACTS AND CRIMINAL PENALTIES

Sec. 6.

(a)   No person may excavate, remove, damage, or otherwise alter or de-
face any archaeological resource located on public lands or Indian
lands unless such activity is pursuant to a permit issued under section 4,

(b)   No person may sell, purchase, exchange, transport, receive, or offer
to sell, purchase, or exchange any archaeological resource if such
resource was excavated or removed from public lands or Indian
lands in violation of —

(1) the prohibition contained in subsection (a), or

(2) any provision, rule, regulation, ordinance, or permit in effect under any other provision of Federal law.

(c)   No person may sell, purchase, exchange, transport, receive, or offer to sell, purchase, or exchange, in interstate or foreign commerce, any archaeological resource excavated, removed, sold, purchased, exchanged, transported, or received in violation of any provision, rule, regulation, ordinance, or permit in effect under State or local law.

(d)   Any person who knowingly violates, or counsels, procures, solicits, or employs any other person to violate, any prohibition contained in subsection (a), (b), or (c) of this section shall, upon conviction, be fined not more than $10,000 or imprisoned not more than one year, or both: Provided, however, That if the commercial or archaeological value of the archaeological resources involved and the cost of restoration and repair of such resources exceeds the sum of $5,000, such person shall be fined not more than $20,000 or imprisoned not more than two years, or both. In the case of a second or subsequent such violation upon conviction such person shall be fined not more than $100,000, or imprisoned not more than five years, or both.

The Black Hills and
Camp Yellow Thunder

1981–1987

Despite the reassurances of the 1978 American Indian Religious Freedom Act (AIRFA), and its promise to usher in a new era of respect and safeguards for native religions, in practice AIRFA provided little legal protection of Indian religious beliefs, sacred sites, or church practices. The struggle to strengthen defenses against assaults on Indian spirituality continued both in the courts and in protest activism. Several issues emerged during the 1980s and early 1990s that revealed the continuing vulnerability of native religious and cultural rights: the U.S. government's failure to return and protect sacred lands, the ongoing desecration of Indian burial remains and sacred objects, and the persistent harassment of Indians for using peyote as a sacrament in the Native American Church and other ceremonial settings.

Two major court decisions in the 1980s showed that the U.S. government's intentions regarding Indian sacred lands were not consistent with the claims put forth in AIRFA. The first strong post-AIRFA indication of the U.S. government's continuing disregard for land claims involving sacred places was the 1980 U.S. Supreme Court decision that affirmed a series of lower court rulings acknowledging that the Black Hills in South Dakota had never been legally ceded to the United States by the Lakota and Dakota peoples but refusing to give back possession of the land. Instead of returning the Paha Sapa, the government offered the tribes money. The tribes declined the offer, and on April 4, 1981, a six-year-long occupation of the Black Hills at "Camp Yellow Thunder" began. In his book *In the Spirit of Crazy Horse* Peter Matthiessen provides the following account of the dispute, the legal and financial machinations involved, and the establishment of Camp Yellow Thunder by American Indian Movement and Sioux activists. Although activists moved away from Camp Yellow Thunder in 1987, the question of the Black Hills remains unresolved.

On April 4, 1981, a caravan of twenty cars, carrying sacred pipes, sweat-lodge materials, tipi poles, cold-weather equipment, stoves, and food, departed from Porcupine, bright red flags waving, and traveled through Rapid City to Victoria Creek Canyon, about twelve miles southwest of Rapid City, in the Black Hills. Here a camp was established on federal

land, in what was perceived as the first step in the reclaiming and resettle-
ment of Paha Sapa. The legal basis of this action was the "undisturbed
use" of the Black Hills guaranteed to the Lakota in the 1868 Treaty, as well
as the American Indian Freedom of Religion Resolution of 1978 and a
federal law (1897) relating to the free use of wilderness sites for schools
and churches.

On a day of light snow, the Indians set up tents in a canyon bend,
where striking red cliffs rose to the ponderosa pines on the spring sky;
there was good running water here, and a small pond. Naming the camp
for Raymond Yellow Thunder, the man from Porcupine killed in Gordon,
Nebraska, in 1972, Dakota AIM proposed to the government a permanent
alternative-energy community for which it would ask federal cooperation,
and on April 6, spiritual leader Matthew King, a descendent of Crazy
Horse, filed a claim with the U.S. Forest Service for 800 acres of surrounding forest. Asked if he thought the Indians would be allowed to stay, King
declared, "This is our land!"

A Forest Service spokesman blustered, "We have the legal muscle and
the law-enforcement muscle to evict them very quickly," and Sheriff "Mel"
Larson conferred with the FBI. For want of a better plan, two vanloads of
heavily armed agents showed up at the camp gates, apparently in a show
of force; asked to state their business, they said, "Turkey-shooting." Other
armed agents in camouflage costumes were seen prowling the rimrock
and high pines, on the lookout for suspicious signs of terrorist activity
around the cook tent. But unlike Wounded Knee, the Camp Yellow Thunder "occupation" had the support of many whites right from the start, not
only those in the Black Hills Alliance, which served the camp as a communications center, but the American Friends Service Committee, several
church groups, and many private organizations and individuals across the
country. With so much attention from the media, the authorities decided
upon an indulgent attitude, not wishing to risk bloodshed on color TV;
Russell Means, who had moved to Yellow Thunder from that "BIA concentration camp at Kyle," had made it plain that the Indians would not
go without a fight.

Dakota AIM's dramatic move revived the spirits of the traditionals,
whose Black Hills land claim had been stifled by the courts. In 1977 —
more than a quarter century after the claim was filed — the U.S. Court of
Claims had finally affirmed the Indian Claims Commission conclusion
that no valid agreement to cede the Black Hills had ever existed, the
"abrogation" of 1877 notwithstanding, and that the Hills had been taken

without compensation, as the Indians said. "The Dakota nation" was promptly offered $17.5 million, the estimated value of the area in 1877, and a modest fraction of the more than $1 billion worth of gold removed from the Black Hills by the Homestake Mine, which to this day accounts for half of U.S. gold production.

The traditional Lakota refused this ignoble offer, having maintained throughout that Paha Sapa was not for sale; they demanded the return of the Hills themselves. The tribal-council chairmen of the seven Lakota bands, persuaded that they could do better, refused it, too. In 1979, the Court of Claims, holding the federal government responsible for "the most ripe and rank case of dishonorable dealing in our history," decided that the Lakota were also entitled to 102 years' interest, or a total of $122 million. This much improved offer — more precisely, a judgment — advertised as the largest settlement ever offered by the Indian Claims Commission, worked out to approximately the equivalent of a second-hand car for each eligible Indian (about sixty thousand people) for land that is estimated to contain billions of dollars in uranium, in addition to gold, copper, molybdenum, and other precious minerals. The Justice Department, protesting that the payment was too high, appealed the decision before the Supreme Court on the basis of its archaic Lone Wolf decision of 1903, in which it was held that Congress had plenary power over Indians and could, in effect, abrogate treaties with Indians at will; the Justice Department also cited the Tee-Hit-Ton decision of 1955, which had catered to the termination mood in Congress by removing all constitutional protection from "Indian title" or "aboriginal title" lands (that is, territories inhabited by an Indian nation before the advent of the Europeans) — in no way applicable to this case, since title to the Great Sioux reservation had been signed over by the U.S. government itself.

The Sioux tribal councils were attracted by the larger settlement, but the traditionals continued to hold out for the return of the Black Hills; more than three-fourths of Paha Sapa, or about 1,320,000 acres, was classified as federal or state land (mostly national forest), which could be returned to the Indians without causing hardship to private citizens. The traditionals' views were ignored, however; it was only because the award had been contested by the Justice Department that the case was turned over to the Supreme Court.

In June 1980, when the Court of Claims judgment was affirmed by the Supreme Court, it was contested by traditionals of the "Oglala Sioux Tribe of Pine Ridge Reservation." (As "Sioux," they were not endorsed by Dakota AIM or the Means family, for whom the word "Sioux" represents wasicu values. "Sioux sold the Black Hills; the Lakota did not sell," says Russell Means.) This group, led by Louis Bad Wound, sought a temporary restraining order prohibiting the government from paying out any part of the award; the request was denied in September 1980. Meanwhile, Washington attorney Arthur Lazarus continued to press for a monetary settlement, even though his own contract with the Oglala Tribal Council had expired in 1977 and had not been renewed, despite his urgent request to be reinstated. Acknowledging that the majority of the people he wished to represent would have preferred land, Lazarus — who was claiming as a fee over $10 million of the Indians' money — expressed great satisfaction with the Supreme Court decision. On May 20, 1981, he and two associates were awarded $10,595,493 — the "nothing short of sensational result" of what Lazarus himself hailed as "a unique accomplishment in the annals of American jurisprudence." The case had been won by the wealthy lawyer and lost by his poverty-stricken clients, and for once, Dakota AIM and the Oglala Sioux Tribe joined forces, threatening a malpractice suit in contesting this immense payment to a lawyer who had "prosecuted the claim for money without proper authorization and without the understanding and consent of the Dakota people." The Indians' complaint, put in the form of a motion before the Court of Claims, was speedily dismissed without hearing or explanation, and on this sordid note, a claim first filed in 1923 came to an end.

Al Trimble, who was head of the Tribal Council when Arthur Lazarus was fired, does not excuse the lawyer's misrepresentation of his clients or the massive fee, but he points out that for many years Lazarus and his firm had done honorable and competent work that had the full support of the tribal councils; most of the people in those days wanted money. Many of the older Indians who now repudiate the money and are holding out for the return of the Black Hills "were pretty shifty characters back in '49, '50; they sold a lot of our land, and I can still remember all the talk about getting our Black Hills money. The AIM people have to be given credit for renewing the people's awareness of what the Black Hills meant."

Lyng v. Northwest Indian Cemetery Protective Association

U.S. Supreme Court, April 19, 1988

Ten years after the American Indian Religious Freedom Act another U.S. Supreme Court decision showed the government's continuing disregard for the importance of native spiritual traditions and the court's ongoing inclination to privilege non-Indian economic and political interests over native religious rights.

The case of *Lyng v. Northwest Indian Cemetery Protective Association* originated in a challenge to U.S. Forest Service plans to build a road (the "G-O road") through the Chimney Rock Section of the Six Rivers National Forest in northern California. The Chimney Rock area has historically been used for religious purposes by the Yurok, Karok, and Tolowa tribes. A government study found that constructing the road "would cause serious and irreparable damage to the sacred areas which are an integral and necessary part of the belief systems and lifeways of Northwest California Indian peoples" and recommended that the G-O road not be built. The Forest Service disregarded this recommendation and proceeded with plans to build the road, and the tribes sued to stop construction, arguing that commercial logging would be enhanced by the road. When the 1984 California Wilderness Act outlawed logging, the Forest Service persisted in its plans to build the road. A series of lower court decisions mainly supported the Indians and prohibited construction of the road. The Forest Service appealed the case to the U.S. Supreme Court, and on April 19, 1988, the Supreme Court decided in favor of the U.S. Forest Service. Ironically, the G-O Road was never built, but the damage to Indian religious rights brought about by the *Lyng* decision remained as a legacy of the case.

The following excerpts are from the Supreme Court's *Lyng v. Northwest Indian Cemetery Protective Association* decision, which was based on a five-three split, with Justice Anthony Kennedy taking no part. Justice Sandra Day O'Connor wrote for the majority, which found the Forest Service had a right to build the road through the sacred Chimney Rock area:

This case requires us to consider whether the First Amendment's Free Exercise Clause forbids the Government from permitting timber harvesting in, or constructing a road through, a portion of a National Forest that has traditionally been used for religious purposes by members of three American Indian tribes in northwestern California. We conclude that it does not. . . .

The Free Exercise Clause of the First Amendment provides that "Congress shall make no law . . . prohibiting the free exercise [of religion]." It is undisputed that the Indians respondents' beliefs are sincere and that the Government's proposed actions will have severe adverse effects on the practice of their religion. Respondents contend that the burden on their religious practices is heavy enough to violate the Free Exercise Clause unless the Government can demonstrate a compelling need to complete the G-O road or to engage in timber harvesting in the Chimney Rock area. We disagree.

In *Bowen v. Roy*, 476 U.S. 693 (1986), we considered a challenge to a federal statute that required the States to use Social Security numbers in administering certain welfare programs. Two applicants for benefits under these programs contended that their religious beliefs prevented them from acceding to the use of a Social Security number for their two-year-old daughter because the use of a numerical identifier would "rob the 'spirit' of [their] daughter and prevent her from attaining greater spiritual power." Similarly in this case, it is said that disruption of the natural environment caused by the G-O road will diminish the sacredness of the area in question and create distractions that will interfere with "training and ongoing religious experience of individuals using [sites within] the area for personal medicine and growth . . . and as integrated parts of a system of religious belief and practice which correlates ascending degrees of personal power with geographic hierarchy of power." (Scarred hills and mountains and disturbed rocks destroy the purity of the sacred areas, and [Indian] consultants repeatedly stressed the need of a training doctor to be undistracted by such disturbance.) The court rejected this kind of challenge in *Roy*:

The free Exercise Clause simply cannot be understood to require the Government to conduct its own internal affairs in ways that comport with the religious beliefs of particular citizens. Just as the Government may not insist that [the Roys] engage in any set form of religious observance, so [they] may not demand that the Government join in their chosen religious practices by refraining from using a number to identify their daughter. . . . The Free Exercise Clause affords an individual protection from certain forms of governmental compulsion; it does not afford an individual a right to dictate the conduct of the Government's internal procedures.

The building of a road or the harvesting of timber on publicly owned land cannot meaningfully be distinguished from the use of a Social Security number in *Roy*. In both cases, the challenged government action would interfere significantly with private persons' ability to pursue spiritual fulfillment according to their own religious beliefs. In neither case, however, would the affected individuals be coerced by the Government action into violating their religious beliefs; nor would either governmental action penalize religious beliefs; nor would either governmental action penalize religious activity by denying any person an equal share of the rights, benefits, and privileges enjoyed by other citizens.

Whatever may be the exact line between unconstitutional prohibitions on the free exercise of religion and the legitimate conduct by government of its own affairs, the location of the line cannot depend on measuring the effects of governmental action on a religious objector's spiritual development. The Government does not dispute, and we have no reason to doubt, that the logging and road-building projects at issue in this case could have devastating effects on traditional Indian religious practices. Those practices are intimately and inextricably bound up with the unique features of the Chimney Rock area, which is known to the Indians as the "high country." Individual practitioners use this area for personal spiritual development; some of their activities are believed to be critically important in advancing the welfare of the tribe, and indeed, of mankind itself. The Indians use this area, as they have used it for a very long time, to conduct a wide variety of specific rituals that aim to accomplish their religious goals. According to their beliefs, the rituals would not be efficacious if conducted at other sites than the ones traditionally used, and too much disturbance of the area's natural state would clearly render any meaningful continuation of traditional practices impossible. To be sure, the Indians themselves were far from unanimous in opposing the G-O road, and it seems less than certain that construction of the road will be so disruptive that it will doom their religion. Nevertheless, we can assume that the threat to the efficacy of at least some religious practices is extremely grave.

The Indian respondents insist that "[p]rivacy during the power quests is required for the practitioners to maintain the purity needed for a successful journey." Similarly: "The practices conducted in the high country entail intense meditation and require the practitioner to achieve a profound awareness of the natural environment. Prayer seats are oriented so there is an unobstructed view, and the practitioner must be surrounded by undisturbed naturalness." No disrespect for these practices is implied when one notes that such beliefs could easily require de facto beneficial ownership of some rather spacious tracts of public property. Even without anticipating future cases, the diminution of the Government's property rights, and the concomitant subsidy of the Indian religion, would in this case be far from trivial: the District Court's order permanently forbade commercial timber harvesting, or the construction of a two-lane road, anywhere within an area covering a full 27 sections (i.e., more than 17,000 acres) of public land.

Nothing in our opinion should read to encourage governmental insensitivity to the religious needs of any citizen. The Government's rights to the use of its own land, for example, need not and should not discourage it from accommodating religious practices like those engaged in by the Indian respondents.

Except for abandoning its project entirely, and thereby leaving the two existing segments of road to dead end in the middle of a National Forest, it is difficult to see how the Government could have been more solicitous. Such solicitude accords with "the policy of the United States to protect and preserve for American Indians their inherent right of freedom to believe, express, and exercise the traditional religions of the American Indian . . . including but not limited to access to sites, use and possession of sacred objects, and the freedom to worship through ceremonials and traditional rites."

Respondents, however, suggest that AIRFA goes further and in effect enacts their interpretation of the First Amendment into statutory law.

The late Justice William J. Brennan was joined by Justices Thurgood Marshall and Harry A. Blackmun in a dissenting opinion:

For at least 200 years and probably much longer, the Yurok, Karok, and Tolowa Indians have held sacred an approximately 25-square-mile area of land situated in what is today the Blue Creek Unit of Six Rivers National Forest in northwestern California. As the Government readily concedes, regular visits to this area, known to the respondent Indians as the "high country," have played and continue to play a "critical" role in the religious practices and rituals of these tribes. Those beliefs, only briefly described in the Court's opinion, are crucial to a proper understanding of respondents' claims.

As the Forest Service's commissioned study, the Theodoratus Report, explains, for native Americans religion is not a discrete sphere of activity separate from all others, and any attempt to isolate the religious aspects of Indian life "is in reality an exercise which forces Indian concepts into non-Indian categories." Thus, for most Native Americans, "[t]he area of worship cannot be delineated from social, political, cultural and other aspects of Indian lifestyle." A pervasive feature of this lifestyle is the individual's relationship with the natural world; this relationship, which can accurately though somewhat incompletely be characterized as one of stewardship, forms the core of what might be called, for want of a better nomenclature, the Indian religious experience. While traditional western religions view creation as the work of a deity "who institutes natural laws which then govern the operation of physical nature," tribal religions regard creation as an ongoing process in which they are morally and religiously obligated to participate. Native Americans fulfill this duty through ceremonies and rituals designed to preserve and stabilize the earth and to protect humankind from disease and other catastrophes. Failure to conduct these ceremonies in the manner and place specified, adherents believe, will result in great harm to the earth and to the people whose welfare depends upon it.

In marked contrast to traditional western religions, the belief systems of Native Americans do not rely on doctrines, creeds, or dogmas. Established or universal truths — the mainstay of western religions — play no part in Indian faith. Ceremonies are communal efforts undertaken for specific purposes in accordance with instructions handed down from generation to generation. Commentaries on or interpretations of the rituals themselves are deemed absolute violations of the ceremonies, whose value lies not in their ability to explain the natural world or to enlighten individual believers but in their efficacy as protectors and enhancers of tribal existence. Where dogma lies at the heart of western religions, Native American faith is inextricably bound to the use of land. The site-specific nature of Indian religious practice derives from the Native American perception that land is itself a sacred, living being. Rituals are performed in prescribed locations not merely as a matter of traditional orthodoxy, but because land, like all other living things, is unique, and specific sites possess different spiritual properties and significance. Within this belief system, therefore, land is not fungible; indeed, at the time of the Spanish colonization of the American southwest, "all . . . Indians held in some form a belief in a sacred and indissoluble bond between themselves and the land in which their settlements were located."

For respondent Indians, the most sacred of lands is the high country where, they believe, pre-human spirits moved with the coming of humans to the earth. Because these spirits are seen as the source of religious power, or "medicine," many of the tribes' ritual and practices require frequent journeys to the area. Thus, for example, religious leaders preparing for the complex of ceremonies that underlie the tribes' World Renewal efforts must travel to specific sites in the high country in order to attain the medicine necessary for successful renewal. Similarly, individual tribe members may seek curative powers for the healing of the sick, or personal medicine for particular purposes such as good luck in singing, hunting, or love. A period of preparation generally precedes such visits, and individuals must select trails in the sacred area according to the medicine they seek and their abilities, gradually moving to increasingly more powerful sites, which are typically located at higher altitudes. Among the most powerful of sites are Chimney Rock, Doctor Rock, and Peak 8, all of which are elevated rock outcroppings.

According to the Theodoratus Report, the qualities "of silence, the aesthetic perspective, and the physical attributes, are an extension of the sacredness of [each] particular site." The act of medicine making is akin to meditation: the individual must integrate physical, mental, and vocal actions in order to communicate with the pre-human spirits. As a result, "successful use of the high country is dependent upon and facilitated by certain qualities of the physical environment, the most important of which are privacy, silence, and an undisturbed natural setting." Although few tribe members actually make medicine at the most powerful sites, the entire tribe's welfare hinges on the success of the individual practitioners.

The Court does not for a moment suggest that the interests served by the G-O road are in any way compelling, or that they outweigh the destructive effect construction of the road will have on respondents' religious practices. Instead, the Court embraces the Government's contention that its prerogative as landowner should always take precedence over a claim that a particular use of federal property infringes religious practices. Attempting to justify this rule, the Court argues that the First Amendment bars only outright prohibitions, indirect coercion, and penalties on the free exercise of religion. All other "incidental effects of government programs," it concludes, even those "which may make it more difficult to practice certain religions but which have no tendency to coerce individuals into acting contrary to their religious beliefs," simply do not give rise to constitutional concerns. Since our recognition nearly half a century ago that restraints on religious conduct implicate the concerns of the Free Exercise Clause, we have never suggested that the protections of the guarantee are limited to so narrow a range of governmental burdens. The land-use decision challenged here will restrain respondents from practicing their religion as surely and as completely as any of the governmental actions we have struck down in the past, and the Court's efforts simply to define away respondents' injury as non-constitutional are both unjustified and ultimately unpersuasive.

Today, the Court holds that federal land-use decision that promises to destroy an entire religion does not burden the practice of that faith in a manner recognized by the Free Exercise Clause. Having thus stripped respondents and all other native Americans of any constitutional protection against perhaps the most serious threat to their age-old religious practices, and indeed to their entire way of life, the Court assures us that nothing in its decision "should be read to encourage governmental insensitivity to the religious needs of any citizen," I find it difficult, however, to imagine conduct more insensitive to religious needs than the Government's determination to build a marginally useful road in the face of uncontradicted evidence that the road will render the practice of respondents' religion impossible. Nor do I believe that respondents will derive any solace from the knowledge that although the practice of their religion will become "more difficult" as a result of the Government's actions, they remain free to maintain their religious beliefs. Given today's ruling, that freedom amounts to nothing more than the right to believe that their religion will be destroyed. The safeguarding of such a hollow freedom not only makes a mockery of the "policy of the United States to protect and preserve for American Indians their inherent right of freedom to believe, express, and exercise the[ir] traditional religions," it fails utterly to accord with the dictates of the First Amendment.

Vine Deloria Jr. noted a number of causes for concern in the *Lyng* decision. The most important misgiving was the precedent set to favor strongly the federal government and its agencies' interests over its trust responsibilities to Indian tribes.

Sandra Day O'Connor, writing the majority opinion, put the construction of the road in perspective; it was the final link of a seventy-five-mile paved road that had been gradually completed over the years by the Forest Service. Leaving the road unfinished would then have left two segments coming to a dead end in what was now a designated federal wilderness area with timber harvesting prohibited in much of the area.

The majority opinion then went down the line of traditional reasoning that government activities could not be disrupted by the religious claims of citizens because of the great variety of possible religious beliefs and activities inherent in American society. The basic "threat" perceived by the high court was that of a "sudden revelation" of sacredness to individuals, as well as the equally necessary task of recognizing and accommodating beliefs. O'Connor seized on the most remote possibility, a revelation at the Lincoln Memorial to one individual, and pretended that this was comparable to the continuing religious practices of three groups of Indians which extended back perhaps thousands of years. Her basic logical structure appeared to be: "Socrates is a man. Socrates is insane. All men are therefore insane." Such thinking is applicable perhaps to the netherworld inhabited by current Supreme Court justices but is hardly relevant to the issue at hand.

At this point in discussing the opinion, it is important to note that O'Connor was using what is called the "old fact situation" to justify her reasoning, since the California Wilderness Act had rendered moot the question of whether or not there would be logging in the area: there would not be. With commercial logging virtually eliminated as a justification for building the road, the issue then became simply a question of whether the Forest Service had to give Indian religious freedom its due. O'Connor decided negatively on this point, arguing that the federal government as a landowner had certain rights that could not be infringed upon by either its wards or its citizens.

In this, O'Connor finally committed the high court to a formal position on a question it had studiously avoided addressing through a whole series of cases involving Indian spiritual rights to land during the past half-century. Examples include the submersion of traditional Cherokee burial grounds in the Tennessee Valley behind the Tellico Dam, flooding of much of the Allegheny Seneca Reservation in Pennsylvania behind the Kinzua Dam, flooding of Lakota burial sites on the Standing Rock Reservation as part of the Missouri River Project, submersion of the Rainbow Bridge formation, sacred to both the Navajo and the Hopi, behind the Glen Canyon Dam in southern Utah, and destruction of Hopi and Navajo sacred sites on the San Francisco Peaks (near Flagstaff, Arizona) during construction of a ski resort. Further, the Supreme Court's ruling in *Lyng* destroyed the basis for several promising religious freedom cases brought by Indians during the 1980s in the effort to protect or regain use of sacred lands. Notable in this regard were Lakota efforts to ensure unrestricted access to and spiritual use of the Black Hills, and litigation designed to prevent wholesale strip mining of sacred areas within the former Navajo-Hopi Joint Use Area in northeastern Arizona. At this point, such endeavors in attaining due process through U.S. courts appear to have been gutted by the "G-o Road Decision."

Once the idea of trust responsibility was negated, and this neutralization could only occur by conceiving of the Indians as a private party petitioning the government, rather than as a people to whom a trust responsibility is owed, it became necessary to attack the practice of religion itself.

Felix S. Cohen once remarked that Indians serve as a sort of miner's canary on the American domestic scene. The idea is that oppression of indigenous peoples indicates at an early stage the general tightening of the administration of justice to exclude and restrict the rights of all citizens. The basis for this statement is the nature of the trust responsibility. Trust requires that the United States act with the highest moral standards in its treatment of a small group of people who have placed themselves or have been placed under its protection. If a special and specific responsibility cannot be discerned and met, there is not much hope that broader and more universal responsibilities are going to be upheld. The minority opinion adequately described the meaning of the *Lyng* decision in its closing remarks: "[T]oday's ruling sacrifices a religion at least as old as the Nation itself, along with the spiritual well-being of its approximately 5,000 adherents, so that the Forest Service can build a 6-mile segment of road that two lower courts had found had only the most marginal and speculative utility, both to the Government itself and to the private lumber interests that might conceivably use it."

The tremendous irony of *Lyng* is that the road construction was later abandoned, as it should have been, so that the case need never had been heard in its own right. In upholding the principle that no citizen or group of citizens — or "wards," if that is what the Indians are — can tell a federal agency through court injunction how it is supposed to manage public lands, the Supreme Court has openly elevated the federal government to a dictatorial position over its citizens, legitimizing it as an entity with oppressive powers instead of a government of, by, and for the people. Three major questions arise from this litigation: (1) What is the nature of the trust responsibility of the federal government toward American Indians and what primacy does it have in the pyramid of federal values and decision making? (2) What is the nature of the relationship between the practice of religion and the administration of government? (3) What is the real nature of government in the United States today? The first question involves Indians primarily and non-Indians only secondarily, but the second and third questions are pivotal inquiries that must be resolved if American citizens are to maintain (or recover) their individual and collective freedoms.

The National Museum of the American Indian Act

November 28, 1989

While there were challenges to Native American religious and cultural freedom during the 1980s, there were also gains made by Indian leaders, particularly in the areas of Indian art and repatriation. The foundation laid by the 1979 Archaeological Resources Protection Act was expanded considerably during the 1990s, beginning with the National Museum of the American Indian (NMAI) Act of 1989. The intention of the NMAI Act was to provide a new home for a major part of the U.S. government's native art and ethnographic holdings, which were spread among the Smithsonian Institution's nineteen museums, galleries, and research centers and the Heye Museum in New York. The new museum was to be constructed on the last available site on the National Mall in Washington DC. Perhaps most important about the new museum was that its leadership and governance were to be predominantly Native American. The NMAI was a museum about Indians run by Indians: Dr. W. Richard West, a Cheyenne-Arapaho, was the museum's first director, Douglas Cardinal, a Blackfoot, was the principal architectural designer, John L. Colonghi, an Aleut, was the national fund-raising campaign director, and the NMAI's founding board of directors included many notable native people, including Vine Deloria Jr., N. Scott Momaday, and Helen M. Scheirbeck.

The 1989 National Museum of the American Indian Act not only established the National Museum itself, it also set in motion a process of repatriating Indian burial remains and funerary objects from the Smithsonian Institution's extensive Indian collection. This section of the NMAI Act represented the culmination of decades of struggle on the part of Indian tribes to regain control over the remains of their ancestors and the return of sacred tribal artifacts. In many ways, the National Museum of the American Indian represented the first successful battle in what was to become a growing moral victory during the 1990s.

To establish the National Museum of the American Indian within the Smithsonian Institution, and for other purposes.

Be it enacted by the Senate and House of Representatives of the United States of America in Congress Assembled,

SEC. 2. FINDINGS.

The Congress finds that —

(1) there is no national museum devoted exclusively to the history and art of cultures indigenous to the Americas;

(2) although the Smithsonian Institution sponsors extensive Native American programs, none of its 19 museums, galleries, and major research facilities is devoted exclusively to Native American history and art;

(3) the Heye Museum in New York, New York, one of the largest Native American collections in the world, has more than 1,000,000 art objects and artifacts and a library of 40,000 volumes relating to the archaeology, ethnology, and history of Native American peoples;

(4) the Heye Museum is housed in facilities with a total area of 90,000 square feet, but requires a minimum 400,000 square feet for exhibition, storage, and scholarly research;

(5) the bringing together of the Heye Museum collection and the Native American collection of the Smithsonian Institution would —

(A) create a national institution with unrivaled capability for exhibition and research;

(B) give all Americans the opportunity to learn of the cultural legacy, historic grandeur, and contemporary culture of Native Americans;

(C) provide facilities for scholarly meetings and the performing arts;

(D) make available curatorial and other learning opportunities for Indians; and

(E) make possible traveling exhibitions to communities throughout the Nation;

(6) by order of the Surgeon General of the Army, approximately 4,000 Indian human remains from battlefields and burial sites were sent to the Army Medical Museum and were later transferred to the Smithsonian Institution;

(7) through archaeological excavations, individual donations, and museum donations, the Smithsonian Institution has acquired approximately 14,000 additional Indian human remains;

(8) the human remains referred to in paragraphs (6) and (7) have long been a matter of concern for many Indian tribes, including Alaska Native Villages, and Native Hawaiian communities which are determined to provide an appropriate resting place for their ancestors;

(9) identification of the origins of such human remains is essential to addressing that concern; and

·(10) an extraordinary site on the National Mall in the District of Columbia (U.S. Government Reservation No. 6) is reserved for the use of the Smithsonian Institution and is available for construction of the National Museum of the American Indian.

SEC. 3. NATIONAL MUSEUM OF THE AMERICAN INDIAN.

(a) ESTABLISHMENT. — There is established, within the Smithsonian Institution, a living memorial to Native Americans and their traditions which shall be known as the "National Museum of the American Indian."

(b) PURPOSES. — The purposes of the National Museum are to —

(1) advance the study of Native Americans, including the study of language, literature, history, art, anthropology, and life;

(2) collect, preserve, and exhibit Native American objects of artistic, historical, literary, anthropological, and scientific interest;

(3) provide for Native American research and study programs; and

SEC. 11. INVENTORY, IDENTIFICATION, AND RETURN OF INDIAN HUMAN REMAINS AND INDIAN FUNERARY OBJECTS IN THE POSSESSION OF THE SMITHSONIAN INSTITUTION.

(a) INVENTORY AND IDENTIFICATION. — The Secretary of the Smithsonian Institution, in consultation and cooperation with traditional Indian religious leaders and government officials of Indian tribes, shall —

(1) inventory the human remains and Indian funerary objects in the possession or control of the Smithsonian Institution; and

(2) using the best available scientific and historical documentation, identify the origins of such remains and objects.

(b) NOTICE IN CASE OF IDENTIFICATION OF TRIBAL ORIGIN. — If the tribal remains of any human remains or Indian funerary object is identified by a preponderance of the evidence, the Secretary shall so notify any affected Indian tribe at the earliest opportunity.

(c) RETURN OF INDIAN HUMAN REMAINS AND ASSOCIATED INDIAN FUNERARY OBJECTS. — If any Indian human remains are identified by a preponderance of the evidence as those of a particular individual or as those of an individual culturally affiliated with a particular Indian tribe, the Secretary, upon the request of the descendants of such individual or of the Indian tribe shall expeditiously return such remains (together with any associated funerary objects) to the descendants or tribe, as the case may be.

(d) RETURN OF INDIAN FUNERARY OBJECTS NOT ASSOCIATED WITH INDIAN HUMAN REMAINS. — If any Indian funerary object not associated with human remains is identified by a preponderance of the evidence as having been removed from a specific burial site of an individual culturally affiliated with a particular Indian tribe, the Secretary, upon the request of the Indian tribe, shall expeditiously return such object to the tribe.

(e) INTERPRETATION. — Noting in this section shall be interpreted as —

(1) limiting the authority of the Smithsonian Institution to return or repatriate Indian human remains or Indian funerary objects to Indian tribes or individuals; or

(2) delaying actions on pending repatriation requests, denying or otherwise affecting access to the courts, or limiting any procedural or substantive rights which may otherwise be secured to Indian tribes or individuals.

SEC. 12. SPECIAL COMMITTEE TO REVIEW THE INVENTORY, IDENTIFICATION, AND RETURN OF INDIAN HUMAN REMAINS AND INDIAN FUNERARY OBJECTS.

(a) ESTABLISHMENT: DUTIES. — Not later than 120 days after the date of the enactment of this Act, the Secretary of the Smithsonian Institution shall appoint a special committee to monitor and review the inventory, identification, and return of Indian human remains and Indian funerary objects under section 11. In carrying out its duties, the committee shall —

(1) with respect to the inventory and identification, ensure fair and objective consideration and assessment of all relevant evidence;

(2) upon the request of any affected party or otherwise, review any finding relating to the origin or the return of such remains or objects;

(3) facilitate the resolution of any dispute that may arise between Indian tribes with respect to the return of such remains or objects; and

(4) perform such other related functions as the Secretary may assign.

(b) MEMBERSHIP. — The committee shall consist of five members, of whom —

(1) three members shall be appointed from among nominations submitted by Indian tribes and organizations; and

(2) the Secretary may appoint to the committee any individual who is an officer or employee of the Government (including the Smithsonian Institution) or any individual who is otherwise affiliated with the Smithsonian Institution.

(c) ACCESS. — The Secretary shall ensure that the members of the committee have full and free access to the Indian human remains and Indian funerary objects subject to section 11 and to any related evidence, including scientific and historical documents.

SEC. 13. INVENTORY, IDENTIFICATION, AND RETURN OF NATIVE HAWAIIAN HUMAN REMAINS AND NATIVE HAWAIIAN FUNERARY OBJECTS IN THE POSSESSION OF THE SMITHSONIAN INSTITUTION.

(a) IN GENERAL. — The Secretary of the Smithsonian Institution shall —

(1) in conjunction with the inventory and identification under section 11, inventory and identify the Native Hawaiian human remains and Native Hawaiian funerary objects in the possession of the Smithsonian Institution;

(2) enter into an agreement with appropriate Native Hawaiian organizations with expertise in Native Hawaiian affairs (which may include the Office of Hawaiian Affairs and the Malama I Na Kupuna O Hawai'i Nei) to provide for the return of such human remains and funerary objects; and

(3) to the greatest extent practicable, apply, with respect to such human remains and funerary objects, the principles and procedures set forth in sections 11 and 12 with respect to the Indian human remains and Indian funerary objects in the possession of the Smithsonian Institution.

(b) DEFINITIONS. — As used in this section —

(1) the term "Malama I Na Kupuna O Hawai'i Nei" means the nonprofit, Native Hawaiian organization, incorporated under the laws of the State of Hawaii by that name on April 17, 1989, the purpose of which is to provide guidance and expertise in decisions dealing with Native Hawaiian cultural issues, particularly burial issues; and

(2) the term "Office of Hawaiian Affairs" means the Office of Hawaiian Affairs established by the Constitution of the State of Hawaii.

Native American Graves Protection and Repatriation Act

November 16, 1990

The National Museum of the American Indian Act's provision that the Smithsonian Institution must return its Indian burial remains and funerary objects was a sure sign that the winds of change were blowing across U.S. natural history museums. These selected entries from the *New York Times* during the period from the 1960s to the 1990s illustrate the decades-long effort by Indian tribes to secure the return of their ancestral remains and artifacts. The stance of the museums can be seen to shift during this period from simple refusals to return objects, to admonitions to the Indians that they were not qualified to take possession, to statements about the conditions tribes had to meet in order for the objects to be returned, to compliance with the 1990 Native American Graves Protection and Repatriation Act (NAGPRA), which ordered museums to catalog and notify tribes of their holdings, and to make arrangements for their return.

March 25, 1967 — "Iroquois League Demands Return of Ancient Belts Locked in Museum." The chief of the Iroquois League . . . is demanding that the state of New York return to Indian custody ceremonial wampum belts. . . . The state says the belts are priceless and fragile.

April 16, 1970 — "Iroquois Are Seeking Return of Wampum Belts Held by State Museum." The Indians want the belts, made of shell beads, returned to them for display at a planned museum and cultural center on Onondaga land near Syracuse. . . . The State Education Department, which administers the [state] museum, opposes the [return] on the grounds it could set a precedent that "could destroy the concept of museums and libraries being collectors of anything."

February 14, 1986 — "Smithsonian in Dispute over Indian Skeletons." Officials of the Smithsonian Institution's Museum of Natural History, criticized by two American Indian groups, say they would turn over to recognized tribal leaders Indian skeletons that have a "clear biological or cultural link" to modern-day tribal units. But the museum officials estimated that this description would apply to fewer than 10 percent of the Smithsonian's collection of 14,000 Indian skeletons.

December 8, 1987 — "Indians Seek Burial of Smithsonian Skeletons." The Smithsonian Institution's collection of skeletal remains of native

Americans is a sore point with Indians who want their ancestors' remains buried properly and treated with dignity. . . . Mr. Adams, Secretary of the Smithsonian, has said that the museum has no problem returning those bones that were stolen from graves or can be traced to living descendants, but that it would like to keep other bones for scientific study . . . "compulsory internment is an irretrievable loss of material of significant scientific and educational value."

August 13, 1989 — "New York Returning Wampum Belts to Onondagas." New York State has agreed to return 12 wampum belts, some of which have been in State Museum since 1898, to the Onondaga Nation of Indians.

August 13, 1990 — "Zunis' Effort to Regain Idols May Alter Views of Indian Art." This is a rare story of American Indians getting back what was taken from them, and it may presage broad changes in the way that Indian artifacts are bought and sold, in how they are studied and exhibited. Zunis have received or begun talks over every war god known to be in the hands of an American museum or collector; scholars and policy makers regard the push to regain an entire category of objects as a turning point in a process that is redefining the concept of ownership of objects sacred to Indians.

February 19, 1993 — Oglala Sioux of South Dakota demand that a small museum in Barre, Massachusetts, return long-held artifacts which were taken from bodies of Indians killed at Wounded Knee in 1890. Curator Audrey Stevens says the museum had no knowledge of the origin of the items, which were donated in 1892 by Frank Root, a local resident who may have bought them from a contractor who worked at the site of the mass graves. A 1990 Federal law requires the return of such artifacts.

To provide for the protection of Native American graves, and for other purposes.

Be it enacted by the Senate and House of Representatives of the United States of America in Congress assembled,

SEC 2. DEFINITIONS.

For purposes of this Act, the term —

(1) "burial site" means any natural or prepared physical location, whether originally below, on, or above the surface of the earth, into which as part of the death rite or ceremony of a culture, individual human remains are deposited.

(2) "cultural affiliation" means that there is a relationship of shared

group identity which can be reasonably traced historically or prehistorically between a present day Indian tribe or Native Hawaiian organization and an identifiable earlier group.

(3) "cultural items" means human remains and —

(A) "associated funerary objects" which shall mean objects that, as part of the death rite or ceremony of a culture, are reasonably believed to have been placed with individual human remains either at the time of death or later, and both the human remains and associated funerary objects are presently in the possession or control of a Federal agency or museum, except that other items exclusively made for burial purposes or to contain human remains shall be considered as associated funerary objects.

(B) "unassociated funerary objects" which shall mean objects that, as part of the death rite or ceremony of a culture, are reasonably believed to have been placed with individual human remains either at the time of death or later, where the remains are not in the possession or control of the Federal agency or museum and the objects can be identified by a preponderance of the evidence as related to specific individuals or families or to known human remains, or, by a preponderance of the evidence, as having been removed from a specific burial site of an individual culturally affiliated with a particular Indian tribe,

(C) "sacred objects" which shall mean specific ceremonial objects which are needed by traditional Native American religious leaders for the practice of traditional Native American religions by their present day adherents, and

(D) "cultural patrimony" which shall mean an object having ongoing historical, traditional, or cultural importance, central to the Native American group or culture itself, rather than property owned by an individual Native American, and which, therefore, cannot be alienated, appropriated, or conveyed by any individual regardless of whether or not the individual is a member of the Indian tribe or Native Hawaiian organization and such object shall have been considered inalienable by such Native American group at the time the object was separated from such group.

SEC. 3. OWNERSHIP.

(a) NATIVE AMERICAN HUMAN REMAINS AND OBJECTS. — The ownership or control of Native American cultural items which are excavated or discovered on federal or tribal lands after the date of enactment of this Act shall be (with priority given in the order listed) —

(1) in the case of Native American human remains and associated funerary objects, in the lineal descendants of the Native American; or

(2) in any case in which such lineal descendants cannot be ascertained, and in the case of unassociated funerary objects, sacred objects, and objects of cultural patrimony —

(A) in the Indian tribe or Native Hawaiian organization on whose tribal land such objects or remains were discovered;

(B) in the Indian tribe or Native Hawaiian organization which has the closest cultural affiliation with such remains or objects and which, upon notice, states a claim for such remains or objects; or

(C) if the cultural affiliation of the objects cannot be reasonably ascertained and if the objects were discovered on Federal land that is recognized by a final judgment of the Indian Claims Commission or the United States Court of Claims as the aboriginal land of some Indian tribe

(1) in the Indian tribe that is recognized as aboriginally occupying the area in which the objects were discovered, if upon notice, such tribe states a claim for such remains or objects, or

(2) if it can be shown by a preponderance of the evidence that a different cultural tribe has a stronger cultural relationship with the remains or objects than the tribe or organization specified in paragraph (1), in the Indian tribe that has the strongest demonstrated relationship, if upon notice, such tribe states a claim for such remains or objects.

SEC. 5. INVENTORY FOR HUMAN REMAINS AND ASSOCIATED FUNERARY OBJECTS.

(a) IN GENERAL. — Each federal agency and each museum which has possession or control over holdings or collections of Native American human remains and associated funerary objects shall compile an inventory of such items and, to the extent possible based on the information possessed by such museum or Federal agency, identify the geographical and cultural affiliation of such item.

(b) REQUIREMENTS. —

(1) The inventories and identifications required under subsection (a) shall be —

(A) completed in consultation with tribal government and Native Hawaiian organization officials and traditional religious leaders;

(B) completed by not later than the date that is five years after the date of enactment of this Act, and

(C) made available both during the time they are being conducted and afterward to a review committee established under section 8.

(2) Upon request by an Indian tribe or Native Hawaiian organization which receives or should have received notice, a museum or Federal agency shall supply additional available documentation to supplement the information required by subsection (a) of this section. The term "documentation" means a summary of existing museum or Federal agency records, including inventories or catalogues, relevant studies, or other pertinent data for the limited purpose of determining the geographical origin, cultural affiliation, and the basic facts surrounding acquisition and accession of Native American human remains and associated funerary objects subject to this section. Such term does not mean, and this Act shall not be construed to be an authorization for, the initiation of new scientific studies of such remains and associated funerary objects or other means of acquiring or preserving additional scientific information from such remains and objects.

(c) EXTENSION OF TIME FOR INVENTORY. — Any museum, which has made a good faith effort to carry out an inventory and identification under this section, but which has been unable to complete the process, may appeal to the Secretary for an extension of the time requirements set forth in subsection (b)(1)(B). The Secretary may extend such time requirements for any such museum upon a finding of good faith effort. An indication of good faith shall include the development of a plan to carry out the inventory and identification process.

(d) NOTIFICATION. —

(1) If the cultural affiliation of any particular Native American human remains or associated funerary objects is determined pursuant to this section, the Federal agency or museum concerned shall, not later than 6 months after the completion of the inventory, notify the affected Indian tribes or Native Hawaiian organizations.

(2) The notice required by paragraph (1) shall include information —

(A) which identifies each Native American human remains or associated funerary objects and the circumstances surrounding its acquisition;

(B) which lists the human remains or associated funerary objects that are clearly identifiable as to tribal origin, and

(C) which lists the Native American human remains and associated funerary objects that are not clearly identifiable as being culturally affiliated with that Indian tribe or Native Hawaiian organization, but which, given the totality of circumstances surrounding acquisition of the remains or objects, are determined by a reasonable belief to be remains or objects culturally affiliated with the Indian tribe or Native Hawaiian organization.

SEC. 7. REPATRIATION.

(a) REPATRIATION OF NATIVE AMERICAN HUMAN REMAINS AND OBJECTS POSSESSED OR CONTROLLED BY FEDERAL AGENCIES AND MUSEUMS. —

(1) If, pursuant to section 5, the cultural affiliation of Native American human remains and associated funerary objects with a particular Indian tribe or Native Hawaiian organization is established, then the Federal agency or museum, upon the request of a known lineal descendent of the Native American or of the tribe or organization and pursuant to subsections (b) and (e) of this section, shall expeditiously return such remains and associated funerary objects.

Passage of the Native American Graves Protection and Repatriation Act in November 1990 did not result in an instant return of burial remains and funerary artifacts to Indian tribes. The process of identifying sacred objects and their tribes, of notifying tribes, and of negotiating the return of objects was time-consuming and laborious. The case of several Diné (Navajo) Nightway masks in the Field Museum of Natural History in Chicago illustrates both the power and challenge posed by NAGPRA for Indians and for museums. In the early 1990s Navajos visiting the Field Museum saw the sacred Nightway masks on display in the museum. They were disturbed by the inappropriate exposure of the masks to public viewing and conducted a brief ceremony at the museum before returning home to Arizona to report the masks to tribal officials. In July 1993 a delegation of Navajos visited the Field Museum, inspected the masks, and determined that the masks should be removed. The museum complied and the masks were removed in a ceremony soon after. The masks were put in storage, and the Navajo Nation officially requested their return in 1996. The Navajos and Field Museum officials continued to negotiate the terms of their return in 1997. The following article from *Indian Country Today* describes the discovery of the masks by Diné chanter Alfred Yazzie.

Repatriation Demanded across the Country
Valerie Tallman

CHICAGO — The sacred beings, human remains and medicine bundles of many Native peoples are suffering as they remain cloistered and imprisoned in boxes and dark basements of museums, private collections and universities around the country.

As federally mandated deadlines for returning sacred objects to tribes approach, many spiritual leaders and tribal officials are calling on America's institutions to demand that their heritage be returned. Inventories of human remains or associated funerary objects must be submitted to the government this fall and to the tribes by Nov. 16, 1995.

During the recent Parliament of the World's Religions — a global gathering of spiritual leaders — many Native people made a point to visit the Chicago Field Museum in search of what is rightfully theirs.

In one such visit, Alfred Yazzie and his wife, Alice, were distressed to see Yeibichai masks hanging in a display case in the Field Museum's extensive Native American collection.

A well-known Diné (Navajo) chanter who prefers not to be called a medicine man, Mr. Yazzie pointed out that these sacred beings should not be on public display. The masks, considered living beings, are traditionally worn to depict Yeis (gods) as part of the sacred nine-day healing ceremony called the "Night Chant," still widely practiced by Navajo people. Mr. Yazzie noted that the masks appeared to have been "abused" and that much of the museum's display was culturally incorrect, a problem that museum staff said they "would research."

"When we saw the sacred masks and the medicine bundles they have locked up here, we were very sad," Mr. Yazzie said. "My wife broke down to see these Holy Ones, who are still living, longing for their people. They need to be reblessed and returned to the people."

Mr. Yazzie and a delegation of native people, including eight Navajos, returned to the museum a second time so they could perform a blessing for the sacred beings and offer sacred corn pollen to feed them. Mr. Yazzie sang several songs from the Night Chant in an abbreviated ceremony to re-bless hundreds of Diné sacred items stored on the shelves.

"These medicine bundles are the heartbeat of the Navajo Nation and they have their origins there," he said. "It's not right to have these bundles locked up here. We need them for our ceremonies. No wonder our people are confused," Mr. Yazzie said.

Jonathan Haas, the museum's vice president, said he was uncertain how the collection was acquired because it was "before his time." However, he acknowledged that the museum had some displays that are "very sensitive" to the Navajo people.

"We'd like to have some communication from the Navajo on what to do with these masks," he told Mr. Yazzie and the native delegation. "I don't want to make that decision without consulting with the Navajo. I hope these things go back to the tribe."

But Mr. Haas also told the group that the museum had the legal right of possession to sacred objects because they had paid for them. He acknowledged that thousands of sacred items, including a large collection from the Lakota people, are in the museum's possession. Some are being returned, he noted.

In response, Mr. Yazzie pointed out that Mr. Haas was talking about legal rights defined by the dominant society's rules.

"You talk about the right of possession under the white man's laws which were imposed on us. But these things were given to us by the gods, so far as we know, and handed down through the centuries. It make me wonder how you got them."

Mr. Haas was uncertain, but insisted that the museum had done its best to care for the thousands of sacred items in their possession.

"We may not be able to take care of things spiritually, but we can take good care of them physically. And we worry what will become of (these things) when we give them back and they don't have a facility to take care of them. They may fall apart in two or three years," he said.

His comments angered Pemina Yellow Bird, a Hidatsa/Arikara activist who has worked for years in the struggle to have sacred objects repatriated to tribes. As a board member of the North Dakota Tribal Reburial Association, Ms. Yellow Bird has heard such comments many times before.

"The fact that they won't return things unless tribes have repositories that meet current museum standards is another example of shoving the white man's paradigms down our throats," she said.

"How do you think these ancient things got in their possession if Native people didn't know how to take care of them? And who are they to tell us how to take care of our own sacred objects?"

Raymond Apodaca, chairman of he Human Rights Committee of the National Congress of American Indians, agreed that museum officials constantly question the integrity of Native people to care for their own ceremonial items.

"They always tell us 'You people don't know how to take care of these things.' What are they talking about? These things belong to us, were created by us, and are highly respected by us," she said.

"We've heard this same line a million times from other anthropologists, museum officials and curators who are protecting their institutions and perpetuating the status quo at our expense," said Ms. Yellow Bird. "Well, we Native people are standing up and saying this is wrong and we're coming after what is ours."

The Native American Graves Protection and Repatriation Act of 1990 requires museums, universities and other institutions to submit to tribes written summaries of what is in their collections by the end of this year [1993]. Then, by the close of 1995, institutions are required to provide to tribes an inventory of human remains in their collections. The process then mandates formal consultations with tribes to determine who has right of possession so that museums can provide clear title to tribal groups for their sacred items.

But already many institutions say they will not make the deadlines imposed by law and will need more money to compile the inventories which will ultimately slow down the return of sacred objects to tribes.

"We are tired of delays," said Ms. Yellow Bird. "This is the theft and appropriation of our heritage and our life, and it's done under the guise of academia and the dominant societies' paradigms.

"What really hurts and angers me the most is all those living beings in museums who are suffering because they don't belong there," she said with great emotion.

"They are lost between this and the spirit world and they can't go back to either one until we bring them home."

This letter from Navajo Nation President Peterson Zah to the Field Museum represented an important step in the process of removing the masks from public view. To illustrate the changes brought on by the Native American Graves Protection and Repatriation Act, the Field Museum displayed a copy of this letter in the empty display case after the masks had been removed and only the labels remained.

September 21, 1993
Dr. Jonathan Haas, Vice President
Museum Affairs
Field Museum of Natural History
Roosevelt Road at Lake Shore Drive
Chicago, Illinois 60605-2496
Dear Dr. Haas:

On July 27, 1993, Richard M. Begay, Alan Downer and Alexa Roberts of the Navajo Nation Historic Preservation Department (NNHPD) viewed your display of the Navajo Nightway masks and other items in your collection. I wish to extend my sincere appreciation for the hospitality your staff extended to the Navajo Nation representatives during their visit.

The Nightway masks are utilized in a sacred ceremony held in the winter months, and should not be seen by uninitiated eyes. As you are aware, the Navajo Nation objects to the public display of these masks and requests that they be removed. Please inform us as soon as possible of a date for removal so we can arrange to have a representative present to oversee the proper handling of the masks during removal and subsequent storage.

Thank you for your prompt attention to this matter. Please contact Alan Downer, Historic Preservation Officer, should you require more information.

Sincerely,
THE NAVAJO NATION
Peterson Zah, President

In 1994 Janice Klein, registrar at the Field Museum, delivered a paper at the Ohio Museum Association's annual meeting in which she outlined the steps the Field Museum now takes to comply with the Native American Graves Protection and Repatriation Act and to respond to tribes' requests for the proper handling, storage, and return of sacred objects.

NAGPRA, Consultation, and the Field Museum
Janice Klein

The Native American Graves Protection and Repatriation Act became law on November 16, 1990. Although it pertains to both newly discovered human remains and objects, and pre-existing collections, museums are, in general, more concerned with the sections of the law which deal with their current holdings.

In the past four years the Field Museum has hosted a number of visits from Native Americans and responded to several requests for repatriation. We have had formal visits — by which I mean those which included tribal and religious leaders or representatives approved by the tribal Council — from native Hawaiians, Iroquois, Blackfoot, Hopi, Ermineskin Cree, Pawnee, Navajo, Arapaho, Shawnee, and Ute, as well as visits from individual Pawnee, Cheyenne, Crow, and Inuit, among others. We have responded to several repatriation requests and have returned human remains to the Blackfoot and native Hawaiians, a Sun Dance wheel to the northern Arapaho, and are in the process of returning bundles to the Pawnee and a wampum belt to the Oneida.

We have also undertaken substantial consultation concerning the appropriateness of our current Native American exhibits. Some consultation has resulted in the removal of objects from view: we have covered over our Hopi kachina altars and removed a case of Navajo Nightway masks and two Iroquois false face masks. In each instance, we have explained to our visitors why these objects are no longer on display. In the case of — and in place of — the Nightway masks, we have posted a letter from Peterson Zah, Navajo tribal President, asking for the removal of the masks because they *are used in a sacred ceremony and should not be seen by uninitiated eyes.*

Consultation regarding the storage of our collection has also taken several forms. Many of the visits from Native Americans result in changes in the way objects are stored, for example, keeping pipe bowls and stems separate, or removing certain items from plastic bags so they can breathe. We are making provisions for *feeding* and smudging, which we feel may need a separate storage area for conservation reasons. As a consequence, we are also learning to address the concerns which result from the concentration of a large number of sacred objects in one place. There are also questions of who should handle — and who needs to avoid — certain types of material. Some objects should not be touched by women, while other objects can be handled by non–Native Americans, but pose problems for members of particular tribes if they have not been initiated into the appropriate religious society.

There are many things that we have learned in the last few years. The most important is that consultation is process. Policies, procedures, and guidelines cannot be cast in stone, but will have to change as we see how they work and as we learn more about each other. It may not be easy and it will certainly not always be comfortable. We are, after all, members of different cultures with different ways of communicating and different perceptions and expectations.

Indian Arts and Crafts Act

November 29, 1990

An interesting chapter in American Indian cultural renewal is the controversy over Indian art. Part of the legacy of the Red Power activist era has been a cultural renaissance on reservations and in urban Indian communities marked by a growing interest in Indian traditional crafts such as basket weaving, pottery making, rug weaving, and wood and stone carving, as well as a vast increase in the production of Indian art — drawing, painting, sculpture, and music. This upsurge of interest in Indian arts and crafts was accompanied by rising prices and sales of art by Native American artists and craftspeople. As more and more artists began identifying their work as "Indian art" and began working in Indian-style artistic mediums, questions arose about the rights and authenticity of Indian artists. It is important to note that the question of who can rightfully claim to be an Indian artist is not a new one. For many years Santa Fe, New Mexico, has regulated and licensed native artists and craftspersons selling their work under the governor's portico in downtown Santa Fe. However, the question of "certifying" Indian artists expanded into a national debate following the passage of the 1990 Indian Arts and Crafts Act, which established an "Indian Arts and Crafts Board" with the power to determine who is and is not an official Indian artist and which makes the misrepresentation of oneself or one's art as "Indian" a criminal offense.

The passage of the Indian Arts and Crafts Act had some dramatic results. Many established Indian artists could no longer claim their art was "Indian art." An example was Bert Seabourn, a Cherokee from Oklahoma City, whose family was not on the tribe's 1906 enrollment list, and who thus could not qualify for tribal membership necessary to be certified as an Indian artist: "I don't know if my ancestors even knew about it [the list]." The following documents are excerpts from the 1990 Indian Arts and Crafts Act followed by a 1994 article by Dennis Fox that appeared in *Native Americas*, in which Fox argued against the certification requirements of the act.

To expand the powers of the Indian Arts and Crafts Board, and for other purposes.

Be it enacted by the Senate and House of Representatives of the United States of America in Congress assembled,

SEC. 102. POWERS OF INDIAN ARTS AND CRAFTS BOARD.

Section 2 of the Act . . . is amended —

(2) by amending clause (g) to read as follows:

"(g)(1) to create for the board, or for an individual Indian or Indian tribe or Indian arts and crafts organization, trademarks of genuineness and quality for Indian products and the products of an individual Indian or particular Indian tribe or Indian arts and crafts organization; (2) to establish standards and regulations for the use of Government-owned trademarks by corporations, associations, or individuals, and to charge for such use under such licenses; (3) to register any such trademark owned by the Government in the United States Patent and Trademark Office without charge and assign it and the goodwill associated with it to an individual Indian or Indian tribe without charge; and (4) to pursue or defend in the courts any appeal or proceeding with respect to any final determination of that office;" and

(3) by adding at the end the following new sentence: "For the purposes of this section, the term 'Indian arts and crafts organization' means any legally established arts and crafts marketing organization composed of members of Indian tribes."

"Misrepresentation of Indian produced goods and products

"(a) It is unlawful to offer or display for sale or sell any good, with or without a Government trademark, in a manner that falsely suggests it is Indian produced, an Indian product, or the product of a particular Indian or Indian tribe or Indian arts and crafts organization, resident within the United States.

"(b) Whoever knowingly violates subsection (a) shall —

"(1) in the case of a first violation, if an individual, be fined not more than $250,000 or imprisoned not more than five years, or both, and, if a person other than an individual, be fined not more than $1,000,000; and

"(2) in the case of subsequent violations, if an individual, be fined not more than $1,000,000 or imprisoned not more than fifteen years, or both, and, if a person other than an individual, be fined not more than $5,000,000.

"(c) As used in this section —

"(1) the term 'Indian' means any individual who is a member of an Indian tribe, or for the purposes of this section is certified as an Indian artisan by an Indian tribe;

"(2) the terms 'Indian product' and 'product of a particular Indian tribe or Indian arts and crafts organization' has the meaning given such term in regulations which may be promulgated by the Secretary of the Interior;

"(3) the term 'Indian tribe' means —

"(A) any tribe, band, nation, Alaska Native village, or other organized group or community which is recognized as eligible for the special programs and services p[rovided] by the United States for Indians because of their status as Indians; or

"(B) any Indian group that has been formally recognized as an Indian tribe by a State legislature or by a State commission or similar organization legislatively vested with State tribal recognition authority; and

"(4) the term 'Indian arts and crafts organization' means any legally established arts and crafts marketing organization composed of members of Indian tribes."

Indian Arts and Crafts Act: Counterpoint
Dennis Fox

At the turn of the century my grandfather, Simon Ridge WalkingStick, a lawyer in Tahlequah, Oklahoma, was hired as a Cherokee interpreter for the implementation of the Curtis Act, which parceled out "Indian Territory" to those individual tribe members who would allow themselves to be numbered and registered. The land that remained after this parceling was then given or sold to white homesteaders and businesses. Indian Territory was no more, and Oklahoma became a state. My grandfather took the job because he saw the inevitability of statehood and wanted to get his tribe the fairest shake possible. He wanted to ensure that those registrants who spoke only Cherokee knew exactly what they were signing.

Many Cherokee, however, didn't sign. Some lived outside Indian Territory and felt they had nothing to gain by making the trip to Tahlequah. Others mistrusted white people — the Trail of Tears was only sixty years in the past. These people were often traditionalists who wanted to retain the old ways. Their tribal lands and their way of life were being taken from them. Furthermore, numbering and registering them was a humiliating process, and its purpose was to control people.

Even so, the only way one can prove one is Cherokee today is to produce the registration number of an ancestor and through such documentation be accepted as a tribal member. The children and grandchildren of those who did not register cannot prove they are Indian.

Now the numbering and registering have returned to haunt us. On November 29, 1990, President Bush signed into law the Indian Arts and Crafts Act, which stated that a person who exhibits Native American art for sale must be able to prove, through tribal membership or certification, that the maker is indeed an American Indian. If a person not certified as an Indian is convicted of selling Native American arts or crafts, or exhibiting them for sale, he or she and the exhibiting space — whether commercial or nonprofit — are subject to a $250,000 fine and up to a year in jail. The members of no other racial group in the United States have ever had to prove their ethnic heritage in order to sell their art.

The goal of the act is to update a law on the books since 1935, its purpose is to promote and protect Indian arts and crafts and to prevent misrepresentation. At present, there are no regulations for defining or imposing the new law — legislators have yet to decide, for instance, how many objects made by Indian artists who are citizens not of the United States but of Mexico, Canada, or South and Central America will be sold here, and whether or not the law applies to film, video, performance, and computer-generated art. According to Geoffrey Steam, of the Indian Arts and Crafts Board (IACB), which will handle complaints, the formulation and implementation of regulations will take about a year. Until then, the chances of anyone being brought to trial are negligible.

Once the regulations are in place, however, individuals will be able to make a complaint to the IACB, and tribes will be able to bring civil suit. And the regulations are not intended to address the basic premise of the law, which is problematic. For there seems to be no consistent rule for tribal membership among the hundreds of tribes in the United States. The conditions of membership are decided by each sovereign tribal nation. To be a tribal member of the Salish of Montana, for example, one must have been born on the Salish reservation. In order to be a Hopi, one's mother must be a Hopi tribal member. This means that if your father is Hopi and your mother is Salish and you were born in St. Louis, you cannot be a member of either tribe, even though you are a full-blooded Native American.

In addition, many tribes are not recognized by the government, some tribes that were formerly recognized are no longer, and some are recognized by their state but not by Washington. The net result is that many people who identify themselves as Indian are not recognized as such by the federal government. (It often happens that Indians in need of the assistance that the government has promised native peoples through treaty cannot prove their Indian identity.) Furthermore, there are Native Americans who reject the whole idea of formal tribal membership to the extent that they see it as a foreign, bureaucratic imposition alien to their own traditions of thought.

This problem in the classification system on which the law is based is accompanied by considerable worry over how it will be applied. A foretaste has been provided by the Native American Art Alliance (NAAA), out of Santa Fe, which has been vociferously leading a fight to prevent unregistered Indian artists from selling their artwork as "made by Native Americans." The NAAA has made accusations against many prominent artists. This July they were able to prevent the opening of an exhibition at Santa Fe's Center for Contemporary Art by the Cherokee artist Jimmy Durham, on the grounds that Durham is not registered — this despite the fact that the NAAA has no judicial power (it is only a political lobbying group); that the Indian Arts and Crafts Board, according to Steam, will not support any civil or criminal charges under the law until the regulations are complete; and that the law allows an exhibition venue to protect itself from civil or criminal suit simply by printing a disclaimer that although the artist identifies him- or herself as Native American, he or she is not regarded as a member of a tribe.

The most convincing voice I have heard in support of the law is that of the Mohawk artist and educator Richard Glazer-Danay. Glazer-Danay doesn't want his culture defined by the art of non-Indians. He doesn't want his grandchildren to pick up an art book and see a painting by a non-Indian who claims to represent Indian culture. The law is intended to prevent this possibility, but its long-term effects may also be negative. We do have to prevent non-Indians from marketing American Indian-style objects as authentic. We must protect collectors of Native American art. We have to stop fraudulent behavior; surely no one would argue against that view. Yet through this law some of our most important artists may be stopped from exhibiting their work and affirming their identity. How are we to get them out of the tribal membership trap written into law?

It is our Cherokee custom to consider the welfare of the next seven generations in all the decisions we make. Grandfather WalkingStick may

have made the wrong decision in taking translation work in Tahlequah —
but he was trying to foster the long-term common good of his tribe,
within the framework of turn-of-the-century federal Indian policy. That
policy was based on the economics of real estate, with little regard for the
individual Indian. This present law is also about economics. Its intention is to protect the individual Indian artist and craftsperson, but it is
crippled and may end up hurting our fellow artists. The law needs to be
re-examined to work for the long-term common good of Native American people.

American Indian Religious Freedom Act Amendments

October 6, 1994

The weakness of the 1978 American Indian Religious Freedom Act was made evident by the U.S. Supreme Court's 1989 *Lyng* decision denying protection to lands considered sacred by several California tribes. Although the 1990 Native American Graves Protection and Repatriation Act reaffirmed Indian tribes' rights to the remains of their ancestors, during that same year the rights of living Indians to practice their religion were once again in jeopardy. In 1990 the Supreme Court, in *Employment Division, Department of Human Resources of Oregon v. Smith*, upheld the decision to deny unemployment benefits to two Native American employees who were fired from their jobs for using peyote in Native American Church ceremonies. The Supreme Court decided that the two Indians' First Amendment guarantee of free exercise of religion had not been violated, since "we have never held that an individual's religious beliefs excuse him from compliance with an otherwise valid law prohibiting conduct that the State is free to regulate."

Despite the ongoing federal "war on drugs," the *Smith* decision so disturbed Congress, which felt that the religious freedom of many Americans was threatened — native and non-native alike — that in 1993 it passed the Religious Freedom Restoration Act and in 1994 the American Indian Religious Freedom Act Amendments, the latter specifically protecting the "traditional Indian religious use of the peyote sacrament." Although in 1997 the Supreme Court found the 1993 Religious Freedom Restoration Act unconstitutional, the 1994 American Indian Religious Freedom Act continued to protect Native American Church members' use of peyote.

To amend the American Indian Religious Freedom Act to provide for the traditional use of peyote by Indians for religious purposes, and for other purposes.

SEC 2. TRADITIONAL INDIAN RELIGIOUS USE OF THE PEYOTE SACRAMENT.

The Act of August 11, 1978 (42 U.S.C. 1996), commonly referred to as the "American Indian Religious Freedom Act," is amended by adding at the end thereof the following new section:

"sec. 3. (a) The Congress finds and declares that —

"(1) use of the peyote cactus as a religious sacrament has for centuries been integral to a way of life, and significant in perpetuating Indian tribes and cultures;

"(2) since 1965, this ceremonial use of peyote by Indians has been protected by federal regulation;

"(3) while at least 28 States have enacted laws which are similar to, or are in conformance with, the Federal regulation which protects the ceremonial use of peyote by Indian religious practitioners, 22 States have not done so, and this lack of uniformity has created hardship for Indian people who participate in such religious ceremonies;

"(4) the Supreme Court of the United States, in the case of *Employment Division v. Smith*, 494 U.S. 872 (1990), held that the First Amendment does not protect Indian practitioners who use peyote in Indian religious ceremonies, and also raised uncertainty whether this religious practice would be protected under the compelling State interest standard; and

"(5) the lack of adequate and clear legal protection for the religious use of peyote by Indians may serve to stigmatize and marginalize Indian tribes and cultures, and increase the risk that they will be exposed to discriminatory treatment.

"(b)

(1) Notwithstanding any other provision of law, the use, possession, or transportation of peyote by an Indian for bona fide traditional ceremonial purposes in connection with the practice of a traditional Indian religion is lawful, and shall not be prohibited by the United States or any State. No Indian shall be penalized or discriminated against on the basis of such use, possession or transportation, including, but not limited to, denial of otherwise applicable benefits under public assistance programs."

References and Further Reading

Champagne, Duane, ed. 1994. *Native America: Portrait of the Peoples.*
   Detroit: Visible Ink.
Deloria, Vine, Jr. 1992. "Trouble in High Places: Erosion of American
   Indian Rights to Religious Freedom in the United States." In *The State
   of Native North America: Genocide, Colonization, and Resistance*, ed.
   M. A. Jaimes. Boston: South End. 267–90.
Evans-Pritchard, Deirdre. 1987. "The Portal Case: Authenticity, Tourism,
   Traditions, and the Law." *Journal of American Folklore* 100: 287–96.
Fox, Dennis. 1994. "Indian Arts and Crafts: Counterpoint." *Native
   Americas* (fall/winter): 114–18.
Karp, Ivan, and Steven D. Lavine. 1991. *Exhibiting Cultures: The Poetics
   and Politics of Museum Display*. Washington DC: Smithsonian
   Institution Press.
Klein, Janice. 1995. "NAGPRA, Consultation and the Field Museum."
   Registrars' Quarterly (fall): 7–8, 16.
Matthiessen, Peter. 1991. *In the Spirit of Crazy Horse*. New York: Viking.
Price, H. Marcus, III. 1991. *Disputing the Dead: U.S. Law on Aboriginal
   Remains and Grave Goods*. Columbia: University of Missouri Press.
Tallman, Valerie. 1993. "Repatriation Demanded across the Country."
   Indian Country Today, September 22, A7.
Trask, Haunani-Kay. 1991. "Natives and Anthropologists: The Colonial
   Struggle." *The Contemporary Pacific* 3: 159–67.

6 Rebuilding Native American Lives and Communities

American Indian Population Trends

U.S. Bureau of the Census, 1960–1990

In 1990, the U.S. Census reported 1,878,285 American Indians in the United States. This figure represented a 38 percent increase in the number of Indians since the 1980 census, which itself showed a historically large growth in the American Indian population, from 792,730 in 1970 to 1,364,033 in 1980 — a 72 percent increase. Table 1 shows the number of Indians (not including Alaska Natives) reported by the U.S. Census Bureau during the three decades during and after the Red Power period.

A number of explanations have been sought to understand these dramatic increases in the American Indian population — increases that cannot be explained using traditional methods of understanding population growth: increased birthrates, decreased death rates, immigration. Although Native American birthrates have risen during this period, especially given improvements in infant mortality, and although Indian death rates have fallen somewhat due to improved Indian health care, these changes are not sufficient to account for this amount of population growth. Since few Indians are immigrants, these increases are not the result of new Indians entering the United States. The most likely cause of the growing Indian population has been the increased willingness on the part of many Indian people to identify themselves as Indians to census takers during this period, particularly those individuals who are of mixed Indian and non-Indian ancestry. Thus, another consequence of the Red Power activist era has been the desire of many Americans of native ancestry to reestablish a connection with their tribal and Indian roots.

Several other trends in the American Indian population combine with the trend in population growth to construct an emerging and very different picture of the Indian population landscape than existed in the first half of the twentieth century. These trends are the urbanization of the Indian population; increasing rates of intermarriage with non-Indians, which has resulted in an increase in the number of children of mixed Indian and non-Indian ancestry; and a decrease in the number of American Indian–language speakers. Table 2 shows the U.S. Census Bureau's reports on these trends for 1960 to 1990.

We can see in table 2 the growth of the urban Indian population, from about a quarter of American Indians in 1960 living in cities to more than one-half in 1990. Intermarriage with non-Indians grew even more dramatically, tripling from 1 in 5 married Indians with non-Indian spouses in 1960 to nearly 3 in 5 in

TABLE 1. *American Indian Population,*
1960–1990

Year	Number	% Change
1960	523,591	46
1970	792,730	51
1980	1,364,033	72
1990	1,878,285	38

TABLE 2. *Changes in the American Indian Population,*
1960–1990

Year	% Urban	% Inter-married	% Native Language Speakers
1960	27.9	15.0	—
1970	44.5	33.0	—
1980	54.6	48.0	26.1
1990	56.2	59.0	23.0

1990. And the number of Indians speaking a native language declined to less than one-quarter in 1990.

What do these demographic changes mean for American Indian identity and community? And what is the relationship among these changes in the Indian population and the rise of Indian activism and the subsequent changes in federal Indian policy during the past thirty years?

Simply put, federal Indian policies during the 1950s and 1960s that were designed to terminate and assimilate American Indians by moving Indian people off of reservations and into cities had some unintended consequences. These policies, along with other factors such as employment opportunities in cities, created an urban Indian population that was bicultural and intertribal, educated, wage-earning, and politically aware. Many of these urban Indians became activists during the Red Power period. The power of the moral claims and national attention that the Red Power activists brought to long-standing Indian grievances captured the attention of many Americans of Indian ancestry, who began to reassess their weakening connection to their Indian back-grounds and communities of origin. The changes in federal Indian policy that brought more autonomy and authority to tribal communities helped to open the door to a cultural, political, and economic renewal in many Indian home-lands, which further attracted urban Indians. The result was the resurgence of Native American self-identification as reflected in the U.S. Census data.

The increase in the Indian population during the past three decades has not been without its growing pains. The urbanization of the Native American population resulted in a widening gap between the life styles and world views of reservation and city dwellers. And as the urban Indian population con-tinued to grow, so did tensions between reservation and urban Indians. Ques-tions arose. Who should receive federal Indian funds — reservation or urban Indians? Who should receive tribal royalty and land claims payments? Who should have access to federal services such as health care or education? Who should represent all Indians on commissions and committees advising and deciding on federal Indian policy? Who should have access to scholarships and jobs set aside for Indians? Who should be recognized as legitimate Indian tribes? Who is an Indian?

These questions represent the most important and most difficult issues that Native America faces in the twenty-first century. The answers are not easy, and there are a variety of opinions about the correct approach to these issues. The documents in this last section of the book represent various ways that policy-makers and Indian people have proposed to answer these and other questions of Indian membership, rights, and cultural authenticity.

Report on Urban and Rural
Non-Reservation Indians

American Indian Policy Review Commission, 1976

U.S. Census Bureau reports have shown that the number of American Indians living in cities has grown dramatically in the past four decades, from less than 13 percent in 1950 to 56 percent in 1990. This massive move of Native Americans from reservation homelands into U.S. cities was the result of several factors, most importantly Indian military service during the Second World War and work in wartime industries, federal termination and urban relocation policies, and economic opportunities on and off reservations.

Like other Americans, Indians participated in the war effort during the Second World War by serving in the armed forces and by working in wartime industries. There were several consequences of this wartime movement of Indians off reservations during the 1940s: an increase in Indian family income, acculturation resulting from intertribal and interracial contact and wage labor market participation, and the formation of intertribal urban Indian communities and organizations.

Participation in the war effort also changed Indian outlooks and perspectives, particularly toward education. Many Indian people during that era were very suspicious of educational institutions, given the history of forced acculturation and abuse that many had suffered in church-run and government boarding schools. Wartime work in urban labor markets, however, made many native people aware of the usefulness of education in obtaining employment and advancing in their jobs. In addition, the benefits of the GI Bill permitted many Indian veterans to receive further education and vocational training after the war.

The relocation of Indians from reservations to cities was further spurred by federal policies designed to terminate Indian tribes. In the 1950s the federal government initiated the Employment Assistance Program and Adult Vocational Training Program. These programs involved the vocational training and relocation of reservation Indians to urban areas, where they were assisted by Bureau of Indian Affairs field staff in finding jobs and housing. During the period from 1952 to 1972, more than one hundred thousand American Indians were relocated to a number of targeted cities, such as Chicago, Cleveland, Dallas, Denver, Los Angeles, San Francisco, Oakland, Phoenix, San Jose, Salt Lake City, Seattle, Tulsa, and Oklahoma City. A large number of these "relocatees" returned to their reservations or moved back and forth between reservation and urban communities, and many found urban life intolerable and returned permanently to their home reservations. However, many remained in the cities to join other Indian urban migrants who had worked in wartime industries, served in the military, worked on the Santa Fe railroad, or migrated to cities on their own in search of work or to join friends and relatives; these reservation emigrants formed the mainstay of the urban Indian population.

The urbanization of the American Indian population created economic opportunities for many native people who had faced high levels of unemployment and often crushing poverty on home reservations. However, these urban Indians also experienced many difficulties in the cities, finding themselves without the rights, services, or connections to family and tradition of reservation Indians. Some urban Indian institutions helped fill this void — urban Indian centers, churches, clubs, and bars served as meeting places for reservation emigrants. However, as the urban Indian population grew during the 1960s and 1970s, the problems became more evident.

The American Indian Policy Review Commission established a special task force to investigate the condition of urban and rural non-reservation Indians and to make recommendations for solving some of the problems confronting this growing segment of the Indian population. The results of the work of the task force, which was chaired by Alfred G. Elgin (Pomo), were published in its final report in 1976.

We have conducted hearings and received testimony from urban and rural Indians throughout the United States. We have also examined the previous studies, reports, and testimony by urban and rural Indians. In general, our conclusions as outlined in detail in this report show:

That Indian people in substantial numbers came to urban areas because of a lack of employment in addition to other social and economic problems existing on the reservation, but have failed to make a desirable transition because of a lack of necessary and sufficient, continued support from the Federal Government, coupled with the indifference and misunderstandings, by and large, existing in the communities in which they have chosen to live. . . .

That these Indian people, as a result, have become victims of a Federal policy which denies services, if not thereby their very existence, while at the same time substantially subsidizing and contributing to an increase in the population of the urban multi-racial poor. . . .

That as a result of their situation and without regard to the slow and agonizing judicial process, the Federal Government must recognize the urban and rural Indians' immediate and undeniable needs. . . .

That the Federal Government must recognize the duality of the American Indians' citizenship and there must be a federal recognition of the trust, protection under the law, and services, the right to which cannot be terminated on an individual basis, without specific congressional action against the entire tribe. . . .

That the need and struggle for much needed services for the urban and rural Indian people has created a national split between reservation and urban Indians which has been exploited and encouraged by the executive departments for their own selfish purposes whenever it suits them. . . .

That the federal Government and the Congress must recognize already existing legal provisions provided by Congress with budgetary action to extend services " . . . for the benefit, care and assistance of Indians throughout the United States. . . ."

A 50-year review of the historical, legal and social developments underlying the urban and rural nonreservation Indian people's relationship with the federal Government and with the States and cities in which they have come to live, has been developed by the members of the Task Force on Urban and Rural Non-Reservation Indians. During those years there has been at first a gradual and then a steadily accelerating concern for the unfortunate circumstances of these transplanted tribal people.

The decades immediately following World War II, accompanied by its fluctuating political philosophies, has produced the policies and administrative mechanisms affecting the tribal people now known as urban Indians.

It has been the events of the last 10 years, however, that have precipitated the most intense American public and national Indian interest in these partially, if not wholly, disenfranchised people. These events and incidents were initiated by the urban and rural Indian people themselves as an act of violent rejection of the national, State, local, and indeed, Indian tribal indifference to their quiet desperation and overwhelming social need. Their history can best be described as a period in which many of them have been "relocated and dislocated" to urban and rural areas. In the case of the rural group, Federal services and even the recognition of tribal governments, with the exception of Oklahoma and Alaska, have been withdrawn gradually as a part of the national "withdrawal" and "termination" policies of the 1950's.

Present Federal program administrators still do not adequately provide for the rights of urban and rural Indian people. The bureaucrats' natural inclination to serve categories rather than people denies the very physical, geographical and legal existence of Indian people in many instances. Ordinarily, if the Federal Government was not inclined to assist an Indian temporarily in transit or permanently relocated from his reservation, then one might expect the local, State or county government to provide assistance. Since the predominant needs at both levels are highly subsidized by the Federal Government, then it is reasonable to assume that we are merely trying to decide from which pocket to pay the bill. Such has not been the case. The Federal Government absolves itself from responsibility when the Indian leaves the reservation, and then the State and local governments deny services when the Indian arrives.

Federal program policies dedicated to the assimilation of Indian people have created a situation in which half a million people now present a cultural and legal paradox; they are neither reservation nor urban, and neither culturally stable nor assimilated. Government policies meant to assimilate, if not eliminate, a portion of an entire race of people have created a large class of dissatisfied and disenfranchised people who, while being subjected to all the ills of urban America, have also been consistently denied services and equal protection guaranteed under the Constitution as well as by their rights as members of Federal Indian tribes.

RECOMMENDATIONS

1. An overall legislative mandate is required to recognize the 500,000 off-reservation Indians and their needs from the two Indian service agencies that Congress appropriates for under the Snyder Act of 1921 and its subsequent amendments. These two agencies are the Bureau of Indian Affairs and the Indian Health Service.

2. Congress should appropriate for 100,000 (20 percent of the off-reservation Indian population) off-reservation Indians' needs in education, housing, and job placement, and training assistance under the jurisdiction of the Bureau of Indian Affairs; an Assistant Commissioner of Off-Reservation Indian Affairs must be mandated under the law to cause

the implementation of the program delivery requirements for this segment of the population; and the recommended sum total should be no less than $40 million.

3. Congress should appropriate for 100,000 (20 percent of the off-reservation Indian population) off-reservation Indians' needs in health under the jurisdiction of the Indian Health Service; an Assistant Director of Off-Reservation Indian Affairs should be mandated under the law to cause the implementation of the program service delivery requirements for this segment of the population; and the recommended sum total should be no less than $50 million.

4. The legislative mandate should continue to provide trust responsibility for off-reservation Indian property owners under the jurisdiction of the Bureau of Indian Affairs.

5. The Assistant Director of Off-Reservation Indian Affairs, IHS, should advocate and coordinate with Federal/State agencies the various entitlements based upon citizenship, and for the proper effectiveness in delivering funds and services.

6. The Bureau of Indian Affairs and the Indian Health Service should recognize and designate a local unit of off-reservation government as chief local service provider for Indian people in need in urban areas.

7. The legislative mandate should require tribal governments and local Bureau of Indian Affairs Superintendents and the Indian Health Service Unit Directors to supply services to its members regardless of residency requirements. These specific programs should include the economic development programs under the Self-Determination Act under Public Law 93-638, 88 Stat. 2203, passed on January 4, 1975; and the Indian Finance Act under Public Law 93-626, 88 Stat. 77, passed on April 12, 1974.

8. Eligibility requirements for BIA's and IHS's services vary according to certain programs. For example, title 25 CFR 32.1 spells out eligibility requirements for the BIA's scholarship assistance for post-secondary education and specifically requires that nonreservation members of federally recognized tribes can receive scholarship grants only after the needs of the reservation residents are met. Title 25 CFR 261.2, which allows assistance for "nontribal Indians" under the new BIA housing and improvement program, spells out eligibility to a person of one-half or more degree Indian ancestry who is a descendant of a member of a tribe that has been federally recognized by treaty or otherwise. For uniformity of defining "Indian" and for purposes of establishing an off-reservation service population base, an Indian should be defined by respective tribal government

processes and an identification card or roll number be verified as the process to service Indians by those administering agents of programs for Indians. Eligibility for program services should be prioritized strictly upon Indian needs wherever an Indian resides.

9. Off-reservation Indians recommend an overall legislative mandate to remove the continual threat of termination of the trust to Indian Nations. This mandate is required to formally affirm the continuing U.S. responsibilities to preserve, protect, and guarantee Indian rights and property. This policy should not permit the liquidation of Indian lands and resources or terminate the trust relationship with any Indian tribe, but should establish a perpetual trust relationship.

10. An independent Indian agency to manage Federal funding and services as required to fulfill the trust responsibilities of the U.S. Government to Indian Nations is required. The independent agency would service the total 1 million Indian population needs whether they come from: (a) members of federally recognized tribes residing on or near the reservation; (b) tribal members wherever they reside; (c) members of all Indian tribes and communities; (d) all descendants of American Indians (including Alaskan Natives).

11. The Federal Government, preferably under the independent Indian agency jurisdiction, should develop a total Indian needs assessment every 5 years to determine policy formation and program development. Representation should come from: (a) members of federally recognized tribes residing on or near the reservation; (b) tribal members wherever they reside; (c) members of all Indian tribes and communities; (d) all descendants of American Indians (including Alaskan Natives).

12. Congress should mandate the Bureau of Indian Affairs to form a Council of Off-Reservation Advisers through a legally established referendum process under that jurisdiction, to develop immediate policy and program requirements that will be consistent with the need requirements under the $40 million appropriation for off-reservation Indians.

13. Congress should mandate the Indian Health Service to form a Council of Off-Reservation Advisers through a legally established referendum process under that jurisdiction, to develop immediate policy and program requirements that will be consistent with the need requirements under the $50 million appropriation for off-reservation Indians.

Definition of Indian: Tribal Membership

American Indian Policy Review Commission, 1977

In December 1973 the U.S. Senate passed a resolution introduced by Senator James Abourezk to establish the American Indian Policy Review Commission: "First, to affirm the unique and longstanding relationship between the Indian people and the U.S. Government, and to recognize that this unique relationship forms the basis to undertake fundamental reform in Indian policies, [and] . . . Second, to admit openly that the Federal trust responsibility for the Indian people has not been fulfilled, and to admit further that by that failure Indian people have been denied full opportunity." The pro-Indian tone of the resolution was weakened by an anti-Indian movement in the U.S. House of Representatives, led by Representative Lloyd Meeds, but the resolution eventually led to the creation of the American Indian Policy Review Commission (AIPRC) on January 3, 1975. The AIPRC established eleven commissions predominantly comprised of Indian members. The commissions held hearings around the United States on such topics as tribal government; Indian education; Indian health, alcohol, and drug abuse; and urban and rural non-reservation Indians.

The final recommendations of the American Indian Policy Review Commission were published in a final report on May 17, 1977. The recommendations strongly emphasized American Indian tribal sovereignty and called for the appropriation of funds for many new and expanded federal Indian programs. Given the opposition in Congress and the complexity and scope of its more than two hundred recommendations, the AIPRC had little real impact on the direction of federal Indian policy. It was, nonetheless, a commission that reflected the activist times that produced it. The AIPRC questioned much of federal Indian policy, pushed for expanded Indian rights, and asked much from the federal government.

The final report provided one answer to a question posed in "American Indian Population Trends": Who is an Indian? The AIPRC's answer stresses official tribal membership, a definition that excluded more and more native people as the Indian population grew during the 1960s, 1970s, and 1980s to include many Indians without formal tribal affiliations.

Who is an Indian? Early judicial decisions held that an Indian is a person who is ethnically or legally part of his or her tribe. Recognition by the tribe, once given, was not easily lost. This Commission has found, for example, that off-reservation Indian people identify themselves in the context of their tribal affiliation. The tribe's power to determine its own membership, that is, individual identity as an Indian, has been repeatedly recognized by the courts; the power derives from the tribe's status as a distinct political party. The tribe's power over its own membership is the starting point for any discussion of Indian identity.

But Congress can, and has, passed laws to define Indian status for some Federal purposes. Although no statute has laid down a general definition of "Indian," Congress has sometimes set standards to define Indian status for special purposes. Older legislation uses various degrees of Indian blood for different tribes, but those standards were often arbitrary and conflicted with tribal provisions. Recent congressional legislation, however, has avoided these conflicts and has given recognition to the primary tribal interest in membership by defining "Indian" as a member of an Indian tribe.

In the area of eligibility for Federal services, the Bureau of Indian Affairs and other Federal agencies must work within definitions given by Congress. For example, the Indian Reorganization Act of 1934 contains a definition of "Indian" for the implementation of that Act. That definition includes all members of federally recognized Indian tribes regardless of degree of Indian blood.

Despite that statutory definition, the Bureau of Indian Affairs and the Indian Health Service for many years defined "Indian" for purposes of employment preference as any person who was a member of a federally recognized Indian tribe and one-fourth or more Indian blood. This administrative criterion was challenged in court as being contrary to the definition in the IRA. The Government conceded in a final judgment that the statutory definition in the IRA controlled. Similarly, a recent Supreme Court case found that the BIA had acted improperly by denying welfare services to Indians living "near" reservations while providing services to those living "on" reservations. Again, the reasoning was that the BIA was acting contrary to congressional direction in denying benefits to tribal members.

In most circumstances, then, a person is an Indian if that person's tribe recognizes him or her as an Indian. That means that the tribe, as a political institution, has primary responsibility to determine tribal membership for purposes of voting in tribal elections, property distributions, exercise of treaty rights, Indian preference, and other rights arising from tribal membership. Many tribal provisions call for one-fourth degree of blood of the particular tribe but tribal provisions vary widely. A few tribes require as much as one-half degree of tribal blood and a small number permit any descendent of a tribal member to be enrolled, regardless of the blood quantum. For tribal purposes, that tribal definition is final. Absent express congressional action, the Bureau of Indian Affairs has no power to alter tribal determinations.

Petitioners for Federal Acknowledgment

Office of Federal Acknowledgment

Bureau of Indian Affairs, 1978–1997

In order for Indian communities to receive federal services, they must be officially designated or recognized by the Department of the Interior. Such recognition permits an Indian community to put land into trust; to contract with the Bureau of Indian Affairs for health care, education, and housing services; to establish tribal government and legal systems; and to put in place economic development projects. While most tribes have been recognized for decades, there are many Indian groups seeking official federal acknowledgment. In order to deal with such cases, in 1978 the federal government issued a set of criteria for tribal recognition to be administered by the Office of Federal Acknowledgment in the Bureau of Indian Affairs in the Interior Department. Indian communities seeking federal recognition had to petition the Office of Federal Acknowledgment to begin the process of proving that they were indeed legitimate Indian tribes and deserved federal services and acknowledgment. By 1997 there were 185 petitions, of which 37 were resolved one way or the other and 148 were still pending.

According to Bureau of Indian Affairs' Office of Federal Acknowledgment criteria, in order to qualify for official recognition, petitioning groups must provide evidence to show that "a single Indian group has existed since its first sustained contact with European cultures on a continuous basis to the present; that its members live in a distinct, autonomous community perceived by others as Indian; that it has maintained some sort of authority with a governing system by which its members abide; that all its members can be traced genealogically to an historic tribe." These criteria emphasize historical, social, and political continuity and stress the importance of a clearly identified continuous tribal membership.

The process of federal acknowledgment is a long and demanding one for Indian communities. During the nearly twenty years of its operation, the Federal Acknowledgment Office has processed only one-fifth of its cases — many of which were decided by congressional or executive action by the U.S. president. This list of petitioners for federal acknowledgment illustrates the diversity of groups seeking federal recognition.

Accohannock Indian Tribal Association, Inc.
Ahon-to-ays Ojibwa Band
Alleghenny Nation (Ohio Band)
Amah Band of Ohlone/Costanoan Indians
American Cherokee Confederacy
American Indian Council of Mariposa County
Amonsoquath Tribe of Cherokee
Ani-Stohini/Unami Nation
Antelope Valley Paiute Tribe
Apalachee Indian Tribe
Apalachee Indians of Louisiana
Apalachiocola Band of Creek Indians
Aroostook Band of Micmacs
Biloxi, Chitimacha Confederation of Muskogees, Inc.
Brothertown Indians of Wisconsin
Burt Lake Band of Ottawa and Chippewa Indians, Inc.
Caddo Adais Indians, Inc.
Cane Break Band of Eastern Cherokees
Canoncito Band of Navajos
Cherokee Indians of Georgia, Inc.
Cherokee Indians of Hoke County, Inc.
Cherokee Indians of Robeson and Adjoining Counties
Cherokee-Powhattan Indian Association
Cherokees of Jackson County, Alabama
Cherokees of Southeast Alabama
Chickahominy Indian Tribe
Chickamauga Cherokee Indian Nation of Arkansas and Missouri
Chicora Indian Tribe of South Carolina
Chicora-Waccamaw Indian People
Chinook Indian Tribe, Inc.
Choctaw-Apache Community of Ebarb
Choinumni Council
Christian Pembina Chippewa Indians
Chukchansi Yokotch Tribe of Coarsegold
Chukchansi Yokotch Tribe of Mariposa
Clifton Choctaw Indians
Coastal Band of Chumash Indians
Coastanoan Band of Carmel Mission Indians
Coharie Intra-Tribe Council, Inc.

Confederated Tribes of Coos, Lower Umpqua and Siuslaw Indians
Consolidated Bahwetig Ojibwas & Mackinac Tribe
Coree (Faircloth) Indians
Costanoan Ohlone Rumsen-Mutsun Tribe
Costanoan-Rumsen Carmel Tribe
Council for the Benefit of Colorado Winnebagos
Cowasuck Band-Abenaki People
Cow Creek Band of Umpqua Indians
Cowlitz Tribe of Indians
Creeks East of the Mississippi
Death Valley Timbi-Sha Shoshone Band
Delaware-Muncie
Delawares of Idaho
Dunlap Band of Mono Indians
Duwamish Indian Tribe
Eastern Pequot Indians of Connecticut
Esselen Tribe of Monterey County
Etowah Cherokee Nation
Federated Coast Miwok
Federation: Moorish Science Temple of America, Inc.
Federation of Old Plimoth Indian Tribes, Inc. Circa 1620
Fernandeno/Tataviam Tribe
Florida Tribe of Eastern Creek Indians
Four Hole Indian Organization/Edisto Tribe
Gabrielino/Tongva Tribal Council
Georgia Tribe of Eastern Cherokees, Inc. (Dahlonega)
Golden Hill Paugussett Tribe
Grand River Band Ottawa Council
Grand Traverse Band of Ottawa and Chippewa
Haliwa-Saponi
Hattadare Indian Nation
Hatteras Tuscarora Indians
Hayfork Band of Nor-El-Muk Wintu Indians
Huron Potawatomi, Inc.
Indian Canyon Band of Costanoan/Mutsun Indians of California
Ione Band of Miwok Indians
Jamestown Clallam Tribe
Jena Band of Choctaws
Juaneno Band of Mission Indians

Kah-Bay-Kah-Nong (Warroad Chippewa)
Katalla-Chilkat Tlingit Tribe of Alaska
Kaweah Indian Nation
Kern Valley Indian Community
Lac Vieux Desert Band of Lake Superior Chippewa Indians
Lake Superior Chippewa of Marquette, Inc.
Langley Band of the Chickamogee Cherokee Indians of the Southeastern
 United States
Little River Band of Ottawa Indians
Little Shell Band of North Dakota
Little Shell Tribe of Chippewa Indians of Montana
Little Traverse Bay Bands of Odawa Indians
Lower Muskogee Creek Tribe—East of the Mississippi
Lumbee Regional Development Assoc. Inc.
MaChis Lower Alabama Creek Indian Tribe
Maidu Nation
Mashpee Wampanoag
Match-E-Be-Nash-She-Wish Band of Pottawatomi Indians of Michigan
Mattaponi Tribe (Mattaponi Indian Reservation)
Meherrin Indian Tribe
Meherrin Tribe
Mendota Mdewakanton Dakota Community
Miami Nation of Indians of Indiana
Mohegan Indian Tribe
Mohegan Tribe and Nation
Monacan Indian Tribe, Inc.
Mono Lake Indian Community
Montauk Indian Nation
Mowa Band of Choctaw
Munsee-Thames River Delaware
Muwekma Indian Tribe
Nanticoke Indian Association
Nanticoke Lenni-Lenape Indians
Narragansett Indian Tribe
Nipmuc Nation (Hassanamisco Band)
Nipmuck Nation, Chaubunagungamaug Band
North Eastern U.S. Miami Inter-Tribal Council
North Fork Band of Mono Indians
Northern Cherokee Nation of Old Louisiana Territory

Northern Cherokee Tribe of Indians
Northwest Cherokee Wolf Band, SECC
Oakbrook Chumash
Occaneechi Band of Saponi Nation
Ohlone/Costanoan-Esselen Nation
Oklewaha Band of Seminole Indians
Pahrump Band of Paiutes
Paucatuck Eastern Pequot Indians of Connecticut
PeeDee Indian Association, Inc.
Piqua Sept of Ohio Shawnee Indians
Piro/Manso/Tiwa Indian Tribe of the Pueblo of San Juan de Guadalupe
Piscataway-Conoy Confederacy and Sub-Tribes, Inc.
Poarch Band of Creeks
Pocasset Wampanoag Indian Tribe
Point Au Chien Indian Tribe
Pokagon Potawatomi Indians of Indiana and Michigan
Pokanoket Tribe of the Wampanoag
Powhatan Renape Nation
Principal Creek Indian Nation
Ramapough Mountain Indians Inc.
Red Clay Inter-Tribal Indian Band, SECC
Revived Oachita Indians of Arkansas and America
St. Francis/Sokoki Band of Abenakis of Vermont
Salinan Nation
Salinan Tribe of Monterey County
Samish Indian Tribe
San Juan Southern Paiute Tribe
San Luis Rey Band of Mission Indians
Santee Indian Organization (White Oak Indian Community)
Schaghticoke Indian Tribe
Seminole Nation of Florida
Shasta Nation
Shawnee Nation U.K.B.
Shinnecock Tribe
Snohomish Tribe of Indians
Snoqualmie Indian Tribe
Snoqualmoo of Whidbey Island
Southeastern Indian Nation
Steilacoom Tribe

Swan Creek Black River Confederated Ojibwa Tribes
Tchinouk Indians
Texas Band of Traditional Kickapoos
The People of LaJunta (Jumano/Mescalero)
Tinoqui-Chalola Council of Kitanemuk and Yowlumne Tejon Indians
Tolowa Nation
Tsimshian Tribal Council
Tsnungwe Council
Tunica-Biloxi Indian Tribe
Tuscarora Indian Tribe, Drowning Creek Reservation
Tuscarora Nation of North Carolina
Tuscola United Cherokee Tribe of Florida and Alabama, Inc.
United Houma Nation, Inc.
United Lumbee Nation of North Carolina & America
United Rappahannock Tribe, Inc.
United Tribe of Shawnee Indians
Upper Kispoko Band of the Shawnee Nation
Upper Mattaponi Indian Tribe
Waccamaw Siouan Development Association, Inc.
Waccamaw-Siouan Indian Association
Wadatkuht Band of the Northern Paiutes of the Honey Lake Valley
Wampanoag Tribal Council of Gay Head
Washoe/Paiute of Antelope Valley
Western (Mashantucket) Pequot Tribe
Western Mohegan Tribe and Nation
Wintoon Indians
Wintu Indians of Central Valley, California
Wintu Tribe
Wukchumni Council
Wyandot Nation of Kansas
Yokayo
Yuchi Tribal Organization

An Open Letter to the Governor of Georgia

Wilma Mankiller

Principal Chief of the Cherokee Nation of Oklahoma, 1993

The petitioning of more than a hundred Indian communities to the Bureau of Indian Affairs' Office of Federal Acknowledgment was accompanied by an increase in the number of petitions to state governments by Indian groups seeking state recognition. Most of these petitions were not successful, but some were. In the spring of 1993 the legislature of the state of Georgia extended state recognition to three Indian communities, two of which claimed Cherokee ancestry. The tribes' petition for recognition had alarmed two federally recognized Cherokee tribes, the Cherokee Nation of Oklahoma and the Eastern Band of Cherokees in North Carolina. The decision of the Georgia legislature to recognize these new Cherokee tribes prompted Wilma Mankiller, then principal chief of the Cherokee Nation of Oklahoma, to write an open letter to Zell Miller, the governor of Georgia, expressing her disapproval of the Georgia legislature's decision and requesting repeal of the recognition legislation.

Dear Governor Zell Miller:

I was shocked and dismayed to learn that the Georgia legislature passed a law recognizing three "Indian tribes," two of them purportedly Cherokee! On Jan. 4, 1993, I sent a letter expressing concern about the questionable activities of these "Cherokee" groups.

Even Jonathan L. Taylor, principal chief of the Eastern Band of Cherokee Indians, had sent a letter urging you not to sign H B 265 in March.

Our concern deals with states creating Indian tribes without specific recognition criteria. We pointed out how the United States Constitution gives Congress "the power . . . to regulate Commerce with foreign nations, and among the several states, and with Indian tribes. . . ." The United States has a complex set of criteria and a federal acknowledgement process each tribe must undergo to determine recognition eligibility. Anyone even minimally versed in Indian legal or political affairs is aware that federal recognition of an Indian tribe is a very serious matter.

You turned our Jan. 4, 1993, letter over to Frank Bates, executive assistant, who in turn, forwarded the letter to Carmeleta Monteith, chairperson for the Georgia Task Force on American Indian Concerns. Ms. Monteith, a member of the Eastern Band of Cherokee Indians, is also very concerned about entities using the Cherokee name and posing as Indian tribes.

After our registrar, Lee Fleming, spoke with Ms. Monteith, we were relieved to know that you had within your administration individuals who are cognizant of Indian affairs and understand the federal-to-Indian tribal relationships. However, it appears that even with Ms. Monteith's concerns, these organizations are now "tribes."

Now Georgia state recognized tribes using the Cherokee name will be seeking federal recognition. The Cherokee Nation and probably the Eastern Band of Cherokees in North Carolina will expend precious time and resources to oppose their future attempts at federal recognition.

On Aug. 11, 1992, the Cherokee Nation and the Eastern Band in joint council passed a resolution to protect the use of the Cherokee name and to do something concerning the 50 groups, clubs, and/or associations that have formed throughout the United States claiming to be the official Cherokee Nation or have been using the Cherokee Nation's name, history, culture, and reputation, giving the appearance of being the official Cherokee Nation.

Perhaps efforts can be made to repeal this recent legislation in the next session of the General Assembly. The Cherokee Nation is offended both by the fact that our earlier concerns were completely ignored and the fact that these "tribes" were created by an amendment to a piece of legislation at the end of the legislative session.

Wilma Mankiller
Principal Chief
Cherokee Nation of Oklahoma
Tahlequah, Oklahoma

Statement of Ethnic Fraud

Association of American Indian and Alaska Native Professors

February, 1993

By the early 1990s the growing number of Americans claiming an Indian ancestry and identity and the increasing number of Indian communities seeking federal recognition began to raise concerns among more established and recognized Indian communities and organizations. There were increasing worries
about the distribution of scarce federal resources to a growing number of Indian individuals and communities. The Republican cuts in the federal Indian
budget during the 1980s had begun to take a toll on reservation programs.
The backlash against affirmative action that had been fueled by the statements and policies of the Reagan and Bush administrations was putting at risk
many of the gains made by Indian people during the Red Power era.

The Association of American Indian and Alaska Native Professors (AAIANP)
expressed what was a growing question about who should and should not
receive preference in scholarships and hiring in colleges and universities. Like
the American Indian Policy Review Commission and the Indian Arts and Crafts
Act, the AAIANP came down on the side of tribal membership as the yardstick
to measure Indianness and Indian rights — a definition of ethnic authenticity
that threatened to label many nontribal Indians as "ethnic frauds."

We, the Association of American Indian and Alaska Native Professors,
hereby establish and present our position on ethnic fraud and offer recommendations to ensure the accuracy of American Indian/Alaska Native
identification in American colleges and universities. This statement is developed over concern about the racial exploitation of American Indians
and Alaska Natives in American colleges and universities.

We think it is necessary to establish our position on ethnic fraud because of documented incidents of abuse. This statement is intended to
assist universities in their efforts to develop culturally diverse campus
communities. The implications of this statement are threefold:

(1) to assist in the selection process that encourages diversity among
students, staff, faculty, and administration, (2) to uphold the integrity
of institutions and enhance the credibility with American Indian/
Alaska Native Nations/Tribes, and (3) to recognize the importance of

American Indian/Alaska Native Nations/Tribes in upholding their sovereign and legal right as nations to determine membership.

Therefore, the following prioritized recommendations are intended to affirm and ensure American Indian/Alaska Native identity in the hiring process. We are asking that colleges and universities:

- Require documentation of enrollment in a state or federally recognized nation/tribe with preference given to those who meet this criterion;
- Establish a case-by-case review process for those unable to meet the first criterion;
- Include American Indian/Alaska Native faculty in the selection process;
- Require a statement from the applicant that demonstrates past and future commitment to American Indian/Alaska Native concerns;
- Require higher education administrators to attend workshops on tribal sovereignty and meet with local tribal officials; and
- Advertise vacancies at all levels on a broad scale and in tribal productions.

Federal Indian Identification Policy

A Usurpation of Indigenous Sovereignty in North America

M. Annette Jaimes

Despite the attractiveness to many Indians of official tribal enrollment as the easiest and most reliable way to determine American Indian rights and ethnic authenticity, there were also many voices raised in opposition to this narrow definition of Indianness.

Some of those voices were coming from inside reservation communities. Due to intermarriage of tribal members with nontribal members and non-Indians, many tribes found themselves having to make membership decisions or deny membership to an increasing number of Indian children whose degree of Indian ancestry was less than tribal law required. In many cases, these Indian children were being raised on the reservation by their mothers and fathers, creating situations where only the parents were tribal members, but not their children. *Santa Clara Pueblo v. Martinez* was a landmark court case upholding the rights of tribal governments to exclude the children of tribal members who did not meet tribal enrollment criteria. In this case, Julia Martinez, "a fullblooded member of the Santa Clara Pueblo" who resided on the Santa Clara reservation in New Mexico, married a Navajo man in 1941. Although their children were raised on the Santa Clara reservation, spoke the Tewa language, and lived there as adults, they were excluded from tribal membership because of the tribe's requirement that only children whose fathers were Santa Claran could be members of the tribe. Martinez's children thus were not permitted to hold tribal office, vote in tribal elections, live on the reservation after their mother's death, or inherit her interests in tribal communal lands. In 1978 the U.S. Supreme Court upheld the Santa Clara tribal ordinance excluding the Martinez children from tribal membership and thus affirmed tribal rights to deny membership on the basis of the gender of the parent.

Alternatives to tribal enrollment as the basis for determining Indian rights and status have run the gamut from complete reliance on self-definition (if an individual claims to be an Indian, then he or she is an Indian) to requirements that an individual must have at least one-half tribal ancestry and reside on the reservation. M. Annette Jaimes, an author and activist, criticizes the current common practice by Indian tribes of measuring and certifying membership by calculating an individual's "blood quantum" or degree of Indian ancestry. Jaimes finds that this emphasis on blood quantum is inherently racist, creates divisions among Indians, and is guaranteed to define Indians out of existence as the rate of intermarriage increases. She argues instead for a view of tribal membership that emphasizes citizenship and that parallels some of the ways that countries around the world determine who their citizens are: by birth, marriage, or naturalization.

By all accepted standards of international jurisprudence and human decency, American Indian peoples whose territory lies within the borders of the United States hold compelling legal and moral rights to be treated as fully sovereign nations. It is axiomatic that any such national entity is inherently entitled to exercise the prerogative of determining for itself criteria by which its citizenry, or "membership," is to be recognized by other sovereign nations. This is a principle that applies equally to superpowers such as the U.S. and to non-powers such as Grenada and Monaco. In fact, it is a tenet so widely understood and imbedded in international law, custom, and convention that it bears no particular elaboration here.

Contrary to virtually universal practice, the United States has opted to preempt unilaterally the rights of many North American indigenous nations to engage in this most fundamental level of internal decision making. Instead, in pursuit of the interests of their own state rather than those of the nations that are thereby affected, federal policymakers have increasingly imposed "Indian identification standards" of their own design. Typically centering upon a notion of "blood quantum" — not especially different in its conception from the eugenics code once adopted by Nazi Germany in its effort to achieve "racial purity," or currently utilized by South Africa to segregate Blacks and "coloreds" — this aspect of U.S. policy has increasingly wrought havoc with the American Indian sense of nationhood (and often the individual sense of self) over the past century.

The eventual outcome of federal blood-quantum policies can be described as little other than genocidal in their final implications. As historian Patricia Nelson Limerick recently summarized the process:

> Set the blood quantum at one-quarter, hold to it as a rigid standard definition of Indians, let intermarriage proceed as it had for centuries, and eventually Indians will be defined out of existence. When that happens, the federal government will be freed of its persistent "Indian problem."

Already, this conclusion receives considerable validation in the experience of the Indians of California, such as the Juaneño. Pursuant to the

"Pit River Consolidated Land Settlement" of the 1970s, in which the government purported to "compensate" many of the small California bands for lands expropriated during the course of non-Indian "settlement" in that state (at less than 50 cents per acre), the Juaneño and a number of other "Mission Indians" were simply declared to be "extinct." This policy was pursued despite the fact that substantial numbers of such Indians were known to exist, and that the government was at the time issuing settlement checks to them. The tribal rolls were simply ordered closed to any new additions, despite the fact that many of the people involved were still bearing children, and their population might well have been expanding. It was even suggested in some instances that children born after an arbitrary cut-off date should be identified as "Hispanic" or "Mexican" in order that they benefit from federal and state services to minority groups.

When attempting to come to grips with the issues raised by such federal policies, the recently "dissolved" California groups, as well as a number of previously unrecognized ones such as the Gay Head Wampanoags (long described as extinct), confronted a catch-22 situation worthy of Joseph Heller. This rested in the federal criteria for recognition of Indian existence to the present day:

1. An Indian is a member of any federally recognized Indian tribe. To be federally recognized, an Indian Tribe must be comprised of Indians.
2. To gain federal recognition, an Indian Tribe must have a land base. To secure a land base, an Indian Tribe must be federally recognized.

As Shoshone activist Josephine C. Mills put it in 1964, "There is no longer any need to shoot down Indians in order to take away their rights and land [or to wipe them out] . . . legislation is sufficient to do the trick legally."

The notion of genocidal implications in all this receives firm reinforcement from the increasing federal propensity to utilize residual Indian land bases as dumping grounds for many of the more virulently toxic by-products of its advanced technology and industry. By the early 70's, this practice had become so pronounced that the Four Corners and Black Hills regions, two of the more heavily populated locales (by Indians) in this country, had been semi-officially designated as prospective "National Sacrifice Areas" in the interests of projected U.S. energy development. This, in turn, provoked Russell Means to observe that such a move would turn the Lakota, Navajo, Laguna, and other native nations into "national sacrifice peoples."

Of late, there have been encouraging signs that American Indians of many perspectives and political persuasions have begun to arrive at common conclusions regarding the use to which the federal government had been putting their identity and the compelling need for Indians to finally reassert complete control over this vital aspect of their lives. For instance, Dr. Frank Ryan, a liberal and rather establishmentarian Indian who has served as the director of the federal Office of Indian Education, began during the early 1980s to reach some rather hard conclusions about the policies of his employers. Describing the federal blood-quantum criteria for benefits eligibility in the educational arena as a "racist policy," Ryan went on to term it nothing more than "a shorthand method for denying Indian children admission to federal schools [and other programs]." He concluded that "The power to determine tribal membership has always been an essential attribute of inherent tribal sovereignty," and called for abolition of federal guidelines on the question of Indian identity without any lessening of federal obligations to the individuals and groups affected. The question of the (re)adoption of blood-quantum standards by the Indian Health Service, proposed during the 80's by the Reagan administration, has served as even more of a catalyst. The National Congress of American Indians, never a bastion of radicalism, took up the issue at its 43rd Annual Convention, in October 1986. The NCAI produced a sharply worded statement rejecting federal identification policy:

[T]he federal government, in an effort to erode tribal sovereignty and reduce the number of Indians to the point where they are politically, economically and culturally insignificant, [is being censured by] many of the more than 500 Indian leaders [attending the convention].

The statement went on to condemn:

. . . a proposal by the Indian Health Service to establish blood quotas for Indians, thus allowing the federal government to determine who is Indian and who is not, for the purpose of health care. Tribal leaders argue that *only* the individual tribe, not the federal government, should have the right, and many are concerned that this debate will overlap [as it has, long since] into Indian education and its regulation as well [emphasis added].

Charles E. Dawes, Second Chief of the Ottawa Indian Tribe of Oklahoma, took the convention position much further about the same time:

What could not be completed over a three hundred year span [by force of arms] may now be completed in our life-span by administrative law . . . What I am referring to is the continued and expanded use of blood quantum to determine eligibility of Indian people for government entitlement programs . . . [in] such areas as education, health care, management and economic assistance . . . [obligations] that the United States government imposed upon itself in treaties with sovereign Indian nations. . . . We as tribal leaders made a serious mistake in accepting [genetic] limits in educational programs, and we must not make the same mistake again in health programs. On the contrary, we must fight any attempt to limit any program by blood quantum every time there is mention of such a possibility . . . we simply cannot give up on this issue — ever. . . . Our commitment as tribal leaders must be to eliminate any possibility of *genocide* for our people by administrative law. We must dedicate our efforts to insuring that . . . Native American people[s] will be clearly identified without reference to blood quantum . . . and that our sovereign Indian Nations will be recognized as promised [emphasis added].

On the Pine Ridge Reservation in South Dakota, the Oglala Lakota have become leaders in totally abandoning blood quantum as a criterion for tribal enrollment, opting instead to consider factors such as residency on the reservation, affinity to and knowledge of, as well as service to, the Oglala people. This follows the development of a recent "tradition" of Oglala militancy in which tribal members played a leading role in challenging federal conceptions of Indian identity during the 1972 Trail of Broken Treaties takeover of BIA headquarters in Washington, and seven non-Indian members of the Vietnam Veterans Against War were naturalized as citizens of the "Independent Oglala Nation" during the 1973 siege of Wounded Knee. In 1986, at a meeting of the United Sioux Tribes in Pierre, South Dakota, Oglala representatives lobbied the leaders of other Lakota reservations to broaden their own enrollment criteria beyond federal norms. This is so, despite recognition that "in the past fifty years, since the Indian Reorganization Act of 1934, tribal leaders have been reluctant to recognize blood from individuals from other tribes [or any one else]."

In Alaska, the Haida have produced a new draft constitution which offers a full expression of indigenous sovereignty, at least insofar as the identity of citizenry is concerned. The Haida draft begins with those who are now acknowledged as members of the Haida nation and posits that all those who marry Haidas will also be considered eligible for naturalized citizenship (just as in any other nation). The children of such unions would also be Haida citizens from birth, regardless of their degree of Indian blood, and children adopted by Haidas would also be considered citizens. On Pine Ridge, a similar "naturalization" plank had surfaced in the 1983 TREATY platform upon which Russell Means attempted to run for the Oglala Lakota tribal presidency before being disqualified at the insistence of the BIA.

An obvious problem that might be associated with this trend is that even though Indian nations have begun to recognize their citizens by their own standards rather than those of the federal government, the government may well refuse to recognize the entitlement of unblooded tribal members to the same services and benefits as any other. In fact, there is every indication that this is the federal intent, and such a disparity of "status" stands to heighten tensions among Indians, destroying their fragile rebirth of unity and solidarity before it gets off the ground. Federal policy in this regard is, however, also being challenged.

Most immediately, this concerns the case of Diane Zarr, an enrolled member of the Sherwood Valley Pomo Band of Indians, who is less than one-quarter degree of Indian blood. On September 11, 1980, Zarr filed an application for higher educational grant benefits, and was shortly rejected as not meeting quantum requirements. Zarr went through all appropriate appeal procedures before filing, on July 15, 1983, a suit in federal court, seeking to compel award of her benefits. This was denied by the district court on April 2, 1985. Zarr appealed and, on September 26, 1985, the lower court was reversed on the basis of the "Snyder Act" (25 U.S.C. s 297), which precludes discrimination based solely on racial criteria. Zarr received her grant, setting a very useful precedent for the future.

Still, realizing that the utility of the U.S. courts will necessarily be limited, a number of Indian organizations have recently begun to seek to bring international pressure to bear on the federal government. The Indian Law Resource Center, National Indian Youth Council, and, for a time, the International Indian Treaty Council, have repeatedly taken Native American issues before the United Nations Working Group on Indigenous Populations (a component of the U.N. Commission on Human Rights) in Geneva, Switzerland, since 1977. Another forum that has been utilized for this purpose has been the Fourth Russell International Tribunal on the Rights of the Indians of the Americas, held in Rotterdam, Netherlands, in 1980. Additionally, delegations from various Indian nations and organizations have visited, often under auspices of the host governments, more than thirty countries during the past decade.

The history of the U.S. imposition of this standard of identification upon American Indians is particularly ugly. Its cost to Indians has involved millions of acres of land, the water by which to make much of this land agriculturally useful, control over vast mineral resources that might have afforded them a comfortable standard of living, and the ability to form themselves into viable and meaningful political blocks at any level. Worse, it has played a prominent role in bringing about their generalized psychic disempowerment; if one is not allowed even to determine for one's self, or within one's peer group, the answer to the all-important question "Who am I?" what possible personal power can one feel s/he possesses? The negative impact, both physically and psychologically, of this process upon succeeding generations of Native Americans in the United States is simply incalculable.

The blood-quantum mechanism most typically used by the federal government to assign identification to individuals over the years is as racist as any conceivable policy. It has brought about the systematic marginalization and eventual exclusion of many more Indians from their own cultural/national designation than it has retained. This is all the more apparent when one considers that, while one-quarter degree of blood has been the norm used in defining Indian-ness, the quantum has varied from time to time and place to place; one-half blood was the standard utilized in the case of the Mississippi Choctaws and adopted in the Wheeler-Howard Act; one sixty-fourth was utilized in establishing the Santee rolls in Nebraska. It is hardly unnatural, under the circumstances, that federal policy has set off a ridiculous game of one-upmanship in Indian country: "I'm more Indian than you" and "You aren't Indian enough to say (or do, or think) that" have become common assertions during the second half of the 20th century.

The restriction of federal entitlement funds to cover only the relatively few Indians who meet quantum requirements, essentially a cost-cutting policy at its inception, has served to exacerbate tensions over the identity issue among Indians. It has established a scenario in which it has been perceived as profitable for one Indian to cancel the identity of her/his neighbor as means of receiving her/his entitlement. Thus, a bitter divisiveness has been built into Indian communities and national policies, sufficient to preclude our achieving the internal unity necessary to offer any serious challenge to the status quo. At every turn, U.S. practice vis-a-vis American Indians is indicative of an advanced and extremely successful system of colonialism.

Fortunately, increasing numbers of Indians are waking up to the fact that this is the case. The recent analysis and positions assumed by such politically diverse Indian nations, organizations, and individuals as Frank Ryan and Russell Means, the National Congress of American Indians and the Indian Law Resource Center, the Haida and the Oglala, are a very favorable sign. The willingness of the latter two nations simply to defy federal standards and adopt identification and enrollment policies in line with their own interests and traditions is particularly important. Recent U.S. court decisions, such as that in the *Zarr* case, and growing international attention and concern over the circumstances of Native Americans are also hopeful indicators that things may be at long last changing for the better.

We are currently at a crossroads. If American Indians are able to continue the positive trend in which we reassert our sovereign prerogative to control the criteria of our own membership, we may reasonably assume that we will be able to move onward, into a true process of decolonialization and reestablishment of ourselves as functioning national entities. The alternative, of course, is that we will fail, continue to be duped into bickering over the question of "who's Indian" in light of federal guidelines, and thus facilitate not only our own continued subordination, expropriation, and colonization, but ultimately our own statistical extermination.

American Indian Population Projections

U.S. Office of Technology Assessment, 1980–2080

The population trends reported by the U.S Census paint a picture of a growing Indian population during the twenty-first century, with increasing numbers of Indians of mixed ancestry. But just how much growth will there be in the number of American Indians, and what will be the ancestry or "blood quantum" of those twenty-first-century Native Americans?

One answer to this question is that there will likely be not only more Indians with less than one-quarter Indian ancestry, but also large increases in the number of Indians with more than one-quarter or one-half Indian ancestry. This was the conclusion reached by the U.S. Office of Technology Assessment (OTA) in 1986 when it prepared a series of Indian population projections for the Indian Health Service.

The OTA's population projection described under Scenario IV below is probably the most accurate of the four projections since it is based on actual numbers of Indians reported in the U.S. Census and since it adjusts birthrates for accuracy. Scenario IV predicts that there will be 12 million Indians in the year 2080. Of those 12 million, the OTA predicts that 57.6 percent will be one-quarter or more Indian ancestry and that 15.6 percent will be one-half or more Indian ancestry. Those percentages translate into 7 million "quarter-bloods" and 2 million "half-bloods" in 2080. The latter figure is more than the total number of Indians in the United States today!

If these estimates are correct, the Indian population will continue to grow in the twenty-first century just as it has in the last century. Although most of these future Indians will have less than half Indian ancestry, by 2080 more than half of Indians will be at least one-quarter Indian ancestry. Despite these projections, Indian America will also continue to become increasingly urban and bicultural because of ongoing patterns of urbanization, intermarriage, education, and employment. The diversity of the twenty-first-century American Indian population will continue to raise important questions about the membership, identity, and rights of these next generations.

Four Projections of the Effect of Intermarriage
on the Number of Indian Descendants
U.S. Office of Technology Assessment
1986

The U.S. Bureau of Census reported in 1985 that both American Indian women and men were marrying non-Indians at rates exceeding 50 percent. Births resulting from unions of Indians and non-Indians, whether consensual or within marriage, will greatly increase the number of persons claiming to be of Indian descent and will decrease the blood quantum of the "average" Indian in the long run. Especially with respect to health care provided by IHS, the implications of this projected growth for tribes in determining who is an Indian and for services provided on the basis of Indian descendancy are that growth must be accompanied by increasing services or by eventually restricting services to fewer individuals.

To show the range of future possibilities in the composition of the Indian population, OTA created four different scenarios, varying the out-marriage rates and distribution of the base population into blood quantum groups. In Scenario I, all Indians are assumed to be full-blooded in the base year, and all unions are presumed to be with other Indians; hence, all offspring would also be full-blooded Indians. In Scenario II, the assumption again is that in the base year all Indians are full-blooded, but the 53 percent outmarriage rate reported by the Bureau of the Census is used to assign probabilities that births resulting from Indian/non-Indian unions will fall into specific blood quantum groups. The use of "marriage rate" and "outmarriage rate" is meant to represent "unions-potential for births," not actual marriages. Marriage and outmarriage "rates" are used to determine potential populations of females to which the fertility rates will be applied to calculate births. In Scenario III, an approximation of the 1950 blood quantum information is used; i.e., that 60.2 percent of all Indians are full-blooded, 26.7 percent are half, 9.5 percent are one-fourth and 3.6 percent are less than one-fourth. These figures have been adjusted by including an approximated blood quantum distribution for Oklahoma area Indians. The Oklahoma area, which comprised 21 percent of the BIA population in 1950, was assumed to have a blood quantum distribution equal to that of Indians in the Sacramento area. A constant outmarriage rate of 53 percent was applied across all blood quantum groups. Scenario IV is almost identical to Scenario III, except that the rate at which births result from Indian and non-Indian unions is lowered to 40 percent. The rate has been adjusted downward to take into consideration births resulting from Indian unions occurring consensually that may not be reflected in the census data on marriage. The information generated by the latter three projections is used to examine variations in the future size of the Indian population at certain blood quantum thresholds.

All of the data for OTA's population projections were made available by the IHS Program Statistics Branch and the U.S. Bureau of the Census. Insofar as the projection model yields results in actual numbers, OTA advises that they be used cautiously. The data on which OTA's projections are based are presented below along with a description of the four scenarios outlined above. Results for 1985 and each 20-year period after the base year through 2080 are printed in a summary table at the end of this section. Twenty-year periods are used to approximate one generation, though in many areas, a generation in the Indian population may be less than 20 years.

SCENARIO I

As a lower bound, assuming a 100 percent blood quantum (all Indians are full-blooded) in the base year and presuming that all births result from unions of Indians with Indians, the 1980 Indian population of 1.3 million doubles in about 45 years and grows to roughly 4.6 million Indians in 2080. The unrealistic aspects of this scenario are that all Indians in 1980 were not full-blooded, and the effect of out-unions is not captured. Subsequent scenarios use assumptions that come progressively closer to representing existing factors likely to influence Indian population growth.

SCENARIO II

We assume again that all Indians are full-blooded in the base year but use an outmarriage rate of 53 percent as reported by the Bureau of the Census for 1980 to assign offspring to one of nine blood quantum groups. For example, the child of two full-blooded Indians remains in the same blood quantum group as his or her parents; the child born of a mother who is one-quarter Indian and a father who is one-half is assigned to the three-eighths group. Assignment of offspring to specific blood quantum groups works correspondingly for succeeding generations.

TABLE 3. *Population Projection Summary*

All Indians and Indian Descendants by Degree of Indian Ancestry,
1980–2080

	Projection Year					
	1980	2000	2020	2040	2060	2080
Scenario I						
Total Indians (100% ancestry)	1,295,450	1,898,428	2,352,991	2,956,629	3,687,594	4,606,002
Scenario II						
Total Indians	1,295,450	2,213,466	3,727,826	6,243,954	10,606,557	17,916,076
% ½ or more	100.0	100.0	81.2	56.9	32.9	15.7
% ¼ or more	100.0	100.0	100.0	92.3	75.7	55.2
Scenario III						
Total Indians	1,295,450	2,213,517	3,691,144	6,061,475	9,929,455	15,767,206
% ½ or more	86.9	77.8	57.4	36.1	18.8	8.2
% ¼ or more	96.4	93.4	87.4	76.0	58.8	41.1
Scenario IV						
Total Indians	1,295,450	2,114,168	3,332,863	5,173,122	8,044,218	12,321,204
% ½ or more	86.9	80.1	64.7	46.6	29.1	15.6
% ¼ or more	96.4	94.2	90.5	83.2	71.5	57.6

Source: U.S. Office of Technology Assessment, *Indian Health Care* (Washington DC: U.S. Government Printing Office, 1986).

SCENARIO III

The third scenario assumes a distribution of Indians in the 1980 base year into blood groups reflecting the findings of the 1950 BIA data with an approximated value for Oklahoma. The total Indian population of all age groups is distributed such that 60.2 percent are assumed to be full-blooded, 26.7 percent are one-half, 9.5 percent are one-fourth, and 3.6 percent are less than one-fourth. For each blood group the outmarriage rates to non-Indians are the same as in Scenario II; we have assumed that the marriage rates, or rather "union" rates which produce children, between Indians in different blood groups are determined by the proportions of Indians of marriageable age in each group.

This scenario attempts to account for births that occur to Indians out of wedlock that might not have been reflected in the census data on marriage. The only assumption changed in Scenario IV from the assumptions in Scenario III is the outmarriage rate, which is lowered to 40 percent. Again, the base population in 1980 is distributed by Indian blood quantum with 60.2 percent of all males and females assumed to be full-blooded, 26.7 percent are one-half, 9.5 percent are one-fourth, and 3.6 percent are less than one-fourth.

References and Further Reading

American Indian Policy Review Commission. 1976. *Task Force on Urban and Rural Non-Reservation Indians, Final Report*. Washington D C: Government Printing Office.

American Indian Policy Review Commission. 1977. *Final Report*. Washington D C: Government Printing Office.

Eschbach, Karl. 1995. "The Enduring and Vanishing American Indian: American Indian Population Growth and Intermarriage in 1990." *Ethnic and Racial Studies* 18 : 89–108.

Harris, David. 1994. "The 1990 Census Count of American Indians: What Do the Numbers Really Mean?" *Social Science Quarterly* 75 : 580–93.

Jaimes, M. Annette. 1992. "Federal Indian Identification Policy: A Usurpation of Indigenous Sovereignty in North America." In *The State of Native North America: Genocide, Colonization, and Resistance*, ed. M. A. Jaimes. Boston: South End.

Johnson, Troy. 1996. *The Occupation of Alcatraz Island: Indian Self-Determination and the Rise of Indian Activism*. Urbana: University of Illinois Press.

Nagel, Joane. 1996. *American Indian Ethnic Renewal: Red Power and the Resurgence of Identity and Culture*. New York: Oxford University Press.

Russell, George. 1997. *American Indian Facts of Life: A Profile of Today's Tribes and Reservations*. Phoenix: Russell.

Sandefur, Gary D., Ronald R. Rindfuss, and Barney Cohen. 1996. *Changing Numbers, Changing Needs: American Indian Demography and Public Health*. Washington D C: National Academy Press.

Snipp, C. Matthew. 1989. *American Indians: The First of This Land*. New York: Russell Sage Foundation.

Sorkin, Alan. 1978. *The Urban American Indian*. Lexington M A: Lexington.

Thornton, Russell. 1987. *American Indian Holocaust and Survival*. Norman: University of Oklahoma Press.

U.S. Census Bureau. 1993. *We the First Americans*. Washington D C: Government Printing Office.

U.S. Office of Technology Assessment. 1986. *Indian Health Care*. Washington D C: Government Printing Office.

Reprint Acknowledgments

Acknowledgment is made for permission to reprint the following materials:

American Indian Warriors: Fishing Rights and the Vietnam War

Woody Kipp's statement is from Kipp, "The Eagles I Fed Who Did Not Love Me,"
American Indian Culture and Research Journal 18, no. 4: 213–32. Reprinted by
permission of the American Indian Studies Center, UCLA. © Regents of the
University of California.

This Country Was a Lot Better Off When the Indians Were Running It

From Vine Deloria Jr., "This Country Was a Lot Better Off When the Indians
Were Running It," *The New York Times Magazine*, March 8, 1970. © 1970 by
The New York Times Company. Reprinted by permission.

Women of All Red Nations

The statement is reproduced with the permission of Lorelei DeCora.

The Longest Walk

From Wilcomb E. Washburn, "An Indian Media Play," *New York Times*, July 20,
1978, and Joseph de la Cruz, "On Knowing What Is Good for the American
Indian," *New York Times*, August 2, 1978. Copyright © 1978 by the New York
Times Co. Reprinted by permission.

The Activist Legacy of Red Power

The statement by Janet McCloud is reproduced by permission of Janet
McCloud. The statement by Dennis Banks is from his foreword to *Native
America: Portrait of the Peoples*, ed. Duane Champaigne (Detroit: Visible Ink
Press, 1994).

Indian Self-Government

From Felix S. Cohen, "Indian Self-Government," in *The Legal Conscience: Selected Papers of Felix S. Cohen*, ed. Lucy Kramer Cohen. © 1970 by Yale University Press. Reprinted by permission.

Indian Child Welfare Act

The statement by Cecilia Fire Thunder is from *The Indian Child Welfare Act:
Unto the Seventh Generation*, ed. Troy R. Johnson, by permission of the American Indian Studies Center, UCLA. © Regents of the University of California.

Nuclear Waste Policy Act

"No Nuclear Waste on Indian Land" is reprinted with the permission of Grace
Thorpe

Indian Gaming Regulatory Act

"Tribal Leaders Want Gaming Bill Withdrawn" is reprinted, with permission,
from *American Indian Report*, August 1994.

Rough Rock Demonstration and Community Schools

"Celebrating 30 Years of Navajo Education" is reprinted with permission of Rough Rock Community School.

Navajo Community College / Diné College

The Diné College Mission Statement is reprinted, with permission, from the Diné College General Catalog 1997–1998.

The Black Hills and Camp Yellow Thunder

The excerpt is reprinted from Peter Matthiessen, *In The Spirit of Crazy Horse*, afterword by Martin Garbus (New York: Viking, 1991), 516–18. Copyright © 1980, 1983, 1991 by Peter Matthiessen. Afterword copyright © 1991 by Martin Garbus. Used by permission of Viking Penguin, a division of Penguin Putnam Inc.

Lyng v. Northwest Indian Cemetery Protective Association

The statements by Vine Deloria Jr. are from Deloria, "Trouble in High Places," in *The State of Native North America: Genocide, Colonization, and Resistance*, ed. M. Annette Jaimes (Boston: South End Press, 1992), 283–87. Reprinted with permission from the publisher, South End Press, 116 Saint Botolph Street, Boston MA 02115.

Native American Graves Protection and Repatriation Act

"NAGPRA, Consultation, and the Field Museum," by Janice Klein, appeared in *Registrars' Quarterly* (fall 1995): 7–8, 16. The excerpt is reprinted with the permission of the author.

Indian Arts and Crafts Act

Dennis Fox's counterpoint is reprinted from Fox, "Indian Arts and Crafts Act: Counterpoint," *Native Americas* (fall/winter 1994): 114ff.

Federal Indian Identification Policy

From M. Annette Jaimes, "Federal Indian Identification Policy: A Usurpation of Indigenous Sovereignty in North America," in *The State of Native North America: Genocide, Colonization, and Resistance*, ed. M. Annette Jaimes (Boston: South End Press, 1992), 123–37. Reprinted with permission from the publisher, South End Press, 116 Saint Botolph Street, Boston MA 02115.

Index

Page numbers in italics refer to illustrations.

Haas, Jonathan, 240
Haida, 283–84
Haines, Herbert, 103
Harris, LaDonna, 136
Haskell Indian Nations University
    (Haskell Indian Junior College), 3
Hatch, Viola, 93
Head Start Program, 18
health care, 90–91, 96, 105, 112–13,
    121, 155, 264
Hickel, Walter, 80, 115
Hill, Clifton, 35
Holappa, Ted, 93
Hollow, Norman, 76–77
Horse Capture, George, 39
House Concurrent Resolution 108
    (1953), 104, 106, 131, 134
House Joint Resolution 1042 (1969),
    127
Howard, Simon, 93
Humphrey, Hubert, 143
Hunter, Robert, 35

identity, 7, 8, 62, 123, 197, 210, 248–49,
    257, 259, 267–68, 275–76, 279,
    280–86, 287
Indian Arts and Crafts Act of 1990, 5,
    245–47, 277
Indian Arts and Crafts Board, 245,
    248, 249
Indian Child Welfare Act of 1978, 5,
    122–25, 126
Indian Citizenship Act of 1924, 25,
    136, 267
Indian Country Today (newspaper),
    238
Indian Education Act of 1972, 5, 126
Indian Financing Act of 1974, 5, 126
Indian Gaming Regulatory Act of
    1988, 4, 128, 165, 166–67, 170
Indian Health Care Improvement Act
    of 1976, 5, 126

Indian Health Service, 128, 263, 265,
    267, 282
Indian Historian (periodical), 3
Indian Law Resource Center, 284, 286
Indian Leader (newspaper), 3
Indian Reorganization Act of 1934, 30,
    36, 56, 58–59, 71, 92, 283
Indian Self-Determination and
    Education Assistance Act of 1975,
    4, 119–21, 126, 129, 131, 175
Indians of All Tribes, 1, 28, 39, 40–43,
    103, 127
intermarriage, 7, 257, 258, 279, 287–91
International Indian Treaty Council,
    284

Jaimes, M. Annette, 279
James, John, 166
Johnson, Lyndon, 24, 185
Josephy, Alvin M., Jr., 78–92
Jourdain, Roger, 76–77
Juaneño Band of Mission Indians,
    280–81

Kennedy, Anthony, 218
Kennedy, Edward, 49, 185
Kennedy, Robert, 185
Kills Enemy, Jake, 50
King, Matthew, 215
Kipp, Woodie, 26–27
Klein, Janice, 242

LaDuke, Winona, 136
LaMere, Angelo, 95
land claims, 3–4. *See also* resource
    rights
Land Consolidation Act of 1983, 4
LaPointe, Frank, 35
Lazarus, Arthur, 217
Limerick, Patricia Nelson, 280
Lomawaima, K. Tsianina, 199
Long, Vern, 49